Recipes for Rearing Children

Mother, oh, mother, come shake out your cloth!
   Empty the dustpan, poison the moth,
Hang out the washing, and butter the bread,
   Sew on a button, and make up a bed.
Where is the mother whose house is so shocking?
   She's up in the nursery, blissfully rocking!

Oh, I've grown as shiftless as Little Blue Boy,
   (Lullaby, rockaby, lullaby loo.)
Dishes are waiting, and the bills are past due,
   (Pat-a-cake, darling, and peek, peekaboo.)
The shopping's not done, and there's nothing for stew.
   And out in the yard, there's a hullabaloo.
But I'm playing kanga- and this is my -roo!
   Look! Aren't her eyes the most wonderful hue?
(Lullaby, rockaby, lullaby loo.)

Oh, cleaning and scrubbing will wait till tomorrow,
   But children grow up, as I've learned to my sorrow.
So quiet down, cobwebs. Dust, go to sleep,
   I'm rocking my baby; babies don't keep.

                                        – Ruth Hulburt Hamilton

Recipes for Rearing Children

Kelly, Kevin, Krysten, and Keith

A book containing creative ideas and
practical principles to help with the
rearing of children from infancy
to married children to grandchildren

by

Pete & Frieda Cowling

All Scriptures used in this volume
are from the King James Bible.

OTHER BOOKS BY PETE & FRIEDA COWLING
Rearing Kids with Character

Understanding Your Husband &
Understanding Your Wife

COVER PHOTOS & DVD PRODUCTION: Dan Mock

Cover Photos:
Top left: Sam, Simon, and Stephen Cervantes
Middle: Trevor, Trey, Trent, and Ashley Cowling
Bottom left: Wesley, Karissa, Ryan, and Derek Vestal
Bottom right: David and Peter Cowling
Top right: Pete and Frieda Cowling with Joseph Cowling

Dedication

This book is dedicated to my parents, Bill and Esther White, who made it possible for me to grow up in a home filled with fun, laughter, and love—for God and for others. From childhood, I wanted a home of my own just like theirs. Truly, *"The lines are fallen unto me in pleasant places; yea, I have a goodly heritage."* (Psalm 16:6)

Frieda White Cowling

The following is a letter written by my mother the day my father went to Heaven.

"A great man died today. He was not a world leader or a famous doctor or a war hero or a sports figure or a business tycoon, but he was a great man. He was your father, Frieda. He was your grandfather, Kelly, Kevin, Krysten, and Keith.

My parents on their wedding day

"He didn't get his picture in the paper for heading up committees. I guess you might say he was a person who never cared for credit or honors. He did corny things—like pay his bills on time, go to church on Sunday and teach a Sunday school class. He always took his kids on a vacation in the summertime, many times to the beach. He enjoyed the simplest things—especially football and basketball games, picnics with his family, just sitting in his front yard watching the cars go by, and telling wild, made-up stories to his grandchildren.

"Tonight is the first time without him. I don't know what to do with myself, so I am writing to you. I'm sorry that I didn't tell him more often just how much I loved him, but I am thankful for many things. I am thankful that God let us live together for over 40 years.

Not many people in this world have enjoyed the happiness, the fellowship, and the love we shared together.

"I am thankful that I was able to let him know how much I loved him. Not many men have suffered so much and for so many years, yet have been so patient and uncomplaining. He died with a smile of love on his face. He knew he was a success as a husband, a father, a grandfather, and a friend to many. I wonder how many millionaires can say that. He trusted in God, and I'm sure he is waiting for us in Heaven."

The following letter was written the first Christmas after my father went to Heaven. My dad loved Christmas! He was under the tree with us shaking presents and guessing what they might be!

"I was trying so hard to make Christmas just the way we had always enjoyed it for everyone that maybe I failed to realize that I couldn't make up for your daddy's empty chair.

"I never leave the house and come back but that I want him to be in his favorite chair or couch. I never fix a meal, but my first thought is what he would have liked. I never wake up in the morning but think I must be quiet so he can sleep longer.

"He was such a part of my life (and a wonderful life it was!) that I wonder why God needed him more than I do, but I know God will help me in the years I have left, and someday, I will understand.

"No one has loved a husband more than I loved Bill. We worked together to see our children grown. Then in these later years, my life was trying to make him happy as well as taking care of him in every way I could. We were so happy, and I'll always have the wonderful memories. I hope you and Pete will have as many happy years together as we did. Bill loved the grandchildren so very much and wanted them to grow up strong and happy.

"Yes, we will always miss him, but I thank God every day that He let us have him so many years.

"Have a happy birthday; I know they pass so quickly."

Love you, Mother

Acknowledgments

Thank you to:

Our children, Rafael and Kelly Cervantes, Kevin and Dawn Cowling, Chris and Krysten Vestal, and Keith and Michelle Cowling, whose lives made it possible for this book to be written and have made I John 4 a reality in our lives. *"I have no greater joy than to hear that my children walk in truth."*

Our grandchildren, Sara, Stephen, Scott, Samuel, and Simon Cervantes; Ashley, Trent, Trevor, and Trey Cowling; Derek, Karissa, Wesley, and Ryan Vestal; and David, Peter, and Joseph Cowling, who spent hours learning and singing songs, listening to stories, and acting as "guinea pigs" for the activities in this book. Thanks for the memories!

Mrs. Marlene Evans, who never gave up her dream that we would write down our experiences with children.

Mrs. Linda Stubblefield, our friend, whose hard work and talent in producing books have helped so many. When I thought this material was only a hopeless jumble, she always found a way.

Mr. Danny Mock, whose smile and patience was still evident after hours of taping for the DVD with our grandchildren. Nothing seemed impossible with Danny.

Mrs. Kelly Cervantes, our daughter, who, in spite of her busy schedule, spent hours proofreading and correcting the manuscript.

Mrs. Michelle Cowling who also helped proofread and made helpful suggestions.

Mrs. Martha Wasson, a veteran educator at Hammond Baptist Schools, who read the book lists and gave valuable suggestions.

Mrs. Nancy Auclair, the enthusiastic librarian at Hammond Baptist Grade School, who also helped with the book list and shared ideas from her years of experience in encouraging children to read and love books.

Mrs. Cherlyn Lukenoff, who was able to take the melody for each fun song and put it in print.

Miss Joan Lindish, my soul-winning partner and our friend, who encouraged us in the writing of this book. She carefully read the manuscript and made many useful suggestions.

Mr. Giancarlo León, who wrote the best children's book, *The Little Emperor,* as a class project for Children's Literature that I had ever seen. I am pleased to say that book is now in print and is listed in the book list section. Because of that project, I knew Giancarlo was an excellent artist and therefore asked him to do some of the template art for flannel board.

Mrs. Christine Santaguida, who helped us decide how to include the music for the songs.

Miss Theresa Leonhardt, who spent hours helping with the research and categorization of the book list.

Mrs. Connie Nesbitt, who helped bring order to the first pages of seemingly unorganized material.

Table of Contents

There was a child went forth every day;
And the first object he look'd upon, that object he became;
And that object became part of him for the day, or a certain
part of the day, or for many years, or stretching cycle
of years.
These became part of that child who went forth every day and
who now goes, and will always go forth every day.

– Walt Whitman

Children Learn What They Live
(Author Unknown)

If a child lives with criticism,
He learns to condemn.

If a child lives with hostility,
He learns to fight.

If a child lives with fear,
He learns to be apprehensive.

If a child lives with pity,
He learns to feel sorry for himself.

If a child lives with jealousy,
He learns to feel guilty.

If a child lives with encouragement,
He learns to be confident.

If a child lives with tolerance,
He learns to be patient.

If a child lives with praise,
He learns to be appreciative.

If a child lives with acceptance,
He learns to love.

If a child lives with approval,
He learns to like himself.

If a child lives with recognition,
He learns to have a goal.

If a child lives with honesty,
He learns what truth is.

If a child lives with security,
He learns to have faith in himself.

If a child lives with friendliness,
He learns that the world is a nice place in which to live.

If a child lives in your home, what will he learn?

DEAR KEITH,
   GOD LOVES YOU AND SO DO YOUR PARENTS. PRAISE GOD & SERVE HIM FOREVER. I WILL SEE YOU WHEN YOUR TEETH FALL OUT.
      LOVE
      GWW.

JOHN 15:26

Foreword

Building Traditions
(Photos on page 13)

Top left:	A note from the "Great White Wolf"
Top right:	Dr. Wendell Evans posed for a picture with some of our grandchildren after they finished caroling at his house.
Center:	The Cervantes family invited us to make a family photo with them at the Christmas Country Fair, held at Hammond Baptist High School.
Bottom left:	The yearly Vestal family outing to find the perfect Christmas tree
Bottom right:	Three generations at the Father-Son Chili Supper at Hammond Baptist Grade School

Foreword

Ever since Adam and Eve, God's plan has been to give a married couple children to rear, to love, and to train to serve the Lord. In fact, if we have children, our greatest opportunity to leave a lasting impression for Christ is to find the will of God for our lives, do it, and encourage our children to do the same.

As an undergraduate in the college of engineering at the University of Tennessee, my husband's dream was to earn his doctorate in mechanical engineering and return to the University of Tennessee campus in Knoxville to teach. Four years later, after receiving a master's degree from Oklahoma State University in Stillwater, Oklahoma, and a doctorate from Georgia Tech in Atlanta, Georgia, this dream became a reality. We built a house on 32 wooded acres, overlooking the Tennessee River in one direction and the Smoky Mountains in the other, and thought we were in a place where we could live "happily ever after." We were extremely active in our Baptist church, but we knew something was missing. God showed us that "something" was soul winning. My husband started sharing Christ with university students, and many received Christ. After a 1975 trip to Pastors' School in Hammond, Indiana, we got into the bus ministry. God was blessing in a wonderful way, but my husband and I decided we could not recommend that our children attend the University of Tennessee even though we both had graduated from there. We desperately wanted to send our children to a Christian school, so my husband asked Dr. Jack Hyles what we should do. He answered, "Do anything you have to do to get your children in a Christian school and in the right kind of church."

My husband and I sent 16 students from our Southern Baptist church to Hyles-Anderson College. Dr. Hyles noticed that and called my husband saying, "Why are all your students here while you are still in Tennessee?" After struggling for a year with this decision which meant moving away from my parents, leaving the bus routes we had started, and the people we had won to the Lord, we moved.

It has been the best life imaginable! I have no idea what our children would be doing if we had stayed in Tennessee, but today all are serving God. All four of them graduated from Hyles-Anderson College, and all four of them married someone they met at Hyles-Anderson College. III John 4 says, *"I have no greater joy than to hear that my children walk in truth."*

The word "enthusiasm" means "filled with God." We have tried to show our children (and now our grandchildren) that being in the will of God is a satisfying, wonderful life—a life that the world cannot understand or enjoy. *"The thief cometh not, but for to steal, and to kill, and to destroy: I am come that they might have life, and that they might have it more abundantly."* (John 10:10)

God does not force us to do anything. He loves us and tells us how we can enjoy His blessings if we obey His commands; but the decision of what we do is left to us by God. This is true with our children as well. We can love them, pray for them, and try to be the right example, but the decision of how they will live their lives must be theirs. If our children see serving God as rewarding, I believe they will be more willing to sell out for God. What the world offers brings temporary thrills, but God gives joy—with no regrets. A Christian can have more fun by accident than others have on purpose. This can become a reality in families, but it requires time, effort, and planning. It does not just happen.

God gives parents children to bring joy and blessing to their lives if they follow God's instructions in rearing them. The Bible answers our every question about rearing children, but we must study the Bible, learn what God wants us to know, and apply God's answers to our individual problems. *"Lo, children are an heritage of the LORD: and the fruit of the womb is his reward."* (Psalm 127:3)

God wants husbands and wives to get along so our homes are peaceful and have an atmosphere that is not filled with yelling, negative remarks, and tension. *"Behold, how good and how pleasant it is for brethren to dwell together in unity!"* (Psalm 133:1)

If this unity prevails in our homes, regardless of who is there, our homes reflect Christ—not because of us, but because of Christ. *"Peace I leave with you, my peace I give unto you: not as the world giveth, give I unto you. Let not your heart be troubled, neither let it be afraid."* (John 14:27)

I was reared in a Christian home and accepted Christ as my Saviour at age nine. However, even though my husband and I were saved and serving God, our home was different when other people were present. It was the difference between being nasty and nice. I remember reading Hebrews 13:8, *"Jesus Christ the same yesterday, and to day, and for ever."* I realized we could fool the world and people who occasionally visited our home, but we could never fool our children. I read this verse and asked God to make this verse a reality in my life so our children could grow up in a home that was Christlike. In less than a month, God sent someone to live with us named John Wilbourne, and many times I regretted praying that prayer. However, it was good for me because John's presence was a constant reminder that the atmosphere of our home could honor God if I stopped demanding my way and tried to prefer others. Romans 12:10 says, *"Be kindly affectioned one to another with brotherly love; in honour preferring one another."*

Time is the best gift you can give a child, regardless of how old he is. When you give a child time, you give your life. If parents are too busy to give time to a child of any age, consider the result as given in Proverbs 29:15 which says, *"The rod and reproof give wisdom: but a child left to himself bringeth his mother to shame."*

Fervent Hope

When I see my little children...On the floor in peaceful play...
It has often made me wonder...Where they'll be some distant
day...And I always hope their future...Constant happiness will
hold...For no greater consolation...Could be mine when I am
old...And, of course, like every parent...I have hopes that they gain
fame...And the nation long remembers...Each one as an honored
name...And I also hope their youngsters...Will grow up to be as
fine...And as healthy and as wealthy...As these tiny tots of
mine...But I hope each one discovers...That the most important
thing...Is the kind of daily living...Which a smile to God will bring.

Introduction

According to Psalm 127:3, which says, *"Lo, children are an heritage of the LORD: and the fruit of the womb is his reward,"* children are given to us by God so we can train them. *"Train up a child in the way he should go: and when he is old, he will not depart from it."* (Proverbs 22:6)

Parents are also to give children back to God. *"What? know ye not that your body is the temple of the Holy Ghost which is in you, which ye have of God, and ye are not your own? For ye are bought with a price: therefore glorify God in your body, and in your spirit, which are God's."* (I Corinthians 6:19, 20)

God plans for us to be an example for our children by our consistent Christian life. Philippians 3:17 says, *"Brethren, be followers together of me, and mark them which walk so as ye have us for an ensample."*

I Corinthians 4:14-16, *"I write not these things to shame you, but as my beloved sons I warn you. For though ye have ten thousand instructors in Christ, yet have ye not many fathers: for in Christ Jesus I have begotten you through the gospel. Wherefore I beseech you, be ye followers of me."*

I Corinthians 11:1, *"Be ye followers of me, even as I also am of Christ."*

The Bible tells us in Luke 2:52 that Jesus grew in this way: *"And Jesus increased in wisdom and stature, and in favour with God and man."*

In addition to helping our children grow mentally, physically, and socially, we need to encourage them by providing them with an example of how to live the abundant life God has promised to us.

John 10:10, *"The thief cometh not, but for to steal, and to kill, and to destroy: I am come that they might have life, and that they might have it more abundantly."* The abundant life is filled with joy and tears, happiness and heartache, victories and defeats; but through it all, we can have a merry heart because of Christ. We have a choice—to complain or to rejoice.

Proverbs 17:22, *"A merry heart doeth good like a medicine: but a broken spirit drieth the bones."*

Proverbs 12:25, *"Heaviness in the heart of man maketh it stoop: but a good word maketh it glad."*

Proverbs 15:13, *"A merry heart maketh a cheerful countenance: but by sorrow of the heart the spirit is broken."*

Proverbs 15:15, *"All the days of the afflicted* (moody) *are evil: but he that is of a merry heart hath a continual feast."*

God wants us to experience a life filled with joy, storing up memories that last a lifetime. However, to build these memories takes time, which is the most important gift we can give. When we give our time to someone as we read a book, play a game, work on a project, or take a trip, we are giving them ourselves. Time is a gift money cannot buy, and if we do not give it away today, the opportunity may be gone forever. If we fail to spend time with our children, we may find that our teenagers do not want to spend time with us, deciding to "punish" us for the neglect they feel. Spending time together can diminish differences and build lasting relationships.

I made many mistakes in rearing our children, but I have no regrets concerning the time I spent with our children and grandchildren. I pray their memories of me will be of a person who was fun to be around. The fun the world offers brings temporary thrills, but God gives lasting joy—with no regrets. A Christian should be able to have more fun by accident then the world has on purpose. This can be true in our families if we are willing to invest time, planning, and effort in our children—regardless of their age or marital status. One way to spend quality time with our children is to build family traditions that can be passed on from one generation to the next.

Family Traditions

1. **Establish a family night.** When our children were preschool age, we established Friday as family night. It is not important to spend a lot of money to have "fun" as a family or to always go out to eat. Children will enjoy a night when you play games, work puzzles, or devote some time exclusively to them. If you can't afford to take the children out for ice cream, buy a half gallon of ice cream, bananas, make or buy chocolate syrup, and sprinkles, and let them make banana splits and ice cream sundaes at home. For variety, you can put on an apron, take their orders, and serve them.

Years ago on a Friday night, my husband told our children he had planned a "surprise." He loaded them all in the van and told them to get under a blanket so they could not see where they were going. He drove around for a few blocks and ended up in our driveway. With the blanket over their heads, he led them into the house where I had transformed our kitchen into an ice cream parlor. Every person made his own sundae, and we had fun. We have done the same thing with our grandchildren on a Monday night.

Family Monday

I grew up in a small town in east Tennessee, and our family visiting was done on Sunday afternoon. Families went to church, ate dinner together, and visited until it was time to return to church on Sunday night. After a large meal, we made homemade ice cream while the children played and the adults talked.

In 1977, my husband left his teaching position at the University of Tennessee in Knoxville, and we moved to Hammond, Indiana, so we could rear our children in the ministries of First Baptist Church. We have served in the church bus ministry of First Baptist Church since 1977. When our four children entered Hyles-Anderson College, they joined the "B" bus ministry which meant they left home at 6:30 a.m Sunday morning, and the girls came home after evening church. Our sons often got home at 2:00 Monday morning after riding the night bus. I missed our family meals—especially after the marriages of our two older children. We decided to have our family "get-together" on Monday afternoon, thereby instituting our family Mondays. These Monday afternoons have become a special time for me—an oasis in the middle of a busy schedule. It has kept us close as a family. We set the following guidelines to make and keep Mondays special.

• **Once my husband and I designated Monday afternoon, nothing changes that set time.**

• **We go on with our plans if everyone comes or nobody comes.** Frankly, I cannot remember a time when no one has come. We don't check with every family every week to see what each family is doing, and we do not get our feelings hurt if a family member has to miss because of other plans. Sometimes they call to say they can't make it, but this courtesy is not required.

- **We eat promptly at 5:00 p.m.** We have the rest of the evening to visit, shop, play games, etc.
- **I plan a simple menu on Friday or Saturday and have all of the ingredients needed on hand.** For an hour we all work together to prepare the food—at least those with culinary abilities help! We visit as we prepare the food. Many Mondays in warm weather, our son-in-law Rafael grills, which is always delicious. His wife, our daughter Kelly, often calls and brings dishes to pass. Our goal is to enjoy each other—not spend the entire day cooking. If any family member has a birthday, we follow our family tradition of allowing that person to select the menu. On these days, I spend more time and effort making sure the wish is granted for the meal of the person's choice so he feels extra special. That birthday person also gets to use a red plate that says, "You are special."
- **Meals are served buffet style from the kitchen cabinet and stove.** I have found this service style makes cleanup easier, and everyone can help himself to seconds.
- **To promote togetherness, I have round or oval tables for meals.** One table in the kitchen seats eight; one in the dining room seats six, and the one in the basement seats twelve. We select the table that accommodates that Monday's crowd. Since I'm not sure of the number ahead of time, some set the table while others prepare food.
- **As we eat, we visit.** Sometimes we talk for over an hour, enjoying each other. It is relaxing to forget life's pressures and problems during our Monday "oasis."
- **After dessert, we share in the cleanup.** We make plates for family members who missed the meal or for our son-in-law who works nights. I always prepare extra food for this.
- **Our grandchildren are included and share in the activities.** I have a high chair, books, and toys and games so they can be occupied while the adults are talking. Whining, crying, and other undesirable behavior on the children's part is uncommon because they are busy and happy. I dearly love my grandchildren, but they are not allowed to be the center of attention which makes it impossible for adults to visit with each other.
- **Sometimes family members leave after we eat.** Other times we play games or puzzles, go shopping, refinish furniture, etc. In the

past, the grandchildren enjoyed bubble baths with special animal towels that I saved just for them so they would be ready for bed when they got home.

I once had an older woman comment, "Every time my son and his family come for a visit, they eat me out of house and home. They walk around looking at my possessions trying to decide what they will get after I die. I don't enjoy their visits at all."

"How sad," I thought. "I plan to enjoy our family Mondays to the fullest—and if they have to stop for some reason, I will have special memories that will last forever."

2. Make birthdays special. The "birthday child" gets to choose his favorite meal and gets to use a red plate that says, "You're Special Today." When our children were preschool age, they could invite as many friends as they were years old, such as three friends at age three, to a birthday party. I planned games, activities, and food so that everyone could feel special. I had a special occasion cake book, and each child selected the cake he wanted for his birthday which I made in honor of the occasion.

The year we moved from Tennessee to Indiana, I went from being a "stay-at-home" mom to teaching full-time at Hyles-Anderson College. All of our children were in school, but it was a difficult time for me. At that time, our son Kevin was in the fourth grade, and his birthday is on February 21. He had enjoyed many birthday parties, but this year he had chosen not to invite friends but to have his party with our family. I still cannot believe this, but his birthday came and went and nobody mentioned it. At our family altar time on the morning after his birthday, Kevin said, "Does anyone remember what yesterday was?" My heart broke as I realized that if I was too busy to remember our son's birthday, I was too busy. I vowed to reorder my priorities to make sure another birthday child was never forgotten. Today, Kevin is married and lives in Mesa, Arizona, with his wife and four children where he pastors the Valley Baptist Church.

Several years ago, I was speaking for a Mother-Daughter Banquet at Kevin's church and told this story as I talked about the importance of spending time with your children. I cried as I told the story, but I noticed the ladies from Kevin's church were smiling. After the meeting, some of them approached me and said, "Pastor Cowling tells that story and laughs." To me it is still not funny, but God used it to help me realize how important it is to make a birthday special.

3. **Go on family vacations.** Each year we went somewhere special for a vacation. If the trip was to visit one of our parents, we planned daily activities while there that the children would remember such as local ball games, zoos, museums, parks, and forest preserves. We have been to Florida, Canada, Niagara Falls, New England, the Outer Banks of North Carolina, and Charleston, South Carolina on vacation with our children and their grandparents.

Planning daily activities always prevents problems if your loved ones do not have your value system and it also gives everyone something wholesome to do. We made pictures so we could remember those special times. Before "Grandma Ginnie" went to Heaven, we took scrapbooks when we went to visit her in the nursing home. The pictures seemed to "trigger" her memory which was dulled by the effects of Alzheimer's, and the pictures gave us something about which to talk.

One year we had no time or money for a vacation, so we did something special one day every week such as riding the train to Chicago, taking a picnic and hiking over the Indiana Dunes to Lake Michigan, visiting the Museum of Science and Industry on "Free Day," going to the County Fair, or attending an afternoon Cubs game.

4. **Attend ball games.** When our children were playing ball of any kind or cheering, we were there to "participate." We drove many miles to attend the "away" games so we could show our support for each other as a family. Now that we have grandchildren at Hammond Baptist Grade School, we are once again attending ball games and attempting to cheer "Gamma" on to victory. (Gamma is one of the six intramural teams in our grade school for which our children played, and now our grandchildren play for the same team.)

My husband has always been a very supportive and vocal fan. When Kevin, our oldest son, played soccer in his fourth-grade year, my husband and I attended his games. I had tried to teach Kevin to be polite and prefer the other person according to Romans 12:10. *"Be kindly affectioned one to another with brotherly love; in honour preferring one another."* Unfortunately for Kevin, my advice did not work on the playing field. When the soccer ball rolled by and a player from the opposing team was trying to kick it, Kevin stepped back and let him have the ball. My husband said, "Kevin, your job is to get the ball and kick it to your team. Get out there and be aggressive!"

Kevin went back out on the field and promptly stepped aside again. My husband called Kevin to the sideline and said, "Kevin, the next time you step aside, I'm going to yell at you."

"Dad, that will be embarrassing," Kevin said.

"Then you be aggressive and get the ball," his dad replied.

The next time Kevin stepped aside, his dad yelled, "Kick shins, Kevin, and get the ball."

Kevin became more aggressive, but the yelling continued. After one of the soccer games, one of the mothers approached my husband and asked, "Are you one of the coaches?"

My husband replied, "No, ma'am, I'm the designated yeller!" His yelling was positive. Today our grandchildren do not always win their games, but they always have "designated yellers" pulling for them from the sideline. It is very exciting to have a "two-generation" family tradition.

5. **Celebrate holidays together.** With some planning and work, holidays can be exciting and filled with fun.

For **Valentine's Day**, I mail valentines to our grandchildren. A small gift can be wrapped in red and white paper. For our bus riders, we get brown or white lunch sacks for all the children to decorate on the way to church. We judge the bags and give prizes for the best-decorated bags, including the adults. The bags are given back to each child on the bus ride home, and every worker on the bus brings candy to put in every bag.

For **Easter**, I save plastic eggs and baskets. On our "Family Monday" for several weeks before Easter, we take turns hiding the plastic eggs and finding them. (Sometimes months later, I find an "undiscovered" egg!)

When our children were at home, we always made each child an Easter basket with presents and treats. We then hid the basket, and they had to find theirs. I remember at times it was hard for them to find the baskets. Once we hid a basket inside a grandfather clock and once on top of a lamp—which required diligent searching.

When our children were grade-school age, I helped them make decorative sugar eggs for their teachers. If these require more time than you have, make Easter cookies with your child, and let the children wrap them with colored cellophane and take them to their teacher. (See Appendix C for the recipe for sugar eggs.)

Holidays are a good time to help the child appreciate his Sunday school teachers, choir leaders, school teachers, etc. Giving is better than receiving, and this will help children enjoy the blessing that comes from giving. *"I have shewed you all things, how that so labouring ye ought to support the weak, and to remember the words of the Lord Jesus, how he said, "It is more blessed to give than to receive."* (Acts 20:35) When thinking of a gift, I tried to plan one the teacher would enjoy and the child could help in making. It seemed as if most teachers received few gifts from those they were teaching, and their gratitude reinforced the lesson we were trying to get into the heart of our child.

For the **Fourth of July**, we planned special activities. When our children were little, my husband and two of our children traveled with a tour group from Hyles-Anderson College. It would have been easy for the three of us who remained at home to feel lonely and depressed, so I made a plan we followed every year. I prepared a breakfast of boiled eggs, applesauce, and sausage balls to take to the Dunes. We stopped at Dunkin' Donuts on the way for a special treat of doughnuts. We got to the Dunes when the gate opened at 7:00 a.m. and hiked across the Dunes to Lake Michigan. We returned to the picnic area and had breakfast, after which we left the Dunes about the time people were coming to the beach.

We went to the Fourth of July parade at 11:00 a.m. where we watched the floats and caught candy. We returned home and went to eat at a buffet that afternoon at 2:00 p.m. Sometimes we played games in the afternoon, but at 9:00 p.m., we went to Hidden Lake Park to watch the fireworks. Of course, I would have enjoyed the day's activities more if our whole family had been together; but since that was an impossibility, I tried to make the day special for those who were "left behind."

I remember one rainy Fourth of July when only our son Kevin and I were home. He was a teenager, and I think he would have preferred "sleeping in" instead of following our family Fourth of July tradition. However, I got up, made the food, and was ready to leave at 6:30 a.m. in the middle of a thunderstorm. Kevin said, "Mom, do you think we can have a picnic in the basement this year and stay out of the rain?" We did, and I still remember it!

For **Labor Day,** I prepare breakfast for anyone who wants to eat after 9:00 a.m. The food is there for those who want to eat at their leisure. Sometimes my daughter, daughter-in-law, and I go to the mall while the men watch the children. We grill and eat about 3:00 p.m. Everyone usually brings a dish to pass. We play ball and croquet in the yard, ride bikes, talk, and make ice cream later in the day.

My husband has never liked the origin of **Halloween,** so we decided to make our own version. We let our children dress up in a costume (not a witch or monster) and went "treating." I made a homemade treat such as cinnamon rolls, banana bread, brownies, or cookies. At first our children were somewhat skeptical of treating, but when they knocked on our neighbors' doors, handed them a treat, and said, "Happy Halloween," they were invited in and were overwhelmed with treats. This is not why we did it, and if our neighbors gave us nothing in return, we were just as happy. One year Halloween was on a Wednesday night, and we went to church instead of "treating." Several of our neighbors said they waited for us, wondering what had happened because Halloween wasn't the same without being "treated." These neighbors could buy anything they wanted for themselves, but they liked being treated to something special. Eventually, we were able to see several of these neighbors accept Christ.

One Monday in early October we take our children and grandchildren who live near us to a pumpkin farm where we visit the farm animals, ride a horse-drawn wagon to the pumpkin field, and where everyone walks in the field to choose his own pumpkin. We put the pumpkins in our van and let our grandchildren ride ponies. They always remember the name of the pony they ride. We sit around a campfire and then return to our house to eat. The following Monday night, we carve a jack-o-lantern from one of the pumpkins and toast the pumpkin seeds. We sing the "Jack-O-Lantern Song" after we put a candle in the pumpkin. (The "Jack-O-Lantern Song" is in Appendix B; a recipe for pumpkin seeds is included in Appendix D.)

On **Thanksgiving** I always cook a Thanksgiving dinner, but I prepare as much of the food as I can ahead of time because we go to church for a Thanksgiving service from 10:00 a.m. to 11:00 a.m. on Thursday morning. We attend with our married children and grandchildren who live in the area. If my brother and his wife come to spend Thanksgiving with us and don't care to go to church, we go without them. I don't feel I have to try to "force" them to attend our church, but I do not feel God would have me stay at home to entertain them.

When our children were little, we left the Thanksgiving service at 11:00 a.m. and went to Chicago to visit the Museum of Science and Industry. Thursday was free admission, and the museum was **never** crowded on this day. This time together was exciting for the children because the many wonderful, hands-on experiences can never be exhausted there. We came home and had lunch about 2:00 p.m. or 3:00 p.m. Usually one of our friends from church named Ben came home with us. We had the traditional turkey dinner, but I also tried to make special favorites such as sweet potatoes for our son Kevin, hot rolls for our grandchildren, pecan pie for our son Keith, and lemon icebox pie for my brother David.

My brother, David White

After dinner, we cover the food so people can snack anytime they want. We play games with the children, and the adults talk. If there is a ball game, we watch that. At night the older children and adults play games such as charades, Trivial Pursuit, or Catch Phrase. (In many of these games, we removed some of the cards and skipped the worldly categories.) While the children watch an educational video, my daughter, my daughter-in-law, and I peruse the ads to check the after-Thanksgiving sales, making a list of what we would like to purchase at each store, and deciding in what order we will visit the stores.

On Friday morning after Thanksgiving, I pick up my daughter at 4:45 a.m. and we go shopping by 5:00 a.m. Usually by 10:00 a.m., we have all our Christmas shopping done and are back home with our treasures. At noon we take our grandchildren who live near to us to the Christmas tree farm to cut down a Christmas tree. We wander through the trees searching for "the perfect tree." When we find it, we cut it down and drag it back to our van. Sometimes, our son Keith gets his tree at the same time. We take the tree to the "shaker" machine and to the "binder." The children receive a coloring book and a snack I bring with me. We go home, set up the tree, and decorate it with the help of our grandchildren. We can always tell who helped with the decorating because the ornaments are always at their height! I never worry if an ornament gets broken because people are more important than things.

My goal is to have the tree decorated, my Christmas decorations in place, and all the presents wrapped by Monday night. I have some small gifts, and sometimes we let the grandchildren open one on Monday before Christmas. As the grandchildren get older, I buy fewer but more expensive gifts. I usually buy each of our grandchildren a game or puzzle for Christmas and let them open this gift so we can play it on Monday before Christmas.

For **Christmas**, I plan carefully. I love all holidays, and I feel the only way you can keep the holiday fun from being hectic is by planning. I find if I am worried about getting everything done, I lose my joy. That is why I always have all of the Christmas presents purchased by the end of November. I shop all year at sales and at secondhand shops. I have all the gifts wrapped and the tree bought and decorated before December 1. I entertain 30 to 40 bus mothers for Christmas dinner at my home the first weekend in December where each lady is given a small gift. This is a "bus family" tradition.

Every Monday in December before Christmas, we plan something special with our children and grandchildren. One week we took the children to see Santa Claus and had their picture made with him.

Another Monday we took them to see the Christmas lights. Another Monday we dressed the grandchildren in Christmas outfits, let them wear Santa hats and took them "caroling" to people in the church. We took baked treats to give as presents. Another Monday, our son and son-in-law, who are both bus captains on our route, chose some families from their bus; and we took baked treats and presents to them. If our children and grandchildren who live out of town come to our house for Christmas, we pick a day when they will all be there and call it Christmas. This way we can have Christmas any day. This is nice because we can shop the "After-Christmas Sales" for last-minute Christmas presents.

Our Christmas tradition includes a big breakfast and our Christmas dinner about 3:00 p.m. in the afternoon. Sometimes I let

Mrs. Esther White with ten of her
great-grandchildren

the children open a present in the morning so they will have something to play with. Christmas Eve 2002 was special with snow on the
ground so the children spent a lot of time sledding, warming up, and
sledding again. We have the traditional Christmas ham dinner, sing
songs, and have the Christmas story read from Luke 2 just as my dad
read it when I was a child. Sometimes the grandchildren will sing.

The only time our whole family is together is at Christmas time
since they live in Oregon, Arizona, and Indiana. When we are all
together, I treasure every moment. One year Kevin's children,
Ashley, Trent, and Trevor, who were nine, seven, and five at the
time, had learned "The Little Drummer Boy" song to sing at the
Valley Baptist Church in Mesa, Arizona, where our son and their
father is the pastor. Ashley played the piano and sang with the boys.
All 23 of our extended family members sat listening to them and
applauded when they finished. Before anyone moved, our barely
three-year-old grandson, Simon Cervantes, walked to the front of
the crowd, stood in front of the piano, and began to sing at the top
of his voice, "Jesus Loves Me." We looked at one another with puz-
zled looks and wondered why this was happening. Then we realized
that if his cousins were going to receive attention by singing, then he

wanted "equal time"—even if it was unsolicited!

I immediately thought of how much children need to be praised for the good things they do. There is a temptation to punish bad behavior and ignore good behavior. Conscientiously watching for ways to praise children will build self-confidence and give them a desire to do the right thing. Any action on the child's part that achieves positive results will be repeated.

I have many "Santa hats" and some "Santa Claus suits." I take any child who wants to be "Santa's Helper" to the basement where we put on their Christmas costumes. As I call out the children's names, they deliver the presents for that child. After all the children have opened their presents, we clear away the paper and put on an educational video for them to watch. The adults then open their presents one at a time so we can see their reactions. After this, we play games.

I try to plan special activities so our grandchildren will not be bored and always feel it is "fun" to come to see Grandpa and Grandma. I have a basket of Christmas stories by the Christmas tree so I can read them to our grandchildren. Sometimes we tell true-to-life stories to them. The following is one of the stories my husband has told year after year.

A Christmas Story

A long time ago in a faraway place (East Tennessee), a man and his wife lived in a house in the woods with three children (eventually four). The time of the annual commemoration of the birth of Jesus was at hand, and the world was in a festive mood. The family had gone into the woods and selected a beautiful cedar tree and had cut it down, taken it home, placed it in their living room, and decorated it. It was beautiful and the focal point of the children's attention. As the children admired it, visions of sugar plums might have gone through their heads; but alas, no visions of Jesus.

The daddy became distressed and began to preach against the pagan imagery of the tree. But the mama—who was quite wise (look whom she chose to marry)—took the daddy aside and suggested that he take a more positive approach and find something better than the tree.

The daddy thought and thought, "Hmmm..." he said. (He could

think better when he said, "Hmmm.") Then he folded his hands and prayed and asked God for help. (He could pray better when he folded his hands.) God helped! "Aha," said the daddy when his prayer was answered.

The next day the daddy took his three children, an ax, and went for a walk in the woods. He carried the youngest child and the ax because they could not walk. (Technically, the youngest child went for a carry in the woods since she could not walk!) They looked and they looked for the answer to prayer. At last they saw it—a large oak bough! The daddy cut it down, and they all helped drag it home.

When they got the bough back to the house, the children watched while the daddy hewed out a seven-foot cross. They placed the cross in the corner of the living room. Then the daddy and the children made a wooden manger which they placed in front of the cross. Next, they cut out angels, Mary, Joseph, and Baby Jesus from poster board. A poster board star was hung by thread from the ceiling above the manger as were the angels. (See the daddy and the children having fun!) Finally, all of the Christmas presents were placed at the foot of the cross. (See Christ-centered Christmas memories being created.)

Years have passed since then. All four of the children have graduated from Hyles-Anderson College and are serving Jesus. The daddy is now a granddaddy. Something worked in rearing the children. Perhaps the wise mother (now a grandmother) was right when she suggested that the daddy take a positive approach to find something better than a Christmas tree to inspire the children's thoughts at Christmas time. In any event, their children's lives have made the parents happier at Christmas time than all of the glitter of the world.

One of the most comical incidents of 2003 involved our grandson Petey, who is two years of age. I have a Santa Claus calendar candy holder with 25 spaces for regular-sized candy bars. After our meal, each grandchild could choose a favorite. Sam excitedly came in one Monday and announced to the adults that Petey had eaten three candy bars. When I went into the room where the candy holder was, Petey was nowhere in sight. However, I saw the curtain move and discovered Petey hiding behind the curtains. I explained, "Petey, you may have only one candy bar each Monday," but it was impossible to reclaim the "stolen" goods! Not long after I had corrected my errant grandson, I glanced into the room and saw him standing one foot from the candy and staring intently at the bars! When he saw me, he quickly backed away.

    6. Go bike riding together. When our children were little, we all had a bike and would ride around our neighborhood. I have many fond memories of these times. I have two grandsons now in Indiana who can ride bikes, and someone gave me a bike so I can ride the bike trails with them on pretty fall days.

    7. Create fun traditions. For instance, the "Great White Wolf" always left a note with some money when our children lost a tooth. He also left a note praising the child for any achievements the child had recently made. At Easter time, the "Great White Wolf" left a note in each Easter basket, mentioning positive traits he had noticed in the child's life.

    8. Cultivate relationships with grandparents and other loved ones. One of the best ways we found to build relationships with loved ones was through letters. Everyone loves to receive letters, but few people make enough time in their schedule to write. When our children were little, I decided that they would write their grandparents every week, but they never seemed to find time to do so. *"As cold water to a thirsty soul, so is good news from a far country."* (Proverbs 25:25)

    One day I told them that they would have their letters ready to mail by Sunday lunch or they would not be allowed to eat according to the admonition of II Thessalonians 3:10, *"For even when we were with you, this we commanded you, that if any would not work, neither should he eat."* When we got home from the bus route on Sunday, each of our four children would rush to their rooms to write their letters while I put the meal on the table.

Keith, our youngest son, loves to tell how he would dash off a quick note as follows:

Dear Mimi,

How are you? I am fine. School is great. You are the best Mimi in the world.

Love, Keith

Keith says he just scribbled the note, not thinking about what he was saying and not writing because he loved his grandparents, but because he wanted to eat lunch! He tells about visiting his grandmother, Mrs. Esther (Mimi) White, and hearing her say with tears in her eyes, "I always knew you loved me because you took the time to write me every week in spite of how busy you were." Keith tells about feeling guilty because the only reason he wrote was so he could eat! He didn't bother to tell Mimi "the rest of the story"!

9. Make time for storytelling. My father told stories to our children as he had told them to me when I was growing up. I told stories to our children, and our older children told stories to the younger children. One night at my parents' home, five-year-old Krysten was telling a story to two-year-old Keith. When I heard Krysten crying, I ran to the bedroom to see if she had hurt herself in some way (or if they had been quarreling). Finding her still on the bed crying and Keith with a surprised look on his face staring at her, I tried to find what was wrong. In a few moments, Krysten, through her sobs, was able to say, "I was telling Keith a story I made up like Grandpa Bill does, and I scared myself." I reminded her that one of the first verses she learned with her brothers and sisters was Psalm 56:3, *"What time I am afraid, I will trust in thee."*

Infancy

Infancy
(Photos on page 35)

Top left: Kelly's first birthday

Top right: Kevin enjoying the great outdoors

Center top: The Cowlings with Kelly and Archie, our dog

Center: Scott Cervantes the night before he went to Heaven

Bottom left: Mrs. Marlene Evans holding Stephen Cervantes

Bottom right: Keith "enjoying" a bus route "Big Day" picnic

My husband and I had been married for four years when God gave us our first child. What a wonderful exciting time! Sin would cause the birth of a child to be dreaded instead of desired when children are conceived without the benefit of marriage. In the 30 years I have been in the bus ministry, I have observed two ways of dealing with a child conceived outside of wedlock. 1) The child is aborted (murdered) because of the inconvenience and the lack of desire to assume responsibility for the actions of the man and woman involved. 2) Everyone wants the child until the child reaches the age of two, and then no one wants the child because no one is willing to invest the time and effort required to train the child the way God intended. My husband and I set the following guidelines for rearing an infant.

1. We would pray daily that our child would allow God to direct his path from birth. Proverbs 3:5, 6 says, *"Trust in the LORD with all thine heart; and lean not unto thine own understanding. In all thy ways acknowledge him, and he shall direct thy paths."*

2. Nothing would be more important than spending time with our children. *"To every thing there is a season, and a time to every purpose under the heaven."* (Ecclesiastes 3:1)

Spending time with an infant does not mean picking him up every time he cries. Doing so allows the child to control the authority instead of the authority controlling the child. Psalm 58:3 says, *"The wicked are estranged from the womb: they go astray as soon as they be born, speaking lies."*

How can an infant speak lies? They cry to be picked up when nothing is wrong. This can be gratifying temporarily when an infant is screaming at the top of his lungs because he is bored and instantly stops crying when picked up. A warm feeling engulfs you as you think, "My child was in distress, and I picked him up and met his needs." Any infant would prefer being held by an adult to being left alone. By rewarding his screaming, you are encouraging the infant to cry every time he wants to be picked up. **Any action that achieves positive results will reoccur.** This constant, incessant crying quickly becomes irritating, and it is the fault of the authority.

If an infant is hungry, feed him. If he is wet or dirty, change him. If he is tired, put him to bed. However, if the infant is crying for attention, wait until he stops crying before responding. If crying is rewarded by the child's being picked up, the older the child gets, the longer he will cry. This behavior quickly becomes a habit that is difficult to break, and it means the infant is controlling the authority instead of the authority controlling him. *"Children, obey your parents in all things: for this is well pleasing unto the Lord."* (Colossians 3:20)

The world tells us that we prove our love to an infant by satisfying his every whim, never allowing him to cry, and sacrificing our lives to make him happy. This attitude produces a selfish, demanding child who will not appreciate anything that is done for him and who will grow to hate parents who neglected God's admonition to train him God's way. (See "Rebellion Will Cost You" in the "Teenage" section.) *"Train up a child in the way he should go: and when he is old, he will not depart from it."* (Proverbs 22:6)

Sometimes people call me and say, "I have been picking up my infant every time he cries," or "My infant cries at night, and I rock him," or "I put my infant in bed with me." The caller then adds, "I realize I have made a mistake because the child is perfectly happy if I am holding, rocking, or sleeping with him. However, when I try to put the child back to bed, he screams and I haven't a clue of what to do. Is it too late to solve this problem?"

NO! However, you must realize you have trained him how to get his own way, and to retrain him will require determination and perseverance to solve the problem. The following solution will work if you are willing to do it.

- A. Put the infant in bed with his blanket, turn on soft music, and provide a night light.
- B. Let him cry for five minutes. You **can** do it because it is the best thing for both of you. Don't give in!
- C. Go into the child's room, but **do not pick him up**. Speak softly, tell him you love him, lay him down, pat him on the back a few times, and leave the room.

D. Wait ten minutes and repeat step C.

E. Follow the same procedure except add five minutes to the time every time you go into the room. **Do not pick up the child.**

An infant who has had his own way by crying in the past may cry for three or more hours the first time this procedure is followed. However, this method will solve the problem if you will be consistent. The infant will cry until it becomes clear that he will not be picked up as a reward for his crying. *"Now no chastening for the present seemeth to be joyous, but grievous: nevertheless afterward it yieldeth the peaceable fruit of righteousness unto them which are exercised thereby."* (Hebrews 12:11)

In case this seems contradictory as far as spending time with an infant is concerned, the difference is that the authority is in control instead of the child. When our children were infants, I kept them near me, talked to them, sang to them, put their playpen outdoors near the older children, and tried to make them feel like a part of the family. I loved to rock them when they were infants, and we had four rocking chairs in our house. However, when it was time for their nap or time for them to go to bed at night, they were put in their crib, given their "special" blanket, soft music was played, and a night light turned on when it was dark. They could happily go to sleep or cry themselves to sleep. The choice was theirs.

3. From infancy our children would be placed on a schedule. They would have a time for the following:

Sara Cervantes at 6 months

A. **Getting up in the morning.** I wanted the infant to eat about 6:00 a.m. I would put the infant back in the crib with soft books that the child could not destroy so he could stay there until around 7:00 a.m.

B. **Play time.** When the infant grew tired of being in the same place for too long, I would put him in an infant seat, swing, playpen, or jumper which I put near me or our other children. An infant cries when he becomes bored, so I would move him often. I did not put the child in his bed until it was time for him to sleep.

C. **Bath time.** An infant gets the most exercise during bath time, so I gave mine a daily bath. At first infants hate the bath and scream; however, they will quickly learn to enjoy this time. The best way to give an infant a bath is with a bath seat that fits across the sink. (These are expensive but try a baby's secondhand store for a more reasonable price.) When the child can sit up at six months, a bath ring is nice. NEVER leave the child unattended in a bathtub! I usually gave the infant a bath in the morning before the morning nap. If the child is having difficulty sleeping at night, you may choose to give him a bath before he is put to bed at night.

D. **Outdoor time.** Fresh air is good for an infant, will help prevent boredom, and will help them sleep better. However, they should be dressed properly for the outdoor weather. My rule was that we went outdoors daily—sun, rain, snow—unless the infant had a fever. Many times it took longer to get the children dressed to go outdoors than the time we spent outdoors. In spite of the time involved, we went outdoors in the morning and in the afternoon because I felt it was an important part of their schedule.

E. **Nap time.** If the bath is given in the morning before nap time, the infant will usually sleep longer during the nap time. An infant can sleep between 8 and 16 hours a day, but he cannot be allowed to sleep all day and then be expected to sleep throughout the night. I practiced the following rules concerning naps:

(1) Never put the child into his bed unless he is expected to sleep.

(2) Have a ritual to remind the infant that it is time to sleep. This ritual can include the blanket, pacifier, music, or night light.

(3) Never whisper or tiptoe around when the child is sleeping because he will be conditioned to wake up when noise occurs. Children can learn to sleep with noise.

(4) Try to have the same schedule for the morning and afternoon naps daily.

(5) Never let him sleep past 4:30 p.m. if you want him to sleep at night. Wake him in spite of the fact that you are enjoying the peace and quiet and getting much accomplished.

(6)   Rock the child but do not rock him to sleep. Always put
      him in the crib before he is asleep.

I believe in a scheduled life, but I will share a story from my life
when I made a ridiculous schedule for our first infant. My husband
had just been hired to teach at the University of Tennessee, and we
had moved to our house in the country with our four-month-old
daughter Kelly. We knew no one, and I was invited to a faculty wives'
luncheon that my husband wanted me to attend. "Who will take
care of Kelly?" I wondered. I decided to ask my brother David to
watch her since he was a student at the University of Tennessee at
the time and was living in a rented house near the campus. Did I do
the sensible thing—get ready, drive the 20 miles to David's house,
feed Kelly, put her down for her nap, and let her sleep until I returned
two hours later? NO! I was determined to follow my schedule.

I dressed myself, loaded the baby bathtub, feeding dish and food,
a change of clothes, towels, soap, lotion, and probably some other
items I have now forgotten. By the time this was accomplished, I was
running late, Kelly was upset and crying, making the 30-minute drive
to Knoxville anything but pleasant. I never will forget my brother's
face as I handed him my screaming daughter and then made three
trips to carry the supplies into his house. (Could this be the reason
why my brother married but never had any children?) Kelly was over-
tired and upset, but I followed my schedule. Two hours later when I
returned, she was still crying and my brother looked as if he had
experienced a preview of the tribulation period. I learned that sched-
ules are important but can be carried to the point of the ridiculous!

   4.   Provide activities so the infant is not bored. An infant has
a short attention span so the activities will need to be changed often.
You can buy toys or you can use the following:
   • plastic measuring spoons
   • rubber spatulas
   • large beads
   • washable stuffed animals
   • musical toys
   • hand and foot rattles
   • baby seat vibrator
   • baby jumper
   • portable swing

An infant likes an improvised toy as well as a purchased one as long as it can be chewed, makes a noise, and has no small parts that would cause him to choke.

5. Provide books that are washable and durable. Use stiff books that cannot be ripped and cloth books with bright colorful pictures. Check yard sales and collection stores for good book buys. Some of my favorites for infants are listed in Appendix E.

6. Use mobiles or any "homemade items" that move, have lights, or make noise to dangle above the child's head. Many times I would set the infant seat in the center of the kitchen table and tie measuring spoons on a shoelace attached to the light over the kitchen table for the child to hit with his hand.

7. Never turn on the television and use that as a "babysitter" to keep your child occupied. Use of the television may seem like a simple solution, but it fills the child's mind with destructive words, music, and values.

8. Take the child outdoors every day unless he has a fever. The fresh air and sunshine will help eliminate boredom and help the child sleep better. Playpens, swings, and jumpers can be used outdoors to keep the child confined and prevent his eating dirt and sticks. If there are older children playing outdoors, position the playpen near them.

9. Play games with the child. A favorite is "Peek-a-Boo." Some favorite finger rhymes are "Pat-a-Cake," "This Little Piggy," "Open, Shut Them," and "Where Is Thumbkin?" Doing these with the child will prevent him from becoming bored and also builds his attention span. (See these rhymes in Appendix A.)

10. Sing to the child and expose him to the right kind of music. For years when I was in charge of a room full of infants, I found "when one cried, they all cried," which led to bedlam. Singing or playing the right kind of music always helped to calm them. Don't worry if you don't have a wonderful voice because infants won't care. Tape and CD players are portable and inexpensive.

11. Take infants with you on trips to grocery stores, shopping, and parks, etc. Plan this trip with the child's schedule in mind because the child will not enjoy the trip if he is hungry or overly tired. Take along a few play things and train the child that crying will not cause him to be removed from his car seat or infant seat.

Remember that you are in control of the infant instead of his controlling you!

An infant should be left occasionally with a competent person other than a family member. I once had a four-year-old child in nursery school who had never been left with anyone but his family. He was taken to church with his parents from infancy instead of being placed in the church nursery, and he never caused a disturbance during the church service. He was a very pleasant child as long as he remained with a family member, but if he was separated from them, he became extremely upset. His mother realized he would have a problem going to kindergarten, so she placed him in nursery school two mornings a week. The first morning she brought him to school, showed him around the room, and left quickly. As soon as the child realized she was gone, he screamed hysterically and nothing I tried calmed him down. He was not crying to get attention but from panic caused by separation from his mother. He became physically ill and vomited.

I called her and told her I could not teach the 14 other children all morning and take care of him, but I felt we could work together to solve the problem. The nursery school was in the basement of our house, so I had her bring him to school and wait upstairs. (He did not know she was there.) I kept him as long as possible before I asked her to take him home—trying to make the time he stayed longer each day. It took a month before he could stay the full four hours without becoming upset. I believe an infant learns security from the person who cares for him—usually the mother. However, if he becomes older and is never left with anyone but family members, he may develop a phobia or unnatural fear when left with anyone else.

I enjoy being around infants, but if I receive an invitation that says, "No children please," I respect the desire of the hostess or stay home. It is rude and inconsiderate to set your own rules for children which disagree with the hostess, thereby putting the hostess in an awkward position. The exception could be a nursing infant, if you make arrangements with the hostess ahead of time and do not just "show up."

12. Make your infant a part of your service to God. An infant can be trained to adapt to any situation if **you** can. Our family has been involved in the bus ministry since 1973. Keith, our youngest son, rode the bus the first time when he was four days old. Today he is a bus captain, and his children ride the bus weekly. Our children never complained about the bus ride being loud, bumpy, or long because my husband and I did not complain.

Our oldest son Kevin was a bus captain and division leader in Chicago for six years after he was married. His wife Dawn and their children rode the bus with him every week; and each time they had a child, the child was the "bus promotion" for the first Sunday the infant rode.

Not long ago my husband was talking to Stephen Cervantes, our nine-year-old grandson. "What was the most exciting thing you did last week, Stephen?"

"Ride the bus to Sunday school, Grandpa," Stephen replied. Stephen's father, Rafael Cervantes, is a bus captain, and the whole family rides the bus weekly.

13. Never use an infant as an excuse for failing to serve the Lord. When our first child was born, my husband and I were faithfully attending and serving in a church. Shortly after Kelly was born, the pediatrician offered some advice when I took her in for her first checkup. He said, "I do not recommend putting your child in a church nursery for at least six months because of the danger of infection from other children." That seemed like an unusual piece of advice since I had not asked for his opinion; however, I did not say anything to him. As I rode home in my car, I thought, "Why didn't he tell me to keep my child home from the grocery store, shopping mall, or laundromat? There must be as many germs in those places as there are in church."

Then I thought, "My child will not be listening to a sermon in the nursery, but if I stay home for six months, I will be disobeying God and will starve spiritually." *"Not forsaking the assembling of ourselves together, as the manner of some is; but exhorting one another: and so much the more, as ye see the day approaching."* (Hebrews 10:25)

My child did not need the nursery as much as I needed the preaching from the Word of God by a man of God. God blessed that effort, and she was a very healthy child. My desire is to please people and obey; but if the authority disagrees with God, I choose to obey God. *"Servants, be obedient to them that are your masters according to the flesh, with fear and trembling, in singleness of your heart, as unto*

Christ; Not with eyeservice, as menpleasers; but as the servants of Christ, doing the will of God from the heart; With good will doing service, as to the Lord, and not to men." (Ephesians 6:5-7)

If a child has a fever and is too sick to be outside, God understands. However, using a child as an excuse to stop serving God is unwise, in my opinion. God has the power to take the child to Heaven and eliminate our excuse if He would choose to do so. God wants to be first in our lives and does not want a child He gives us to replace Him. *"But seek ye first the kingdom of God, and his righteousness; and all these things shall be added unto you."* (Matthew 6:33)

When taking an infant to the nursery, kiss him, hand him to a worker, and get out of sight. If he cries, give the worker a chance to calm him down. Please do not wait five or ten minutes and look in the door, allowing your child to see you and make him feel you have come to get him. When you leave again, the child must go through the separation from you again—since you represent his security. This will make it more difficult for both the child and nursery worker.

14. Have fun with your infant and treasure every stage of your child's life. As a parent, I can focus on the work involved in rearing an infant such as bathing, feeding, changing diapers, or changing the child's position to prevent boredom, or I can accept this as a necessity in the rearing of a child to love, serve, and live for the Lord. *"And Jesus increased in wisdom and stature, and in favour with God and man."* (Luke 2:52)

If I constantly anticipate the day when the infant will walk, talk, sleep through the night, feed himself, and be "potty trained," I will miss the joy of watching the child change and develop daily. Once these days are past, they can never be recaptured, and the memories God desires for every parent will be lost forever.

Our first granddaughter was named Sara Esther Cervantes. When she was born, her parents lived 70 miles from us on the north side of Chicago. In order to visit, we had to drive through Chicago, which we did every Thursday afternoon. Sometimes as we were creeping along in the traffic on our way to see her, my husband would say, "We must be the world's silliest grandparents to drive all this way to spend two hours with Sara." However, when we got there, it was worth it because Sara was a happy child who loved everyone (however, we always knew she loved us best and looked forward to our visits). Of course, she could not talk and tell us, but there are some things grandparents just know!

Rafael, Sara's father, celebrates his birthday in January, and our daughter asked if they could bring Sara to spend Friday night with us so they could spend the evening together to celebrate Rafael's birthday. We agreed, and Sara arrived on Friday afternoon. Our two youngest children, Krysten and Keith, were still at home. We had a wood fire in the den, and we had all enjoyed playing with Sara. It was getting late, and my schedule said I should iron. I took out the ironing board and clothes, carried them to the den, and got ready to iron. Krysten said, "Mom, what are you doing?"

I felt the question was unnecessary, but I replied, "Preparing to iron."

"Mom," Krysten said, "You can iron some other time. Sara won't be here often. You can iron later."

I am a scheduled person, so I continued in my ironing preparations. Without saying a word, Krysten unplugged the iron, folded up the ironing board, carried the clothes back to the laundry room, led me to the rocking chair, and put Sara in my lap. "Sara needs to be rocked now. You can iron another time," she added. I rocked her, and soon Sara was asleep.

The next day Sara went home, and we anticipated many more delightful visits with our first grandchild. We never dreamed that the following Friday Sara would go to Heaven as a victim of SIDS. I never had another chance to rock her or hold her. How thankful I am that Krysten encouraged me to spend time with Sara instead of following my schedule. It is a memory I will cherish forever.

Angel of Love

A tiny angel came to earth—
For just a little while.
She brought to us so much fun
But first it was "that smile."

With wings of sweetness
Around us she flew;
She brought us life and love
For she was never blue!

Ne'er a stranger did she meet
She loved each and every one.
For our little Sara gave
A smile that outshone the sun.

When in church with Mom and Dad
She'd hum along and sing.
I guess this earth was not the place
For one who made bells ring.

And so one day it was meant to be
Sara took a long flight,
Leaving us alone and sad—
It's been a dark and lonely night

But, methinks, Heaven resounds
With shouts of joy and glee,
That one so lovely; so full of life
Can with our Jesus be!

Grandpa Cowling said of her,
"Sara was never sad,
So it is she'll never know
Sorrow or sin or bad!"

And now we say goodbye, dear one,
Who waits with Jesus above;
A special reunion to be held
With our smiling angel of love.
– Carol Frye Tudor

(Kelly inspired Carol to write this poem by her description of Sara as a little angel on earth.)

Baby Used of God
by Dr. Pete Cowling

On January 8, 1992, my first granddaughter, Sara Esther Cervantes, went to Heaven at eight months of age, a victim of crib death. Nothing in my life ever hurt me more, and it was a thousand days before I did not cry every day.

All grandchildren are special, but Sara had several traits that set her apart from other children I have known. I never heard Sara cry during our weekly visits to see her. Often my wife would say on the trip home, "Sara seems too good to be true." She was genuinely glad to see everyone and never met a stranger. Leaving church every Sunday took a long time because everyone wanted to hold Sara, and she loved the attention.

Psalm 119:75 tells me that God, in His faithfulness, has afflicted me. "*I know, O LORD, that thy judgments are right, and that thou in faithfulness hast afflicted me.*" Psalm 119:71 states that it is good for me to be afflicted. "*It is good for me that I have been afflicted; that I might learn thy statutes.*" While I do not understand God's ways, He has shown me some good lessons as a direct result out of Sara's death.

Our church cemetery just happens to be on my bus route, and God has given me my first bus call every Saturday morning. I go there, lay on Sara's grave, and tell God that I love Him, tell the Devil that I hate him, and that I will try my best to make him sorry he messed with me. Since Sara did not live long enough to send many treasures to Heaven, I resolve to work harder to send some up for her. God has honored this resolution in many ways.

At the time of Sara's death, my wife and I were running three buses on our bus route. We resolved to add a fourth bus for Sara. Sara's mom and dad started that route; Sara's dad is the captain and they are still in charge of that bus ten years later. How many people will go to church because of Sara? God knows, and He is keeping a perfect tally.

Though my sister only knew Sara for a few hours, in that time and through her death, Sara helped resolve a strained relationship between my sister and me.

My mother-in-law, age 80 at the time of Sara's death, decided to take on a new zeal for life and has flown to Chicago, Phoenix, and

Portland to be present at the birth of subsequent great-grandchildren. Several times she has flown to visit her grandchildren and great-grandchildren. That's not bad for a lady who had previously announced that her traveling days were over.

Sara was buried on a bitter cold day in January. The grave-side service was well attended in spite of the weather. A high school senior named Molly Studebaker was there. We had watched Molly grow up in the church and were pleased to see her at the funeral. I thanked Molly for coming and told her that I had waited a long time for her to come to Hyles-Anderson College and was looking forward to having her in my classes. She was caught off guard by this remark but thanked me for my interest. Two years passed before I had Molly in my class, and I mentioned how glad I was to have her there. Later that day she handed me a note. In the note she mentioned that at the time of Sara's funeral, she had no intention of attending Hyles-Anderson College. She decided that if it was that important for me to be concerned about her when I was really hurting, that it would be important to her, too.

I read Molly's note in class the next day. Jennifer Paugh raised her hand and said that Molly Studebaker was the reason why she was attending Hyles-Anderson College. Shannon Weiss raised her hand and gave Jennifer Paugh the credit with getting her to Hyles-Anderson College. Molly worked several years in student recruitment while attending college. How many students will be trained for full-time service because of Sara? God is keeping a perfect tally.

At this writing, Molly taught several years at Hammond Baptist Schools. She married a young man she met at Hyles-Anderson College, who is now teaching at Hammond Baptist Junior High School. Won't it be exciting if he gets to teach Sara's three brothers, Stephen, Sam, and Simon?

If one little girl in eight months can influence so many lives, what should we be able to do? Sara did all of this without saying one word we could understand. But we could all understand her bright eyes, happy smile, and genuine interest in everyone she met. We could all learn from Sara.

Treasures

A wealthy man had traveled far
    O'er many a troubled land,
To find the greatest treasures
    And hold them in his hand.

Yet through all his many travels,
    And in all the countless lands,
He never found the treasures—
    Never touched them with his hands.

The man sat down on a lonely hill,
    For now he was old and wise;
"I'll never find the things I seek!"
    Then a light came in his eyes.

Why these are the dearest treasures!—
    These are the things I prize:
A dewy rose, the sunset's glow,
    The light in a mother's eyes.

– Frieda White Cowling

Toddlers

Toddlers

(Photos on page 51)

Top left:	Rafael and son Stephen enjoy the zoo.
Top center:	Trevor (l) and Trent Cowling covered with kisses
Top right:	Rafael and Stephen
Center top:	Keith Cowling
Center:	Kevin Cowling with Ashley, Trevor and Trent
Bottom left:	Keith
Bottom center:	Grandma playing with Simon and David in a pile of leaves
Bottom right:	Derek and Karissa saying "Cheese!"

Children are constantly learning, and this learning can be Bible-based or based on man's philosophy. The choice is the responsibility of the parents as the Bible directs in Deuteronomy 6:4-7 which says, *"Hear, O Israel: The Lord our God is one Lord: And thou shalt love the Lord thy God with all thine heart, and with all thy soul, and with all thy might. And these words, which I command thee this day, shall be in thine heart: And thou shalt teach them diligently unto thy children, and shalt talk of them when thou sittest in thine house, and when thou walkest by the way, and when thou liest down, and when thou risest up."*

If the Bible command is followed, a child will grow as Jesus grew because He is our example. *"And Jesus increased in wisdom and stature, and in favour with God and man."* (Luke 2:52)

Several years ago, I read an article in the newspaper where parents had written a child psychologist and asked the question: "What should we do with our two year old who refuses to do anything he is told to do? We have been told if we love him, we won't spank him; and when we try having a 'time out,' he won't stay in the chair."

The "expert" incorrectly said that this was normal behavior for a two year old and added that spanking would cause a child to exhibit violent behavior. He then offered this solution: When the child disobeys, place him in a chair and say, "Sit there until I tell you to get up." Quickly take a step back and say, "You can get up." This series of commands should be given before the child gets up. In this rather clever way, you have demonstrated that you have control of the child, yourself, and the situation as well. (And if you believe this, I would like to sell you a used car!)

God has a different view from this child psychologist as given in Proverbs 22:15: *"Foolishness is bound in the heart of a child; but the rod of correction shall drive it far from him."* You may wonder what correction has to do with your having "fun" with your toddler. God's plan from birth is for the parent to be in control of the child instead of the child learning how to control the parent and get his own way. The following story is an illustration.

Grocery Shopping Can Be Fun

When our children were young, we lived in the country at least ten miles from a large grocery store. I took our four children with me to the store, and this outing was something we all enjoyed because of the following rules I set.

1. I prepared a menu weekly. I also made a grocery list to include everything I needed. My list was made in the order the food appeared in the store so I went down every aisle until my shopping was completed.

2. I scheduled my grocery shopping on the same morning each week. We could leave after breakfast, and the children would not be tired and grumpy.

3. I did not plan to do anything else that morning. I did not have to "rush" the children. It is my experience that the more children are hurried and rushed, the slower and more frustrated they become.

4. I taught the older children to walk beside the grocery cart while the younger children rode in the cart. To me, grocery shopping is not fun for me or the other shoppers if the children are running wildly around the store, racing shopping carts, screaming, or begging for items I did not intend to buy.

5. I expected them to behave properly. If they did not behave as I expected them to behave, I parked my cart, walked them back to the van where they were corrected, and then returned to the store. I never remember having to do this, but I would have, and they knew it. In our society now, it might be best to take the child home for private correction. If we are afraid to correct our children, we are deliberately disobeying the scriptural commands of God to correct our children because we love them.

6. I tried to make the shopping fun and an adventure. If they were toddlers and learning the colors, I would hold up a fruit or vegetable and let them name the color. You can let your older children hold them up, making sure they do not bruise the item. You can also teach them the names of fruits and vegetables and how they grow. When children are older, they can be taught how to tell which can of vegetables is the best buy by figuring the price.

7. Sometimes I would let one of the children pick out a box of cereal. I decided before we entered the store if this would be allowed, but the child had to wait until we reached the cereal aisle before he could choose. However, if the child started whining or became impatient before we reached the cereal aisle, he was not allowed to choose. The rule was, "If you whine or cry for something, you lose it." If you are consistent with this rule, your grocery store experience will be enjoyable. Once we reached the cereal aisle, I gave the child as much time as he needed to select the cereal even if we had to walk up and down the aisle several times.

8. I did not buy candy and gum from the rack near the checkout. I told them this ahead of time. However, there is nothing wrong with buying the child candy or gum if you decide to buy it instead of the child coercing you to do so.

9. When the shopping was completed, I provided some treat for them. Many times it was a trip to a small hamburger shop near the grocery store. If I could afford it, I bought them a hamburger. If not, I bought a large order of curly fries and a large cold drink which the five of us shared. If someone complained, he received nothing, and the rest of us enjoyed more. Sometimes I would take them to Baskin-Robbins and let them each pick out a flavor for a one-dip cone.

10. If time remained before lunch and nap time, we went by the park on the way home.

We all enjoyed "Shopping Day." However, I had some friends who would say, "I would rather endure the Tribulation period than take my children to the grocery store." The problem is not the children, but the lack of rules which establishes the authority of the parent that is necessary to make a trip anywhere enjoyable.

It is sad; but almost every time I go to the grocery store, shopping mall, etc., I see children in control of their parents which results in anything but fun. Not long ago, I was in the grocery store checkout lane behind a woman with a two year old and a six year old. The two year old was screaming, and the six year old was angrily demanding a large candy bar from the rack by the checkout counter. The mother was trying to ignore both while she unloaded her groceries, but her frustration and embarrassment was obvious as she felt the disapproving eyes of all within hearing distance upon her. She shoved the two year old down who was attempting to climb out of the cart and selected a small candy bar which she handed to the six year old. "I don't want that," he screamed as he threw it on the floor of the store. The mother then grabbed the large candy bar and threw it on the counter. "If I buy this, you had better shut up," she yelled. Momentarily he did—until he had the large candy bar in his hand. However, by the time they were going out the grocery store door, both children were screaming again. No one could call this fun! This behavior is the fault of the authority and not the child. The immaturity of a child pushes the authority to "give the child his way" because of the child's sin nature. When the authority gives in, the child feels no one loves him enough to correct him. He is insecure due to the absence of parental rules, will not respect an authority who cannot control him, and will probably never learn to control himself.

Schedule

In order for anyone to enjoy being around a toddler, the following should be true:

1. The toddler should obey the authority as God has commanded in Ephesians 6:1. *"Children, obey your parents in the Lord: for this is right."* Making the following excuses for your toddler will cause him to be rebellious as he gets older.

- "He doesn't understand."
- "He's overly tired."
- "He's had too much sugar."

2. Never laugh at a toddler for saying "No!" If he says it exactly the way you do and is adorable as he does it, it is still not appropriate to laugh. ***Any action that achieves positive results will reoccur.*** When he tells you "No!" at age 12, it will no longer be funny.

3. Establish a schedule for your toddler so he will be fun to be around instead of hungry and fussy or overly tired and grumpy. For me having a toddler was fun, but physically exhausting. At 8:30 p.m. every night unless we were at church, I gave them a snack, took them to the bathroom, helped them brush their teeth, gave them a drink, read a short story, prayed with them, kissed them, and told them I loved them. After that, if they got out of bed, whined, or cried for no reason, I spanked them because I needed some time with my husband and away from our children.

4. Make it clear that a toddler must come the first time he is called. If he doesn't, try a ten-inch plastic hot glue stick and apply it to the bottom! It leaves no marks and is a "rod" as God advocates. *"The rod and reproof give wisdom: but a child left to himself bringeth his mother to shame."* (Proverbs 29:15) If you feel this is impossible, you have not invested in your child the time needed to train him.

5. A toddler will obey if you have built a relationship of consistency with him. He must realize the punishment is always worse than the pleasure of having his own way. Correcting the child one moment and ignoring his bad behavior the next because you are tired, busy, or distracted always encourages the child to misbehave.

6. Work is "fun" for a toddler. Show him how fun work can be by making a game out of a simple task like making his own bed. For instance, I told him to "drive" the sheets and blankets over the pillow, making sounds like the roar of an engine. Praise him for efforts as long as you know he did his best even though the bed may look rumpled and not meet your expectations.

At this age, it is much easier to do everything for him; but he will miss the fun of doing any number of jobs and he will enjoy the praise he receives. It may not be so much "fun" to take the time to teach him now, but in five to ten years, it will be "fun" to have a child who works without being told to do so. *"The way of the slothful man is as an hedge of thorns: but the way of the righteous is made plain."* (Proverbs 15:19)

7. Teach a toddler that it is fun to pick up his own toys. Have baskets or tubs or bins for them so he can easily pick up the toys. Pick up toys several times a day and praise him for his hard work. When my children were little, we picked up everything before we went outdoors in the morning, before lunch and nap time, before my husband came home in the late afternoon, and before bedtime at night. It never took long to "clean up."

Clean Up...Clean Up...
Everybody Clean Up!

My husband needed some white shirts so we went to the men's department at Penney's and took along our two and one-half year old grandson, David Cowling. David thought this was a great adventure because he had been promised a trip to the mall play area and food after the shopping. My husband and I were trying to find the correct size and kind of shirt in the disorder created by the big sale that was currently in progress. I heard a small voice behind me singing, "Clean up, clean up, everybody clean up." I turned around to see David with his hands filled with cardboards from shirt packages and plastic covers that had been dropped and left lying on the floor. David said (as he clutched his trash tightly in both hands), "Grandma, this is a big mess, and I'm helping clean it up!"

I led him to a cashier and explained my grandson had a contribution for his trash can. The man looked surprised and then pleased. He praised David for making the store so clean, and David responded to his praise by making three more trips to the trash can in the time it took my husband to select and purchase his shirts.

With children, praise of a job well done is much more effective than becoming frustrated and doing it yourself or yelling at the child because he is not "cleaning up."

8. Other people will enjoy being around your toddler if the same rules apply at home with the family, at home when company is present, or when visiting others. When other people are present, the child will misbehave because he realizes he is not the center of attention. His misbehavior forces people to notice him, and he has brought everyone's attention to himself. When company was present, we told our children they would either behave or go to their room and do what they wanted to do alone. We warned them once and enforced the rule. The child quickly learned it was better to behave and be included.

Time

Time is the most valuable gift you can give your toddler, but it will not become a reality unless planned. Five minutes of giving your toddler your undivided attention will prove your love for them, build the relationship, and make them feel important. If a child does not receive this time, he may whine, cry, or exhibit other undesirable behavior to force you to give him your time. The problem with this is that the child is in control instead of the authority. Instead of scheduling an hour with your toddler, schedule several five-minute periods throughout the day, using some of the following ideas.

Indoor Activities

1. **Crayon and paper.** Children scribble (a design that cannot be identified) at this age, but it helps develop their motor coordination skills. People have said to me, "I would never give crayons to my two year old. He would mark on everything."

To this declaration I respond, "Children will do whatever they are permitted to do by the authority. If you teach them to color only on paper or have their crayons taken away for a time, they will scribble only on paper." If a toddler is allowed to walk around the house holding a crayon, parents should not be surprised when he colors the wall.

When Kelly, our oldest child, was two, she loved to color with crayons on paper. One day I moved the crib to clean the wood floor and noticed two crayon marks the length of the crib on the oak floor board next to the wall. I decided she knew it was wrong to color on the floor, since she crawled under the crib to do it. I got a rag and scouring powder and had her scrub the crayon marks off the floor. That was the last time I remember her coloring on anything but paper.

Paper is not very expensive, but if you have a friend who works in an office or uses a copy machine, you can get paper that is printed on one side only for free—my favorite price! You can encourage the children to use all the paper they want.

2. **Glue objects on paper.** I have made glue with flour and water, but I find this kind unsatisfactory because as soon as it is dry, everything falls off. Elmer's liquid glue and the Elmer's glue bottles are worth the extra cost because items stay on the paper and you can close the top of the bottle. Try letting your child glue the following on paper or cardboard. (You can cut squares from cardboard boxes using a box cutter.)
- small pebbles
- macaroni and all shapes of pasta

- dried beans of all kinds
- small sticks
- leaves gathered in a lunch sack from your yard
- scraps of colored paper or material scraps
- old buttons

At this age, make sure you stress that this is very strong glue and watch the child closely, or he will be so interested in the glue pouring from the bottle that all the glue will be on the paper. Then, if he picks up the paper, glue is everywhere! Show him that only one small dot is needed to glue an item. A child this age will have more fun gluing than admiring the finished product.

3. Tempera paint. The easiest paint to use is liquid tempera which can be purchased in a school supply store. (It is worth it to me to buy it already mixed instead of buying the liquid powder that has to be mixed with water.) Cover the child with a man's short-sleeve shirt with the buttons in the back, and no paint will get on the child's clothes. If you don't have such a shirt, frequent a yard sale or collection store. Your toddler should paint with supervision, and you can use old newspapers to cover the floor and prevent drips. For paper, I have used pieces of newsprint that are left on the end of a roll which the newspaper office gave to me, scrap paper from an office, or the pages from a discarded wallpaper book. Remember where there is a will, there is a way! The toddler can paint with a paintbrush of hair from the school supply store, a cheap narrow paintbrush, or cotton-tipped swabs. I put two or three colors of paint on plastic container lids (such as the lid from a Cool Whip container) or plastic saucers. This way there is no paint to spill and if the colors are mixed together, the whole bottle will not be ruined. (When all colors are mixed together, a muddy brown results.) It is also fun to fold a paper in half, sprinkle several colors of liquid paint on one side, fold, smooth, and open. The design will be printed on each side. The child will need to be instructed and have limits set for him.

4. Play dough. My favorite recipe is homemade, and it will last indefinitely if you do not get it wet or leave it uncovered. (This recipe is included in Appendix C.)

When a toddler plays with play dough, it is best to put him at a child-sized table or on a table outdoors. He should not be allowed to carry it around the house. Be sure to check the bottom of his shoes when he is finished playing because play dough does not make an acceptable addition to carpet. If the toddler has never played with play dough, you take a piece and give him a piece. Start rolling a snake, a ball, etc. It can be rolled with a small rolling pin and shapes cut with cookie cutters.

This play dough can be saved, so when the child finishes playing, separate the colors, and store it in plastic containers.

5. Chalk on paper. Any kind of chalk (white, colored, sidewalk) will do. If the chalk is white, use it on colored paper. Since a toddler will scribble, and chalk smears, use a short-sleeved man's shirt as a cover if you do not want chalk on his clothing. If the chalk picture is sprayed with any cheap hair spray, it will not rub off as easily. A toddler is more interested in making the picture than saving the picture after it is made.

6. Wooden puzzles. These puzzles should contain three to five individual picture pieces per puzzle. To get your toddler started, place the puzzle piece beside the hole and let him slide each piece into its place. If he has a hard time, help him so he will be successful. Praise him when the piece goes into place, and he will love puzzles. Working puzzles will help develop his motor coordination and build his attention span.

7. Baby dolls, strollers, etc. for girls. Put these where the toddlers can reach them and put them away when playing is completed.

8. Cars, trucks, and balls for boys. I prefer putting these in plastic dishpans, buckets on low shelves, or plastic containers with snap lids in closets so the toddler can get them out and pick them up.

9. A pot (kettle), a pan, and a spoon. These items can entertain your toddler while you are cooking. He can learn which cabinets to open and which to leave alone (if you teach him).

10. Colored blocks. These are about the size of shoe boxes and are reinforced so the toddler can stand on the block. A toddler will love to stack up two or three blocks and then knock them down. These blocks, which are wonderful for your toddler, can be purchased at a school supply store.

11. Cardboard boxes. Children like to get inside, sit on them, and slide them across the floor. Any size will do, and when the box is "trashed," it can be discarded.

Outdoor Activities

1. **Sand.** All children have a natural affinity for sand—whether it is in a purchased sand box or a homemade one. If purchased, the sandbox should drain so it is not a "sand puddle" when the children want to play. If it is warm outdoors, children can mix water with sand and mold castles from buckets, tin cans, or sand molds. Add a few cars and trucks, and sand will entertain your toddler often because it is a creative material.

When our children were little, I taught them to ring the back doorbell when they had been playing in the sandbox. I kept a whisk broom by the door, and I brushed them off as well as emptied the boys' pant cuffs. It is possible to let children enjoy sand without their tracking it throughout your house and leaving grit on your floor.

2. **Riding toys.** If there are older children in the family, the toddler can ride a "push" toy and feel a part of the excitement. He can also learn to pedal a tricycle and push a small scooter. (Yard sales are great places to buy inexpensive riding toys.) With our first child, we bought bigger riding toys that she could ride later. However, we found it was frustrating for Kelly to try to ride a toy that was too big for her. We learned it was better to buy the right size, then buy larger ones

Kevin and Kelly

later. Turn off the videos and television and get your children outdoors.

3. **Water.** Children and water go together if the weather is warm. They can learn to play with water without getting soaked if you will set limits.

A. Fill a plastic container with water and let them use small buckets to play in the sand, water plants, or wash riding toys.

B. Give them a small plastic bucket with a handle and an inexpensive paint brush. They can "paint" toys, the side of the house, or the sidewalk with water, leaving no marks.

C. Turn on the sprinkler and let them jump over it or run through it.

D. If it is raining with no lightning, give them an umbrella and let them walk in the rain. You can also let them run in the rain and get wet. Our children loved to run and slide in the puddles in front of our house during or after a rain. If they got muddy, I would wash them off with the hose before they came inside. (I would rather have some extra laundry after the children play in the water then see them bored and dry inside, just watching the rain.)

4. **Bubbles.** Toddlers enjoy bubbles. Take a bottle outdoors and let the children blow and catch the bubbles on a sunny day. Take a flat-bottom cup outdoors on a child-sized table and fill the cup one-fourth full with warm water. Give the toddler a straw and let him show you how he can bubble the water. After he has successfully demonstrated he can blow bubbles in the cup instead of sucking, add a small amount of dishwashing liquid and let him make a "mountain" of bubbles. The sun will make rainbows on the bubbles if the table is near a window on a sunny day.

5. **Playsets, climbing towers, and swings.** Your toddler will love these if they are his size, and they can be bought or made. Our children spent hours playing on a tire swing, a swing set, and a climbing tower. My husband had part of a large oak tree sawed into four circles. One circle was one foot tall, one was

Kelly

two feet tall, one was three feet tall, and one was four feet tall. He tied a large rope with a knot on the bottom around a tree limb. The child climbed to the top of the circles, someone would hand him the rope, and he would swing off. This was their favorite activity—from toddler to grade school age.

6. Science. Introduce science to your toddler by exploring the world around him.

A. If you have anthills outdoors, give the toddler a small bag of granulated sugar or a slice of bread. Drop one grain of sugar near the ants and watch them work to take it into their hole. Do the same with a slice of bread, making the crumbs bigger. If the crumb gets too big for one ant, he will signal for help until they take the crumb away. Remind the child that God wants us to work hard like ants, without having someone to watch us. *"Go to the ant, thou sluggard; consider her ways and be wise: Which having no guide, overseer, or ruler, Provideth her meat in the summer, and gathereth her food in the harvest."* (Proverbs 6:6-8)

B. When it has rained, turn over a rock and try to find an earthworm or a "roly-poly" (a small bug that rolls into a ball when you hold it). The earthworm will feel cool to your hand, but it is harmless.

C. Toddlers can learn to be kind to animals and can accept some responsibility for their care. At this age, probably the favorite animals of our children were dogs, cats, guinea pigs, and rabbits.

7. Books and stories. There is a great difference in the attention span (time a child will sit and listen) of a toddler. If a child is read to from birth, a toddler will have a long attention span. If the toddler has an above-average intelligence, he will not learn effectively until he can sit and listen. Build this attention span by reading colorful books with a few words on a page, books with flaps that can be lifted, and "feel" books. Books that were favorites of our children and grandchildren are *The Very Hungry Caterpillar* by Eric Carle; *Pat the Bunny* by Dorothy Kundhardt; *Hop on Pop, Green Eggs and Ham*, and *The Foot Book* by Dr. Seuss; *Cars and Trucks and Things that Go* by Richard Scarry; and the Spot books by Eric Hill. More books can be found in Appendix E.

8. Songs and finger rhymes. Build a toddler's attention, number concepts, and relationship with you by doing songs and finger rhymes with him. Some of our children's favorites are found in Appendix A and B.

Every summer in August, we visit our son and his family in Arizona and our daughter and her family in Oregon. I plan things that I can do with our grandchildren because I want them to love and remember the fun we have during our visit. When Derek was two, one of his favorites was "Five Little Monkeys." We did it repeatedly, and he loved it. Not long after our visit, I called our daughter and asked to speak to Derek. I heard Krysten say, "Derek, Grandma wants to talk to you."

As he came to the telephone, he said, "Is it the 'Five Little Monkeys' grandmother?"

I am glad to be the "Five Little Monkeys" grandmother instead of a grumpy, complaining, or grouchy grandmother. It doesn't take a lot of planning on our part to be perceived as a "fun" person by children we love.

Some of our children's favorites (and now our grandchildren's favorites) are "Two Little Blackbirds," "I Have a Little Turtle," "Teddy Bear," "Grandma's Glasses," "Ga Goom," "Jack-O-Lantern," "The Wheels on the Bus," "Here Is the Church," and "Here's a Ball." (All of these rhymes are included in Appendix A and Appendix B.)

The first week in October, I put a ceramic pumpkin in my living room window with a candle inside. Every Monday when our grandchildren, who live near me, are at our house, we go into the living room, turn off the lights, light the candle, and sing the "Jack-O-Lantern" song. We usually sing it several times until everyone has an opportunity to blow in the nose and blow out the candle.

When telling any story, it is necessary to lose yourself to keep the toddler's attention. You can do so by changing your voice and letting the children help if there is a line repeated many times, such as found in "The Pancake Man," "The Big Turnip," and "The Bremen Town Musicians" in Appendix F. If you do not enjoy reading or telling a story and cannot keep your own attention, you will never be able to keep the toddler's attention. The best way to tell a story to a child is to tell it aloud in front of a mirror while you look at and listen to yourself. Storytelling is an art that can be learned by practice and can provide hours of fun for the child and the storyteller.

I have many flannel board stories that I told to our children. As they got older, they would act them out and tell them to each other. I put each story in a manila folder with the name of the story on the front. I made a pocket for the manila folder by cutting another folder into three parts on one side only. I glued the pocket into the folder on the bottom right when the folder is opened. Be sure to only glue the bottom and right edges of the pocket being made. The flannel board figures were stored in the pocket I had fabricated, and the story was stapled on the left side of the folder. If you prefer, you could buy a folder with two pockets, putting the story on the left and the figures on the right. See flannel board stories in Appendix F.

To make a flannel board, use a large cardboard box. Cut a rectangle 24 x 72 inches with a box cutter from the side of the box. Bend the 72-inch piece in half and cover both sides with a piece of neutral (white, cream, or tan) felt. Put four holes in the bottom corners of the felt board and use two 14-inch pieces of heavy string to connect the front and 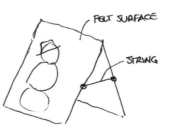 back of the boards. (The string will need to be tied in the front and the back.) This will keep the felt board from collapsing. This felt board will stand up on a table or on the floor when the story is told and will fold when not in use.

To make the felt figures, I cut animals directly from felt by pinning the paper patterns to the felt. If the felt is a light color, you can draw features on the animals with a permanent felt marker. (A washable marker will smear and ruin your felt figures.) If the felt is too dark for the marker to show up, cut out bits of colored felt, such as red for the mouth or yellow for eyes, and glue on with Elmer's glue. Glue eyes and mouth on both sides so you can use animals on either side.

For people I color the paper with a colored marker (any kind will color paper) and use bright, intense colors so they will show up at a distance. Pale colors tend to fade into the felt board. Color the paper figures, glue them on the felt with rubber cement, and block cut or cut out each individual character, cutting the paper and the felt at the same time. Make sure the entire figure is covered with felt or the legs and arms of people and the legs and tails of animals will tear off.

Yes, it does take time to create flannel board stories, but I have some that are "as good as new" after 40 years of use.

The best stories for the flannel graph have a simple plot, a lot of repetition, and a minimum number of characters. It is much better to tell the story than to read it because it is impossible to read the story, put up the flannel board figures, look at your audience, and lose yourself while you are telling the story. Once you master the story, you can tell it with or without the felt board. Make sure you ask a question or have the attention of the child before telling the story.

One of our children's favorite stories was "The Pancake Man," which is an illustration of Proverbs 16:18 which says, *"Pride goeth before destruction, and an haughty spirit before a fall."* Any story that lasts is based on truth. This story and the flannel board templates are included in Appendix F. Certainly, if you do not want to make the flannel board figures, you can tell the story or have the children act it out as you tell it. Other favorites are found in Appendix F. Usually if you tell this story once, the children can act it out, using their own words. Props and costumes can be used but are not necessary. For very young children, the adult can tell the story and let them act it out.

These stories and many like them were told by word of mouth during the Middle Ages, as a way of entertaining adults. Usually there would be a family member or a person in the village who was known as "the storyteller," and he would pride himself in telling the stories the same way each time they were told. The stories were built around a truth or lesson the people shared, and they were a common bond to unite them. The stories also reflected the values the people held as a group.

Trips

Simple trips are a treat for toddlers. Traveling long distances will usually mean the toddler is tired and exhausted before you reach the destination.

1. Trips to parks. In the summer or as long as the weather was pleasant, I took our children to the park one morning a week for three hours. I had lots of play equipment in our yard, but going to the park added variety. I would take a picnic lunch, and by the time we got home, they were tired. Since we had already eaten, they were ready for a nap. There were several parks in our area, and I visited different ones with the children. As you visit the park, you are having "fun" with your children and building memories.

   2. **Trips to pick fruits or vegetables.** When our children were little, we had several "U-pick" places where strawberries, blueberries, raspberries, apples, and vegetables could be picked. We made this a yearly event, and the children loved it. When we planned our trip to pick strawberries, we would get up early; and I would buy doughnuts so we could eat breakfast on the way to the field. Every child would have his own container and could pick, but he could also eat as many berries as he wanted. Keith was our toddler at the time, and he loved strawberries. We would all tease him that the people lost money when he came to the field due to the number of strawberries he ate! We picked for two hours, had our strawberries weighed, then returned to the van for a cold drink I had brought in the cooler and snacks. When we got home, the older children would help me prepare the strawberries for freezing. Keep in mind if you want to freeze strawberries for strawberry shortcake, slice the strawberries into a large freezer bag, add ½ cup sugar, shake, and freeze flat. For jam, smash the strawberries, measure two cups of them, and freeze flat. (A delicious recipe for "Strawberry Freezer Jam" is in Appendix D.)

   We made baskets of fresh strawberries for all our neighbors, and the younger children delivered them while we were processing the strawberries. It was a time we all enjoyed, and I had the strawberries I needed for another year.

   When we picked blueberries, we tied little buckets around our waists with string. Again the children picked and ate their fill. We came home, made baskets for the neighbors and then froze the extra blueberries in the buckets (adding the lids) just as they were picked. I washed them frozen as I used them throughout the year. We often enjoyed blueberry pancakes and blueberry muffins, so blueberry picking became a yearly tradition.

   3. **Seasonal trips.** As I mentioned previously, two of our seasonal trips center around a pumpkin farm and getting the yearly Christmas tree at a Christmas tree farm. We also plan an evening to take baked goods to friends and neighbors and sing Christmas carols. Each one of the grandchildren wears a Santa hat.

Riding the wagon to the pumpkin patch

4. **Museums.** Many museums are too large, too crowded, and have too much information that a toddler cannot understand. However, we are fortunate to have the Chicago Children's Museum, which has a special toddler section where everything is geared to toddlers; and even our one-year-old grandson loved it. The Chicago Museum of Science and Industry also has a "hands-on" section for toddlers. Indianapolis, Indiana, also has a wonderful Children's Museum. Perhaps the area in which you live has a comparable facility. If so, be sure to visit!

Church and Service to God

Your toddler will feel about church the way you do, and if you love serving God, so will he. Our toddlers grew up riding buses to church, and I think they felt everyone did that. If they got tired, they went to sleep, but we always made serving God a "family affair."

We made sure our children were a part of every opportunity the church provided for their age group. If the toddler started to cry on the way to his class, I kissed him and he went into the class crying. We wanted to make sure the toddler realized that crying would not allow him to have his own way. Our philosophy was, "If you cry for it, you lose it." We asked the teacher to let us know if the child was rebellious or created a problem in the class. We praised the child profusely if he received the "Best Boy" or "Best Girl" sticker. Praising a toddler will create a desire within him to do the right thing again. To have your child sit with you in church instead of going to the class provided for him is tearing down the authority over them, and ultimately, tearing down your own authority. It is also causing the child to miss the influence a godly teacher can have on a toddler's life.

Our grandson, David Cowling, had a teacher in Sunday school named "Miss Dot" Barr who wrote to him often. When he would go with his mother to the mailbox, often his mother would say, "David, you have a letter."

Without thinking twice, David would say, "It's from Miss Dot!"

What a wonderful testimony to a faithful Sunday school teacher who took the time to make a difference in a toddler's life. Personally, I don't believe David will ever forget "Miss Dot."

I Go to School, Too!

One summer my 87-year-old mother, Esther White, was visiting her great-grandchildren, Stephen, Sam, and Simon Cervantes. They had enjoyed a wonderful visit—talking, playing games, and buying treats at Wal-Mart. It was August and almost time for school to start at Hammond Baptist Grade School where Stephen would be in the third grade and Sam would be in kindergarten. Taking two dollars from her purse, "Mimi" gave a dollar to each boy, telling them to use it to buy milk for lunch at school.

Determined not to be left out, two-year-old Simon walked up to Mimi and held out his hand for a dollar, too.

"Simon," Mimi said, "I didn't realize you were going to school this year."

"I go to **Sunday** school," was his reply, and Mimi gave him his dollar!

We all laughed at Simon's creative answer, but I realized again how important it is to make every child feel special—whether he goes to **grade** school or **Sunday** school.

Pre-School

Preschool
(Photos on page 71)

(Photos on page 71)

Top left:	Derek and Karissa Vestal hunting for Easter eggs
Top center:	Kelly painting at the easel
Top right:	Kelly playing dress up
Center top:	Derek, Karissa, and Wesley Vestal at a park
Center left:	Derek and Karissa enjoying their jack-o-lantern
Center right:	Petey, David, Stephen, Sam, and Simon (l to r) at Santa's Village
Bottom left:	Kevin and Kelly with their miniature horse
Bottom center:	Kevin and Kelly singing and "playing" the piano
Bottom right:	Kevin creating a masterpiece at the easel

L ife can either be boring or fun regardless of what we are doing. When working with children, this difference is determined by the attitude of the authority because children will reflect this attitude. *"For he that will love life, and see good days, let him refrain his tongue from evil, and his lips that they speak no guile: Let him eschew evil, and do good; let him seek peace, and ensue it."* (1 Peter 3:10, 11)

Someone has said, "Life is a banquet, but most people are starving to death." We wanted our children to see that life involved work, hard times, and disappointments, but to see that God was in control, and we could get through anything God allowed and rejoice. *"And we know that all things work together for good to them that love God, to them who are the called according to his purpose."* (Romans 8:28)

Schedule

I believe God is a God of order and schedule; therefore, our children were taught to have scheduled lives. *"The steps of a good man are ordered by the Lord: and he delighteth in his way."* (Psalm 37:23)

Getting Up in the Morning

We did not make all the children get up at the same time, but we had breakfast at 6:30 a.m. My husband told them they could choose the time they wanted to be called to get up, but by 6:30 a.m. they had to be dressed, have their bed made, and room clean. If this was not done, they would work to do it while the rest of us ate breakfast. We felt this was God's plan because of II Thessalonians 3:10. *"For even when we were with you, this we commended you, that if any would not work, neither should he eat."*

Very rarely did any of our preschool children miss breakfast because they knew my husband did not make idle threats, and "no work meant no food" until the work was done. They also loved to eat. When it was necessary for them to miss breakfast, we did not scream or yell at them and accuse them of being lazy. They did not become angry and whine or cry when the rule was enforced because they knew the rule applied to all. I could probably count the total number of times our children collectively missed a meal during all their years at home on the fingers of my two hands.

When our children decided what time they needed to get up, my husband would call them once. If they did not respond to his call, he threw water on them. This worked very well, and all he had to do was turn on the water and start up the stairs before feet were hitting the floor. My goal was to create a pleasant atmosphere in our home—not one of yelling, confusion, rushing, and chaos.

I have never welcomed the sound of my alarm clock telling me it is time to get up in the morning, but it is necessary. (Even today at this writing, to make sure I get up when the alarm sounds, I put the clock across the room behind the door so I have to get out of bed to turn it off!) When our children were young and still at home, I got up early and made a hot breakfast we would eat together at 6:30 a.m.

After our oldest son Kevin was married, he and Dawn gave us our second grandchild, Ashley. One day when they were visiting our house, Kevin said, "Mom, what is the song you always sang when you cooked breakfast? I want you to teach it to Dawn so she can sing it to Ashley in the morning."

I do not think of myself as a singer (unless I am leading bus songs), and I did not remember greeting every morning with a song like, "Oh, What a Beautiful Morning." I was mystified until Kevin said, "It was a song about cereal, Mom. You sang it all the time."

A light dawned on me, and I remembered a commercial that went like this:

Cream of Wheat is so good to eat that we have it every day.
We sing this song; it will make us strong and make us shout
    "Hooray!"
It's good for growing babies and grownups too-to eat
For all your family breakfasts, you can't beat Cream of Wheat!

"That's it, Mom! That's it!" Kevin exclaimed.

The mystery of the morning song was solved. I am sure singing a "Cream of Wheat" commercial in the morning will not make a lasting impression for good and God. However, I would prefer Kevin remembering a song (any song) than a mother who screamed and yelled and made life miserable for everyone. *"Make a joyful noise unto the LORD all ye lands. Serve the LORD with gladness: come before his presence with singing."* (Psalm 11:1, 2)

This takes work and planning, but it is worth the effort. When children are preschool age, it seems as if they will always be there. However, just the opposite is true. A blink of the eyes and they are now grown and gone—at least that is how it seems to me.

Going to Bed at Night

I enjoyed every stage of development as our four children grew to maturity, but when it was bedtime I was ready for a "breather." Unless we were at a church activity, 8:30 p.m. was the established time for bed each night. I established a ritual for them as follows:

1. Bathe. They bathed daily, but boys and girls did not bathe together. Bath time can be "fun" with bubble bath, bath toys that are stored with suction cups on the wall above the tub in a net, bath crayons, boats, and a variety of other items. Children do not "rush well" so allow time for them to enjoy the bath. When it was time for the children to leave the tub, my daughter Krysten always told her children to "tell the water goodbye," and one child pulled the plug. They should put away their dirty clothes, rub on powder, spray, and "smell good" (lotion).

2. Eat a snack. After the bath, the children always had a snack before going to bed. We would sit at the kitchen table and talk.

3. Brush teeth.

4. Have a drink of water.

5. Use the bathroom.

6. Read a book to the child.

7. Pray.

8. Kiss him and say, "I love you."

This whole procedure should take 30 to 45 minutes. However, once this was completed, I told the children I loved them and would see them in the morning. They did not get out of bed or whine and cry for attention in their beds. I always told them they could stay awake all night as long as I didn't see them or hear them.

Work

Play is a child's work, and I quickly found that "a busy child was a happy child." At the preschool age, it takes longer to teach a child to work than to do the job yourself. However, as the child gets older it will be a help to you as well as the child if your child knows how to work the Bible way. "*Go to the ant, thou sluggard; consider her ways and be wise: Which having no guide, overseer, or ruler, Provideth her meat in the summer, and gathereth her food in the harvest.*" (Proverbs 6:6-8)

God is telling us a child should work hard to the best of his ability without being constantly reminded, watched, and checked upon. If the child doesn't do the job satisfactorily in the time allotted, he should work while others are eating to complete the job. "*For even when we were with you, this we commanded you, that if any would not work, neither should he eat.*" (II Thessalonians 3:10)

Kelly vacuums with her baby and wears high heels!

My husband and I had the following guidelines to encourage our preschool children to work:

1. Each preschool child was given special jobs. These jobs include making their bed, picking up toys, hanging up clothes, feeding the animals, or drying dishes. The child was given a time limit to do the job. For example, they had to make their bed and have their room clean before breakfast at 6:30 a.m. If I told them to pick up toys, I would set the timer to see if they could get the job done before the timer sounded.

2. **I tried to make the work fun by helping them and singing as we worked together.** I didn't want to appear to be a "drill sergeant" standing over them as they worked, but I also wanted them to work just as well when I wasn't helping them. Jesus is always watching; we are working to please Him. Colossians 3:23, "*And whatsoever ye do, do it heartily, as to the Lord, and not unto men.*"

3. **I planned so the work would be easy for them to do.** I put toys in buckets on low shelves they could reach, put a double rod in the closet so they could hang up their own clothes, put book shelves low so they could reach books, and installed low hooks on the wall so they could hang up their own coats.

4. **I never assumed the child could do the job without taking the time to teach him, and re-teach him, and re-teach him until I knew he could do the job easily.** In teaching a preschool child to put on his jacket, coat, or sweater, I had the child put his jacket on the floor in front of him with the back side of the jacket against the floor and the collar of the jacket by his feet. He would bend down, reach over the collar, put his arms into the jacket sleeves, and flip the jacket over his head. At times, he would put the collar by his legs and he would have the coat on upside down. We practiced until each child from two and a half years old and older could put on his own coat. Sometimes I had to help start the zipper, but they soon learned to manipulate that as well.

5. **I praised the child liberally when he did his best.** I knew praise creates within the child a desire to do the job again. When they had worked hard, I praised them to others and I didn't mind if they heard it. Any action that achieves positive results will reoccur.

6. **If the child made a mistake in doing the job, I didn't punish him.** By the time our oldest daughter Kelly was five, she was setting the table for dinner each day. I would set the plates and glasses on the kitchen table and she could reach the silverware and the napkins. One afternoon I was getting the plates for her when one of the

children called me from another part of the house. I quickly set the dinner plates on the kitchen counter and went to solve the problem. I had not been gone long when I heard the sound of breaking glass. Kelly had tried to carry the dishes to the table, had dropped them, and a pile of glass lay on the floor instead of my dinner plates. Kelly was standing beside the glass with a horrified look on her face. I hugged her and said, "That's okay, honey; accidents happen." If she had intentionally broken the plates or if I had told her to leave them on the counter and she had disobeyed, I would have punished her. Now if you feel I was a perfect mother and never lost my temper, you're wrong. However, I did try to learn from my mistakes and learn to correct God's way because Proverbs 15:1 says, *"A soft answer turneth away wrath: but grievous words stir up anger."* Any angry authority produces an angry child.

   7. **When our preschool children did a job the wrong way, I didn't make them feel like a failure and do the job for them.** I wanted them to realize they had simply discovered one way that would not work.

   From the time Kelly was two, we cleaned the bathroom together. When she was five, she decided she wanted to clean the bathroom by herself and "surprise me." I was somewhat reluctant, but I never wanted to discourage a child from working. I got out the cleaning supplies and explained that the scouring powder was for the tub, commode, and sink, the spray was for the mirror over the sink, and the bar soap was for the floor. She was confident she understood everything perfectly and said, "Don't open the door until I'm finished."

   I waited 15 minutes and went to check on her. She said, "Don't come in yet." I waited five minutes more and she said, "I'm not finished. Don't come in."

   I waited another five minutes and asked if I could come in. This time a trembling voice said, "No." I opened the door and was "surprised." At least two inches of water covered the floor along with the entire can of white scouring powder that had turned blue. The bathtub was covered with scouring powder, and it looked as if she had been shaking the can, watching the powder fly. The mirror had been cleaned with a rag covered with scouring powder and nothing could be seen in it. Kelly was standing in the water holding a dripping rag and looking scared.

I wanted to be angry, but I realized most of the blame for the mess was mine since I allowed her to clean alone. It took us about two hours to clean the bathroom as we mopped up the wet floor with towels. I did not praise Kelly for making a mess, but for wanting to do something difficult. However, after that we continued to clean together. When Kelly was in the second grade, she had become so proficient in cleaning bathrooms that our neighbor across the street hired her every week to clean her bathroom. One mistake does not mean the child cannot learn to do a job with patience and teaching.

8. Praise the child for wanting to do a difficult job. Preschool children who are encouraged to work usually want to do a job they do not do well as opposed to one they have mastered. For example, when a child has learned to dry the dishes, he would prefer to wash them. I let them try because I want to encourage work even though the dishes were washed in cool water, and sometimes a grease film was left on the dishes.

Time

I made many mistakes as a parent, but I have no regrets concerning the time I spent with our children. I wanted the children to see that life was "fun" whether we were working or playing. Every day I scheduled time to sing, read, tell stories, play games, and have fun indoors or outdoors. I have listed and explained many of these in the next section. However, in addition to spending time with all the children, I wanted to have a "special time" with each individual child on a weekly basis. If you have only one child, this section would not apply but it requires planning with four or more. To accomplish this goal, I gave each child a morning and if he wanted a "special time" between 6:00 a.m. and 6:15 a.m., he would need to get up early when I woke him. This was never a requirement, but a choice. Usually they always chose to get up. I would make hot chocolate, and we might talk, read a book, or play a game. I know I enjoyed this time, and I feel my children did as well. Morning is not the only time this can be done; this time worked best for me because there were no interruptions.

I did not spend all day programming the lives of our children, but when they said, "Mommy, what can I do?" I could always think of something to tell them. (Many of these ideas are included in the appendixes.)

Church

My husband and I enjoyed church, and we wanted our children to feel the same way. We set the following guidelines:

1. **The children would participate in every activity provided for their age group, and we supported the program.** They went to Sunday school, Sunday night Bible lesson, and choir. If we had a negative feeling about any of these areas, we did not discuss them in front of our children.

2. **We praised the teachers in these classes.** We encouraged our children to write notes of appreciation to them.

3. **We always looked for the positive.** If one of our children had a Sunday school teacher who visited them and another child had a teacher who never visited them, we found something positive to say about both teachers.

4. **We made sure our children knew we expected obedience to all authority placed over them at church.** When the authority made a mistake, we took the side of the authority because we realized that failure to do so would tear down our own authority in the eyes of our children.

5. **We rode the church bus as a family.** We did not complain about the bus ride being too long, the children too noisy, or the temperature on the bus too hot or too cold. If we refuse to complain, our children will follow our example. *"And when the people complained, it displeased the LORD: and the LORD heard it; and his anger was kindled; and the fire of the LORD burnt among them, and consumed them that were in the uttermost parts of the camp."* (Numbers 11:1)

I taught the children that when they complained, it was as though they were wearing a sign that said, "I am not right with God."

6. **At age four when the children left the nursery to sit in "big church," we expected them to sit and listen to the preacher.** They did not talk to one another, draw pictures, or squirm around. They sat next to an adult instead of each other. We praised them when they followed these guidelines.

7. **Our children sat with us instead of with their friends because we wanted to make sure they were a part of the service.** If your children are on the pew with you, you know they are not in the bathroom, hallway, and around the rebels you can find in both of these places. (They still sit with us now that they are married and

have children of their own. I guess habits are hard to break.)

8. They were not allowed to run wildly around the church before the service started because we have always gotten to church early. They were allowed to take a book to read before, but not during, the service. They did not go to the platform to test the microphones or chase one another up and down the aisles. They did not sell items at church.

9. We took them to the bathroom before the service started. They were not allowed to leave the service to go to the bathroom unless they were vomiting or experiencing some type of an emergency. If they chose not to go to the bathroom before the service, they would wait until the service was over.

10. If an activity conflicted with church, we went to church. *"But seek ye first the kingdom of God, and his righteousness; and all these things shall be added unto you."* (Matthew 6:33)

Activities for Preschool Children

I have used all these activities with children. They require some extra effort, but "a busy child is a happy child," and I found the extra effort worthwhile. If an activity is messy, cover an area with old newspapers and then throw them away when finished.

Art Activities

• **Blow bubbles outdoors.** Use straws, cups, or other plastic containers with warm water and a small amount of dishwashing soap. If blowing bubbles indoors, cover a table with an old towel and let the children blow bubbles using a straw. If bubbles spill, it will be absorbed by the towel. (Let younger children show you how to blow bubbles with water before you add the soap so they will not suck soap through the straw.)

• **Drop colored yarn into liquid starch or white glue thinned with water.** Make a picture by arranging yarn on heavy paper or cardboard. The pages of an outdated wallpaper book work well and are free.

• **Make a collage picture.** Let children glue pasta, ribbons, seeds, scraps of ribbon, etc. on paper with Elmer's glue. You can make glue with flour and water, but I have found that the items fall off the paper as soon as the glue dries. Elmer's glue is worth the added cost.

You can use only one or several of the following materials to let children make pictures.

When Kelly was four years of age, she made a self-portrait, using collage materials. She chose to use only red buttons on her stick figure. I wrote her thoughts after her picture was completed. The time spent writing on the picture makes a child feel more important and teaches the child to be more meticulous and more observant.

Collage Materials

fur scraps	burlap sacking
sand paper	seeds
excelsior	pipe cleaners
leather	corrugated paper
velvet	twigs
feathers	acorns
felt	egg carton dividers
corduroy	pebbles
cotton	shells

Patterned Materials

wallpaper samples
catalogues
magazines
printed gift-wrapping papers
printed percales or other fabrics
greeting cards

Transparent and Semi-Transparent Materials

net fruit sacks	lace
thin tissue paper	paper lace doilies
onion sacks	organdy
metal screening	veiling
nylon net	
colored cellophane	

Collage picture by Kelly (age 4)
She chose to use red buttons on her picture.

"It had been raining all day; and in the afternoon, the sun came out. When her brother was asleep, she went out to play in the beautiful sunshine."

Shapes

buttons
cork
rubber bands
drinking straws
bottle caps
tooth picks
wooden applicators
styrofoam (florist foam)
beads
spools

tongue depressors
fluted candy cups
uncooked macaroni
uncooked spaghetti
cupcake cups
gummed stickers
scrap sponge
heavy cotton rug yarn
wood chips
string

Sparkling or Shiny Materials

sequins
paper from greeting cards
glitter*
Christmas tinsel
mica snow
tin foil
aluminum foil
ribbon
Christmas wrapping paper
metallic paper

Scattering Materials

sand
twigs
sawdust
salt
tiny pebbles
rice
shavings

*Have children make a design with glue, shake on glitter, then dump the excess on a cake pan to keep glitter off the floor, and let the picture dry.

Glue

I have found that the best glue is Elmer's School glue because it keeps the items on the paper. Stress to the child that Elmer's is very strong glue, or the child will become enchanted at seeing the glue pour out on the paper creating a "glue lake" which makes a big mess when the child tries to pick it up. Also, stress to the child that "a dot will do when using glue."

4. **Make a sewing card for the children.** Punch simple geometric shapes such as triangles, squares, or rectangles into a shirt or hosiery cardboard using a hole punch. I let the children "sew" with

colored yarn. Keep the yarn from "coming apart" when sewing by planning ahead and dipping the end of the yarn in Elmer's glue the day before and letting it dry on waxed paper. If you fail to do this, stiffen the end of the yarn by putting a piece of Scotch tape around it. Put a large knot in the end of the yarn, so it will not pull through the first hole in the cardboard.

5. **Give the child a lunch sack and have him gather small rocks.** Add liquid starch or white glue to liquid or powdered tempera paint and paint rocks on old newspaper. Put a man's short-sleeved shirt on the child with the buttons on the back to make a cover for the child's clothes, but plan to use this shirt for painting only. Dry rocks on waxed paper for several hours or overnight. The next day children can make "Pet Rocks" by gluing buttons or other items from the collage box on the painted rock.

6. **Make cooked pasta and spaghetti pictures.** Cook pasta or spaghetti, drain but do not rinse, and while warm, let the children make pictures or designs on cardboard or paper. The starch from the pasta will cause it to stick to the paper if you don't rinse the pasta. If you are using natural pasta, the children can glue it on colored paper and dry flat. If you choose to use colored pasta, use white paper or cardboard. While warm, put pasta on a glass plate and let the children create their own designs.

7. **Use washable magic markers instead of crayons to draw pictures.** Crayons are still fun for all ages, but I have found markers inspire children to create detailed pictures. When using markers, stress to the child the importance of replacing each marker cap so the marker is not ruined. The marker tip should not be tapped on the picture as a felt tip will disappear, and the marker is useless. (The use of crayons is discussed in the previous section.) Coloring and drawing are wonderful ways to help a child develop his small motor skills.

8. **Let child make a book on the seasons, his family, etc.** Make one page a day. It could take up to three months for the books to be completed, but I found the children were very proud of these books they worked so hard to complete. After the books were completed, I bound them by punching two holes on one side of the book and tied yarn or string through the holes. I found that brads tended to pull through, and the book fell apart. Silver rings could also be used. Stapled books tend to pull apart. With the availability of lami-

nation, you may want to preserve your children's creations.

The following are ideas I included in some of the books our children made. Do not limit yourself to using only these categories. These books can be made in groups or individually. It doesn't matter how long it takes, but clip all the child's pictures together and save until ready to assemble. It has been over 30 years, and I still have many of these books our children made. They are priceless, and I wish I had saved more of them.

A Story About Me Book

The following are categories I included in this particular book.

My House. Let the child draw a picture of his house and put it in his book whether or not it looks like his house.

My Family. Have the child draw his family, and you write the names of the family members by the pictures.

My Address. When the child could tell me his address and telephone number, I wrote it on this page for him if he could not write.

My Hands. Let the child dip his right hand in red tempera and print this on the paper. Have the child dip his left hand in green and print on the paper. Write "right hand" and "left hand" below the prints. I found if I always used red for right and green for the left, it was easier for the child to distinguish the right from the left. (Put a red rubber band around his right wrist and ask him which is right.)

My Feet. Do the same as "my hands" but with feet instead. Have a pan of water nearby to wash feet with a newspaper underneath. You can do this particular page outdoors. (*The picture to the right is white tempera on blue construction paper. Kevin made these when he was four.*)

Myself. Let the child draw a picture of himself by letting him lie on the floor on white paper, such as a tablecloth cover or butcher paper. Measure his height, weigh him, and put these facts in the picture. He can draw on his features and his clothing.

My Friends. Let the child tell you about his friends and print his words on a paper. He can draw a picture of these friends.

My Parents. Let the child tell you what his parents do and you write what he tells you on his paper. When our daughter Kelly was four, I asked her about her parents. She said, "I have a daddy who teaches at the University of Tennessee. I have a mother. She washes dishes."

What I Like to Eat. This can be cut from magazines or drawn.

What I Like to Do. The child should draw what he likes. When Kelly was age four, she drew a picture of the five of us at the grocery store on our weekly trip.

Shapes, Colors, Numbers, Alphabet, or Letters Books

Each of the following categories represented a page in this book.

A. Cut shapes out of pieces of wood and let children trace around them. When the child can tell you the names of the shapes, you print them in the center of each shape.

B. Let the child color red, blue, yellow, orange, green, and purple on a page to see if he knows the colors. You can also let the child cut the colors from magazines.

C. Let the child count as high as he can without missing a number and write numbers on his paper.

D. When a child can put the alphabet letters in order, write "I know my alphabet," and let the child print his name.

The Story of Creation Book

Make a page for each day of creation.

1. Light and dark. Let the child glue white on one half side and black on the other half side of the paper.
2. Day and night. Let child glue sun and moon on paper.
3. Waters and earth. Have blue paper for water and brown for earth.
4. Seeds. Let child glue seeds on brown paper.
5. Fish. Draw or glue fish on blue paper and put plastic wrap over like water.
6. Animals. Let child draw animals or cut them out.
7. People. Have child draw his family.

Seasons Book

For the "Seasons" books I made with our children, I liked to add the following rhyme in the front of the book:

> Sing a song of seasons
> Something bright in all
> Flowers in the summer
> Fires in the fall.

A. Spring. Have the child draw a tree and glue colored art tissue on the page for flowers.

B. Summer. Have the child draw picture of something he likes to do in summer.

C. Fall. Let the children draw a picture of a fall tree using orange, yellow, or red crayons or use these colors of tempera paint.

D. Winter. Let the child make a tree of twigs to show a tree without leaves.

9. **After a field trip or walk outdoors, let each child draw a picture of what he liked best.** Ask him to tell you about the picture and print what he says on the picture. Encouraging a preschool child to do this will help to make him more observant. A child feels important when you ask him to tell you about his picture and print exactly what he says. Sometimes a 11x17 size of paper is better.

10. **Let the children make "rubbings" of items in the room.** Place a paper over a pair of scissors, a brick wall, etc. Rub over the item with a pencil or crayon, and the item will be printed on the paper. Leaves work well, but some items may need to be taped down so they don't move as the child is trying to make "rubbings." Take a field trip to a cemetery to make rubbings from some of the tombstones.

11. **Make play dough.** My favorite recipe is included in Appendix C. All ages love play dough—even the college students I teach!

12. **Make mud dough.** This recipe is also included in

Play dough entertains Ashley, Trent, Trevor, and Trey Cowling

Appendix C. Keep in mind that mud dough cannot be saved.

13. Make soap fingerpaint. The recipe is included in Appendix C. Shaving cream can be used instead of soap. Color may be added in a bowl or as the children paint.

Cover the child with a man's short-sleeve shirt that is buttoned down the back of the child. Use a baking sheet with edges all around the baking sheet. Put a spoon of foam on the baking sheet and let the child make designs with his hands. Use only white until the child is familiar with finger painting. Print the design a child makes on a piece of colored paper. When child has mastered this, add some colored tempera and let the child make colored designs. Print on white paper by laying the paper on top of the design which will pick up the design. The want-ad section of the newspaper is free and works as well as a page from a wallpaper book. If you want to teach children how colors are mixed, use the following formulas:

- Red + Blue = Purple
- Red + Yellow = Orange
- Blue + Yellow = Green

Creating a new color seems like "magic" to a child. Use a child-size table. Have a dish pan nearby so the child can easily wash the paint off his hands. Print the child's design by laying the paper in the center of the baking sheet and picking it up. Print the child's name on every paper he makes and hang on a line with clothes pins or place on a wooden clothes rack to dry.

14. Make pudding fingerpaint. Make any kind of pudding by following the package directions. Cover the child with a man's shirt for an apron, put a spoonful of prepared pudding on the baking sheet, and let the child make a design. When he has finished the design, print on paper, making sure you print the child's name on his art work.

15. Make soap bubbles. Mix 2 tablespoons liquid dish soap such as Dawn or Joy with 1 cup of warm water. Use a circle bubble blower or put a flat-bottomed cup one-fourth full of soap mixture on an old towel to absorb drips or spills. Tell the child to make a mountain of bubbles using a straw. Remember to make sure the child knows to blow rather than suck soap into his mouth by making him bubble the water before the soap is added. If bubbles are blown in the sun, you will see rainbows in the bubbles. (I have included another bubble recipe called "Super Bubbles" in Appendix C.)

Bubbles and children go together. On a warm day, take a bottle of bubbles outdoors, blow bubbles, and let the children chase and break them.

16. Work puzzles. If a child learns to do two- or three-piece puzzles as a toddler, he will be ready for wooden five- to ten-piece puzzles as a three year old. By the time he is five, he can complete 60- to 100-piece cardboard puzzles. Puzzles help build a child's attention span and help them learn to finish what they start. Puzzles can be purchased at second-hand stores or yard sales, but I have learned to count the pieces unless the puzzle has not been opened. I hate working puzzles with missing pieces, so if we work a puzzle and find pieces are missing, we throw it away.

The following rules helped our children learn to work puzzles:

• Work one puzzle at a time and never dump out several puzzles at once. Doing this makes it impossible for the child to work the puzzle, and he wants to quit before the puzzle is finished.

• Encourage the child to work a puzzle that he is able to finish.

• Stress that the child finish the puzzle if he begins it—even if you have to help him when he gets "stuck." Help the child select a puzzle he is able to finish so he will not become frustrated when the puzzle is too difficult for him.

• Praise the child when he finishes the puzzle.

• Reinforce puzzle boxes so it is difficult to loose puzzle pieces. Use clear tape on corners of the puzzle box or cut out the picture of puzzle and put the puzzle pieces in a sturdy plastic storage bag along with the picture and seal the bags.

• Use a marker or crayon to color the back of each puzzle piece that goes to a specific puzzle or write then number "1" on all the pieces to a particular puzzle. On the next puzzle, number all the pieces on the back with a "2" and so on until all the pieces are numbered in each puzzle. Using this method will make it easy to know where a stray puzzle piece goes.

Music

1. Invite someone to play an instrument for your children. Tell them God loves music because the longest book in the Bible,

Psalms, is a song book. Some instruments are played by blowing and some by plucking strings. *"Make a joyful noise unto the LORD, all ye lands."* (Psalm 100:1)

2. **Use a tape recorder to let the children hear their individual voices as well as the sound of the whole group.** Ask for each child to give his name, his favorite thing to do, or let the group sing a song. Our children made tapes to mail to their grandparents, often with every child speaking. (My only regret is that we taped over these and no longer can hear them.) Our children would read books on the tape recorder and ring a bell when the page was to be turned. They preached sermons and spent hours making tapes.

3. **Have child put his hand on his throat to feel the vibration as he makes a sound.** Discuss with the child that we are *"fearfully and wonderfully"* made by God.

4. **Hum a song that is familiar to the children or play it on an instrument and let them guess what it is.** My children and I spent hours doing this. I would play one note at a time of a hymn or children's song until they were able to guess the song or hymn.

5. **Clap out a child's name in rhythm.** Example: "Ash-ley Cow-ling"—"clap-clap-clap-clap" or "Ste-phen Cer-van-tes"— "clap-clap-clap-clap-clap."

6. **Teach a new song or use a new tape.** Music is an important part of a child's education. Rhythm and singing play an important part in preparing a child to learn to read, possibly more than learning the alphabet. Research studies have shown for years that a child's coordination skills have more to do with his reading development than his memorization of the alphabet letters, even though knowing the letters is important.

Children have a natural love for singing and have not reached the stage where they are self-conscious. If tension is present because of the necessary correction of a child or children, or it has been a trying day, a few songs will lift the spirit. A merry heart enjoys singing. *"A merry heart doeth good like a medicine: but a broken spirit drieth the bones."* (Proverbs 17:22)

Learning the Alphabet

Make a set of 3- to 4-inch tall alphabet letters and teach "The Alphabet Song." Make the letters from colored poster board, using as many colors as possible so the child can be encouraged to name the color if they do not know the letter. (You can use a computer to print out the large letters to trace.) Put the letters in a circle on the floor, and let the children march around them singing "The Alphabet Song."

You can also use "The Alphabet Song" to teach the child his colors by selecting several colored letters and putting them in the lunch sack. Let the child draw out one letter, tell you the color, or both the color and the letter.

Variations of the song for older children to enjoy are included in Appendix B. Use a manila folder with a pocket to store "The Alphabet Song," putting the words of the song on the left side of the folder and a lunch sack to hold the alphabet letters in the right side pocket.

Finger Puppets

Songs can be sung with or without finger puppets, but children enjoy the variety and interest when they are used. They are best stored in a manila folder with four envelopes glued inside it with the envelope flaps out to keep the finger puppets in the envelopes. Put the words to the song on the outside of the envelope.

To make a finger puppet, fold a triangle into a circle and glue the finger puppet to the tip of the triangle. Flatten each finger puppet to make it fit in envelope. Patterns and four finger puppet songs, "Five Green Speckled Frogs," "Five in the Bed," "Five Little Ducks," and "One Elephant," are included in Appendix C and samples are included on page 359.

Rhythm Instruments

Children love noise and rhythm instruments that allow them to be noisy—within the limits you set for them. These instruments may be bought or made, and the child will not care which. Stress that the instrument should not be played continually, but you should keep time with the music. The children can march as they play an instrument. Tell a story and remind the children you will select the best five listeners to play an instrument when you sing a song after the story. A good song to use with rhythm instruments is "Band of Angels," which is included in Appendix B.

How to Make
Rhythm Instruments for Children

The following are some of the rhythm instruments I have made. These instruments may be purchased at a school supply store; but in my opinion, children do not care if the instrument is made or purchased as long as it makes a sound.

* **Rattler**

Materials needed: a round salt carton, tape, dowel rod, some dry beans, rice, or pebbles

Pour some beans into the spout of a salt carton. Close the spout and seal it with tape. Make a small hole in the center of each end of the salt carton. Push a dowel stick that is as long as two salt cartons through both holes. Put tape at the places where the stick goes through to hold it tightly. Add tassel if desired.

* **Tom-Tom**

Materials needed: a large, round cereal carton, such as an oatmeal container; string; something to punch holes; clothes pins

Remove the lid from a round cereal carton. Just below the open end, punch a hole in the side of the carton. Punch another hole directly opposite the first. Run a string through the holes and tie the ends. You can now hang the box around your neck. Put the lid back on the carton. Decorate any way you wish. Use clothes pins or dowel sticks about six inches long for drumsticks.

* **Sandpaper Blocks**

Materials needed: two easy-to-hold building blocks, scissors, coarse sandpaper, staple gun, or wood glue (It is best to use a soft pine block about three inches wide, ¾ inches thick and 4½ inches long.)

Cut two pieces of sandpaper, each a little larger than the side of the block. Use a glue gun, Elmer's glue, or a staple gun to attach the pieces of sandpaper to the blocks.

* **Tambourines**

Materials needed: 2 five-inch circles of ½-inch plywood or a pie plate, roofing caps, nails

Drive a nail through one piece of plywood, 3 roofing caps and into a second piece of plywood. Shellac or paint. Two tin pie plates can also be used by cutting a 3-inch piece of coat hanger, put roofing caps on the coat hanger, put one end of coat hanger through each plate and fasten with duct tape.

- **Jingle Sticks**

  Materials needed: roofing caps, lids or smooth ends of small cans, and 8-inch dowel stick

  Secure the caps to the dowel with them hanging loosely but nailed securely. Jingle sticks can also be made by using sleigh bells. These should be tied securely or held by straps and tacks to a stick.
- **Rhythm Sticks**

  Materials needed: dowel sticks, latex paint or shellac

  Rhythm sticks may be made of dowels of various thickness; but they should be made in matching pairs. Saw dowels into 12-inch lengths. Sand the ends. Paint with latex paint or shellac. Children strike two sticks together.
- **Bells**

  Materials needed: 4 or more jingle bells, elastic, thread

  Cut a piece of elastic 1 inch longer than the distance around four fingers of the hand held together. Overlap the ends and sew the elastic into a loop that will fit over the four fingers. Sew bells on one side of the loop. A child can put the bells over his fingers and shake.
- **Shakers**

  Materials needed: cardboard tube, newspaper, gummed tape, latex paint, rice, split peas, beans, or small pebbles

  Use any kind of cardboard tube of any length such as the inside of a roll of aluminum foil, paper toweling, or toilet tissue. Cut strips of newspaper ½ inch wide and about 1½ inches longer than the distance across the end of the tube. Dip the strips into thin wallpaper paste or white glue and water to cover the end of the tube. At least five layers of overlapping strips will be needed. Allow the paste to dry overnight. Put a small amount of split peas, dried beans, rice, or small pebbles into the tube. Cover the other end in the same manner. Paint the tube with latex paint.
- **Rhythm Blocks**

  Materials needed: scraps of wood, spools or other handles, latex paint

  Any scrap of wood can be cut into rhythm blocks as long as you cut two blocks the same size. (It is easier to play with blocks less than an inch thick.) Use a cross-cut saw and make your blocks square, round, oblong or triangular. Sand them smooth. Shellac or paint them if you wish. For handles, use drawer pulls, strips of an old leather belt, pot cover handles, spools or narrow blocks of wood which can be purchased in the craft section at Wal-Mart.

- **Kitchenware Cymbals**

  Materials needed: used pot covers, string, dowel stick

  Homemade cymbals can be made from pot covers. Test the cover to find one or two of proper ringing tone. If you find one with a bright ring, you can couple it with a less satisfactory pot cover, or strike it with a drumstick. Holding the lid will dim the sound. You can tie a string about the knob on the lid. Hold it by the string and strike with a dowel stick. (Try secondhand stores or garage sales to purchase these.)

- **Sandpaper Sticks**

  Materials needed: sandpaper and one-inch thick doweling stick, glue

  Wrap rough sandpaper around 12-inch lengths of doweling. Tack or glue them in place using Elmer's glue. Scrape the dowels back and forth across each other.

- **Jingle Ring**

  Materials needed: embroidery hoop, roofing caps, hammer, nails, yarn, safety pins, coat hangers

  A wooden or metal embroidery hoop will provide a ready-made frame. You can fashion a hoop by using the plastic ring on a coffee can, cutting the center and removing any sharp edges. Put the ring back together with duct tape. You will need 10 to 14 wooden roofing caps which are available at any home improvement store. Drill a hole in the center of each or use hammer and nail. Attach them in pairs to the hoop with colorful yarn, safety pins, or loops made from wire coat hangers. Shake to jingle.

- **Bell Stick**

  Materials needed: doweling, paint, bells

  Decorate a 6-inch length of doweling ($\frac{1}{2}$ to 1-inch in diameter) with colorful paint. When it is dry, staple on a tiny bell or two at each end of the stick. One can play the bell stick by shaking. Tap the two halves lightly together in rhythm.

- **Rattles from This and That**

  Some of the best-sounding rattles can be made from scraps. Consider using a plastic ice cream carton, a match box, a baking powder can, a pepper tin, a cleanser container, a plastic mayonnaise jar, etc. Test them with pebbles of beans, rice, pebbles, or small nails.

- **Beater**

  Materials needed: 1/8-inch dowel, glue, 1-inch round wooden bead or small rubber "jack ball" or tinker toys

  Dip the end of a 1/8-inch dowel into glue and force it into the hole of a 1-inch round wooden bead. Or sharpen the end of a dowel dipped in the glue and force it into the center of a small rubber ball—the kind used to play jacks.

- **Sleigh Bells**

  Materials needed: keys and rings

  Keys strung from a key ring jingle like sleigh bells. The solid one-piece ring is better than the link-type chain. The larger the keys are the louder the bells sound.

- **Coconut Halves**

  Materials needed: a coconut, handsaw, and sandpaper

  Use a sharp saw to cut a coconut in half. Drain out the milk, pry out the meat, and clean the inside thoroughly. Sand the edges smooth.

- **Coconut Rattles:**

  Materials needed: coconut, drill, handsaw, doweling, glue, rice

  Drill a hole at one end of the coconut and let the juice run into a glass. Then bore a good-sized hole (not more than an inch in diameter) on the other end of the coconut. (I always let the children throw the coconut on a concrete floor until it would crack.) Saw the coconut in half between the two holes you have bored. Pry the coconut meat out of the shell with a knife until the hard, brown inside is completely exposed. After the coconut shell is thoroughly cleaned, dry it in the sun. Keep the edges of the shell clean as you are going to glue the halves together again. You can also leave the coconut halves separate and hold each piece in your hands and clap together for the sound of a horse clip-clopping. Use a large dowel (1x12 inches). Whittle the end of it to fit the hole on top of the shell. About an inch down from the top, bore a small hole from side to side. Put a handful of rice or split peas into the shell. Fit the handle so that your hole is exposed at the top. Carefully glue the two halves together around the handle, let set overnight. Make a 10-inch peg of a piece of pencil or clothespin. Ease it into the hole. Shellac the shell or paint it.

L ISTEN TO THE SOUNDS of your various instruments. Does the tapping sound from bell sticks sound like galloping? Try placing a sheet of paper between the two coconut halves and rubbing in time to music. Does it sound like walking through the snow? Play the jingle ring by holding it in one hand and striking it with the other hand. Shake it, if you prefer, or put a short stick through the hoop and swing it round and round in a small circle.

Dramatic Play

1. **Provide materials for a barber shop.** Some items that could be included are a white apron or an old sheet, tissue, razor without blade, soft brush, soap (if desired) or try a beauty shop complete with combs, brushes, barrettes, clips, spray, spray bottles (with water to mist), scarves, ribbons, and a mirror.

These supplies do not have to be left out all the time, but they will provide fun for children as a change of pace. If you have storage space, put all the supplies in a snap-top square plastic container, label, and store on shelf.

2. **Provide dress-up clothes for boys and girls in a place where the children can reach them.** Have a big sale with play money. I kept these out all the time in the play room, but I put low hooks on the wall so the children could get them down and hang them up. The hats for both boys and girls and high heels were on a low shelf. Provide a long mirror so children can look at themselves when they are "dressed up." A play cash register and play money can be used in many ways.

3. **Play doctor and nurse.** Make kits from old purses and bottles filled with cereal, candy, raisins, and cotton balls. Make band-aids from cotton and masking tape stuck on waxed paper. Children do not have to be constantly entertained, but adults must have a lot of ideas to keep them busy and happy.

4. **Have a picnic on the floor inside, under a table, or take the snack outdoors.** One of our favorite activities was covering our kitchen table with blankets and putting a clamp light on one of the table

Our son Kevin and his son Trent

legs. They would put their dolls, trucks, books, etc. under the table and call it a "tent." Many times they would spend the morning playing under the table, especially on a rainy day. At lunchtime we would put all the toys back where they belonged and would eat lunch under the table. The same peanut butter and jelly sandwich tastes better under the table, and I ate with them. After lunch we folded up the blankets, and everything was back in order before their nap. When the weather was nice outdoors, I would spread a blanket under a tree and take the lunch outdoors occasionally to provide variety.

5. **Have a puppet show.** My children loved making puppets, and I kept the supplies on hand. I encouraged them to make all of the characters for a story such as "The Three Bears." With only five characters in this story, each child could choose a character. When the characters were finished, I would tell the story first, then turn over a child-sized table for them to get behind, letting them "act out" the story using puppets. If one child was too young to speak, I would say their part while they held up the puppet. Children enjoy puppets of all kinds. I made some puppets and collected others from yard sales or from collection stores. Any of the stories included in Appendix F would adapt well to using puppets. The following are ways I have made puppets with children. (Check Appendix B for information on puppets.)

Paper Bag Hand Puppet

Paper bag hand puppets are creative, inexpensive, and helpful in keeping children busy and occupied. Remember that the mouth opening is created by the fold of the bag, and the underside of the flap is the inside of the mouth. Some children enjoy adding interesting collage materials to the puppets being created like yarn for hair. An example might be adding real straw to a bag to create a scarecrow.

Sock Hand Puppets

A sock can serve as both the body and head of a puppet. Buttons, sequins, yarn and bits of felt can be added to bring out the puppet's facial characteristics.

To get ears, make two v-shaped slits at the heel on each side, and poke up to the desired angle. Cover the openings made by the cuts with a wig made of yarn or a hat.

When you want a big mouth that will open and close, fold the bulge of the heel to the inside, and stitch the edge of the fold together.

If the nose of the puppet is very important, the heel of the sock will again serve your purpose. The pointer finger may be inserted to extend the nose and make it move.

Stick Puppets

A stick puppet is a picture or an object attached to a stick. It is animated by moving the stick up and down or from side to side. Usually a puppeteer speaks for each puppet, but one person can take several parts by changing his voice if needed to illustrate a story.

Whole figures attached to sticks may be used for puppets, or the children may be able to find appropriate pictures in old magazines or catalogs. Figures may also be drawn, then colored with crayons or painted, and cut out for mounting.

Types of Sticks	Objects to Use on Sticks
Dowel sticks	Pictures (full figures, heads)
1" wide plywood	Drawings
Tongue depressor	Silhouettes
Ice cream sticks	Torn paper figures
Yardsticks	Stuffed toys
Sticks found outdoors	Balls
Broomsticks	Fruits, vegetables
Old curtain rods	Paper-made heads
Pencils	Paper bags (stuffed)

These puppets can help children express their feelings. Double circles of cardboard glued together may be given exaggerated expressions to indicate strong feelings such as joy, sorrow, fear, anger, and suspicion. Decorate them with crayons, paper, paint, or felt; add a bow under the chin, or a hat, but keep them very simple.

To encourage flexibility, hold up puppets showing different faces and ask the children to say "Good Morning" in the tone of voice indicated.

Paper Bag Stick Puppets

Large paper bags become puppets when they are stuffed with crumpled newspapers and tied to sticks. Broomsticks, dowel sticks, or yardsticks are good to use. Pictures are painted on the bags, and the faces may be decorated with yarn, construction paper, and so forth. Large features such as a trunk or ears can be taped or glued in place for animals. Attach a garment to the neck, if desired. Hats can do wonders for these characters.

An advantage to making this kind of puppets is that quantities can be produced quickly, inexpensively, and easily by children.

Finger Puppets

Attach heads cut from paper to rings which fit around the fingers. A variation is to cut a head double, and glue the front and the back together along the edges, leaving the neck section open for the finger. Staple head and torso of a paper doll to the paper ring. Insert index and middle fingers through the ring. These become the doll's legs and feet. (Some templates for finger puppets are included in Appendix B.)

Self-Portraits

For an art experience, children often draw self-portraits. These can be cut and mounted as stick puppets. A child could give an autobiographical sketch by talking for his own puppet.

Box Puppets

Close the open end of an empty one-serving cereal box. Cut the box almost in two, so as to make two open-sided squares attached by a hinge. The finger (or fingers) goes in one opening and the thumb goes in the other. Keeping fingers above the thumb, open and close the two box halves to suggest a puppet talking. (The lower "jaw" should be shorter than the upper.) Paint the box, making the inside of the mouth red. Add ears and eyes. If the puppet is an animal, add feelers, horns, or other characteristics such as feathers.

6. Secure a large packing box or small box from a grocery store and let the children design a "house," "car," or "cave." Every time we went to the grocery store when our children were preschool age, I made sure we had several cardboard boxes. While I was putting away my weekly groceries, the children would spend time transforming the boxes into a variety of objects with washable markers, pillows, dolls, etc. Before their nap, they put away everything. If you have a washer, dryer, or refrigerator box, children can make a house or a cave with markers. I always helped cut out the windows and doors with a box cutter, but they created everything else.

7. **Cover a card table or any other table with blankets and provide flashlights for a "hideout."** Children are attracted to hiding places and our card table was used a lot more for making a "hideout" than serving as a table. At times, I would put their "hideout" outdoors, and I had some old blankets they used. Make sure you get inexpensive flashlights for the children and teach them how to turn them "off" as well as "on." Do not let them use your husband's "prize" flashlight.

8. **Make blocks.** Our children spent hours playing with "unit blocks" my husband and I made from 2 x 4's we purchased at the lumber company. We made the sizes as follows by sawing across the 2 x 4:

> Half Unit—3 ½" x 3 ½"
> Unit—7" x 3 ½"
> Double unit— 14" x 3 ½"

The size of the above blocks can vary, but it is much easier for the child to build with them if they are uniformly sized. We added some large round dowel sticks, some flat pieces for roofs, and our children spent hours playing with blocks. They were stored by size on low shelves. I traced around the block on the shelf, so it was easy for our children to pick up the blocks and put them in the proper place. After my hus-

With grandson Stephen Cervantes

band cut the blocks, I sanded them with help of the children, and we rubbed linseed oil on them before they were used.

9. **Play with cars and trucks.** These were stored on shelves near the blocks. I bought good-quality cars and trucks so the wheels would stay on after continuous use. No one wants to play with a rolling toy that was "cheap" and no longer rolls. At this point, I threw

away the toy. Check garage sales for more expensive toys like Tonka that stand up to continuous use.

10. Be creative with Legos or other creative building sets. I kept these in plastic dishpans that were on low shelves and accessible to children. The child must be taught how to fit the pieces together and enjoy praise when he has completed a "masterpiece." This is a wonderful way to build the child's motor skills, concentration, and attention span. These will also teach the child to play with one item at a time.

Science

1. Take your child to see an animal such as a kitten, a dog, or a bird. Make sure the animal is friendly and that your child knows how to treat it. If the preschool child is afraid of the animal, you can talk about how friendly the animal is. I often let the child feed the animal. Some preschool children are afraid of animals and trying to "force" the child to touch the animal may create a "phobia" or an unnatural fear of the animal. Patience and understanding work better than force. Building a child's confidence will generally solve the child's fear, whether it is imagined or real. Of course, people should have a natural fear of some animals.

2. Have several kinds of apples, oranges, grapes, etc. for snacks. Let each child taste each kind and compare flavor, skin, color. Talk about how and where the different fruits grow. Polish the outside of the apple and explain to the child that the apple shines because of the natural wax God puts on each apple to make the apple beautiful and to act as a natural preservative so the apples keep during the winter.

Read the true story of Johnny Appleseed. (See Appendix E.) Explain that a worm gets inside an apple by laying an egg on the apple blossom in the spring. The tree has to be sprayed before the apple starts forming from the blossom. If the apple tree is not sprayed, the worm eats its way out of the apple. If a worm is in the apple, it is small and misshapen, but an apple from a sprayed tree is large and beautiful. I always taught our children that this was what sin would do in our hearts when we are not right with God because the Bible says, *"Eat thou not the bread of him that hath an evil eye, neither desire thou his dainty meats: For as he thinketh in his heart, so is he: Eat and drink, saith he to thee; but his heart is not with thee."* (Proverbs 23:6, 7) Some of the best lessons for children are simple ones, if we take the time to take advantage of the teaching opportunities.

3. **Help a child understand what objects sink or float.** Place a pan of water on a low table with a variety of objects next to it such as a sponge, a rock, a pencil, paper, a block of wood, and so forth. Sit with the child and explain that items that are heavier than water sink and those that are lighter float. When an item, such as paper, becomes saturated with water, it will sink.

4. **Put an ice cube in a pan and explain why it melts.** Teach the child that water can be a solid, liquid, or gas. When it is below freezing outside, put about ½-inch of water (liquid) in a metal pan. Put the pan outside and show the child how it becomes a solid (ice). Bring the pan inside and place on a stove or hot place to show how water becomes steam (gas). You can also use a freezer to do this demonstration.

5. **Grow seeds in a cup.** If you want to see overnight growth, use rye grass. Sprinkle rye grass seed on a damp sponge, and it will grow grass quickly if you keep the sponge damp. A bean seed takes longer, but it is more interesting to watch its growth. Use a permanent marker to write the child's name on his cup so he can watch his own plant. If you have space to plant a garden, let the child help and show him how the plants grow. Planting a garden is far better than using cups.

Have a contest to see which bean seedling grows the tallest. Teach the child that if the seed is planted too deeply, it will take longer to grow. Plant the seed too shallow, and the roots will not sustain the weight; the bean seedling will tip over. If watered too much, the seed rots and does not grow. Not watering the seed will result in no germination. You may want to plant a seed illustrating each of the previous conditions as a lesson.

6. **In the spring, "force" a tree or shrub to bloom by bringing a few branches indoors where it is warm.** This activity is for an area where the seasons change. Blooming bushes such as like forsythia, bridal veil, lilac, and trees like a pussy willow are a reminder that spring is on the way. Every spring we brought in a pussy willow, and I taught our children "The Pussy Willow Song" which is included in Appendix B.

7. Make a terrarium with the children. The materials needed include a one-quart mason jar or one-gallon glass jar, pebbles, sand, charcoal, black soil, mosses, small shade-loving ferns, and any other little plants which you find growing beside a shady stream or in the woods. The purpose is to gain a better understanding of how plants grow.

A. In the bottom of the jar, put a small handful of pebbles.
B. Add a handful of sand and a few pieces of charcoal to keep the soil sweet.
C. Add a layer of good black soil, such as potting soil or the soil obtained from a wooded area.
D. Plant the shady plants in the jar, and then sprinkle them until the earth is moist but not soggy.
E. Punch four or five holes in the top of the jar lid with a nail and hammer and then screw the lid on the jar. Your terrarium will need only a few drops of water every few weeks.

The children will be able to see and care for plants growing indoors, learning that a terrarium needs little water from the outside to grow. They can see that a terrarium is an "unnatural" garden planted indoors. They can learn that most indoor plants and gardens need to be watered every day or two, but a terrarium is a garden which waters itself. The water which evaporates from the soil and from the plants condenses into droplets on the sides and top of the terrarium and falls back to the soil. The children will see that shady plants grow best in the terrarium. Adding the charcoal helps to keep soil sweet.

8. Make "feel" boxes to encourage observation and conversation. Lay different types of material such as fur, velvet, suede, silk, coarse wool, etc., in boxes for children to explore by cutting holes in each end of the box for the child's hands. Let him identify what is in each box. If you do not attach the items to the box, they can be interchanged.

A variation of the "feel" box is to use paper bags containing different substances such as sawdust, dirt, flour, salt, sugar, sponges, wood, plastic, leather, sandpaper, or other materials. Let them feel the contents of the paper bags and identify the items.

Another variation is to use a square cardboard box with the flaps folded on the bottom. Cut holes in the sides of a box, glue several items to the sides of the box, let the children insert their hands to see how many items they can identify.

9. **Adopt a tree.** Look at it every day in the spring and note the changes during the year. Every tree has a flower, seed, and fruit. Discuss the different kinds of trees. Some have leaves that die and fall off and others have needles that remain on the tree year around. Teach the child the names of the common trees in your area. Give the child a lunch sack to collect leaves and needles. Let them make a collage picture with the items they have collected. Each item should be identified by writing the name on the child's paper.

10. **Study insects.** Turn over big rocks outdoors and look under the bark of a dead tree to see insect life. Some of the best science lessons are simple and require only an observant adult to teach the child. Under rocks you can find earthworms, roly-polys, ants, beetles, etc. Pull the bark off a dead tree, and you will see armored beetles, and all kinds of insects God is using to return the dead tree to the soil to enrich the earth.

11. **Encourage language development.**

• **Put an assortment of objects in a paper bag** such as a rubber band, comb, ball, toy soldier, brush, hair clip, etc. and let the children guess what the bag contains after letting them feel inside it.

• **Take a walk around the school or in the woods and talk about changes in the trees, bushes, etc.** You can show the child how the buds appear in the spring, how the leaves die and drop off the trees in the fall, and how God made them for us to enjoy.

• **Find a picture of the child when he was younger and talk about how he has grown.** If you have baby pictures, see if he can guess which is his picture. If you kept a "baby book," he will enjoy seeing how he has changed. If you have a scrapbook of when he was young, look at it together and talk about how big he has gotten.

• **Put several common objects on a tray.** Let the children look at the tray, remove one or more objects, and see if they know which object or objects were removed. This activity will develop their power of concentration, build their attention span, and encourage language development. Use only a few objects at the beginning because you want the child to be successful.

• **Have children act out nursery rhymes and familiar folk stories.** Start with the nursery rhymes such as "Humpty Dumpty" or folk stories such as "The Three Little Pigs" or "The Three Bears." Check the book list in Appendix E for ideas. The flannel board stories in Appendix F would adapt well also. Children can act out the same rhyme over and over again. Use the child's name in the rhyme, if possible. If you tell the folk stories often and the children are familiar with the story, they will enjoy being "actors." If the children have trouble remembering what to say, you talk and let them act out the story.

• **Make an experience chart or booklet with your child.** Let him share what he enjoyed most during a holiday or field trip. Children of this age draw "stick figures," and I would write on the picture what the child told me. Every time we took a trip with the child's grandparents, we had the children each draw one or more pages of things they remembered about the trip. I put the pages in a notebook and gave it to the grandparents. The child will be more observant if you write on his picture, and your writing what he says will make him feel important.

• **Sit in the woods and listen.** Help the child identify the wind rustling through the trees, the birds singing, and the squirrels scampering among the leaves. Teach them how Indians wore moccasins so they could walk through the woods silently without snapping twigs and making sounds to tell others that they were coming. Explain how an Indian's ability to move in silence could be a matter of life and death.

• **Teach shapes by naming them.** Cut the shapes from different colors of felt. I make them about 6 inches wide or tall and use Elmer's glue to glue the rhyme on the back of the shape figure. Draw the faces on the figures with a permanent marker so they will not rub off. Children can remember the shapes much better if they have names. You can make a bulletin board with these felt shapes, use them on the flannel board, put them on a stairway so the children can name them as they go up and down the stairs, lay them on the floor so the children can stand beside "Suzy Circle" or hop once beside "Sandy Square," etc. I store these shapes in a manila folder with a pocket to hold the shape. Templates for these shapes and their corresponding rhymes are in Appendix A.

Use the children as a variation to teach the shapes. Four children can lay on the floor to make a square; three for a triangle, six for a rectangle, two for a circle, four for a diamond, and two for an oval. The children do not need to touch to create the shape.

• **Encourage the child to follow instructions.** Make a game of teaching your child to follow directions. Preschool children will learn quickly if they feel they are playing a game. Give oral directions for the child to follow. Preschool children will need help in differentiating between right and left. For that reason, designate a reference to help them in remembering right and left. For instance, I put a red rubber band or a red mark on the right hand with a felt-tip marker. If a child knows which is right, he will automatically know the left. These are some of the directions I used with preschool children:

1. Hold up your right hand.
2. Hop on your right foot.
3. Point to the person who is standing next to you on the right.
4. Touch your right ear with your left hand.
5. Place your left hand on your right elbow.
6. Hop on your left foot.
7. Bend your left knee up.
8. Touch your left eye with your right hand.
9. Touch your right eye with your left hand.
10. Touch your leg with your left hand.
11. Put your right hand behind your back.
12. Put your left hand behind your back.

Cooking

1. **Let children husk ears of corn, remove silk from the corn, and boil for a snack.** If possible, let the child see how the corn grows. Show them we pick the corn when it is soft to eat, but if animals are to be fed the corn is left on the stalk to become hard.

2. **Pop popcorn with children.** Note the appearance of the kernels before and after popping. Explain that popcorn "pops" and all other corn does not because God put a drop of water in popcorn. The water heats, turns to steam, and turns the kernel inside out. Once the water is gone from the kernel, the popcorn will not pop.

Let the children make a collage picture by gluing both the popped and "unpopped " popcorn on a paper with Elmer's glue.

3. **Make applesauce.** Put quartered, unpeeled apples in a saucepan with a small amount of water. Cover. Cook until soft and

put through a colander or a Foley mill. Add sugar, cinnamon, and butter to taste. Let the children eat the applesauce they made on toast or bread.

When Stephen, one of our grandsons, was preschool age he came to our house every Monday. In the fall, we would gather apples from our yard. I cut out the wormy places, and we would cook them. He helped me put the cooked, unpeeled apples through the colander, and we would sweeten to taste. Cinnamon and butter can be added, and the applesauce can be frozen, pressed flat in a freezer storage bag or in an airtight container. Usually by the time our grandchildren ate the applesauce, there was none left to freeze.

4. **Shake whipping cream in a jar to make butter.** Use a clear plastic jar in case it is dropped. It takes a lot of shaking, but it is exciting when the butter appears. Remove the butter from the whey, wash, and salt. Serve with crackers. Let children take turns shaking the jar, and the time will pass much more quickly. Children always enjoy eating what they make themselves.

5. **Make toast using different kinds of bread.** Let the children spread on butter, sprinkle on cinnamon sugar, or spread with jelly. This can be done every morning, and it takes a little longer than doing everything for them, but it builds the child's self confidence. Soften butter, put cinnamon sugar in a shaker, and jelly that is easy to spread. A child should be allowed to make choices, but never given the choice of whether or not to obey his authority.

6. **Make pancakes using an electric skillet or griddle on a low table.** With help, the children can put the pancake batter on the griddle, turn them over, and remove them when cooked. Teach them that when the bubbles appear, it is time to turn the pancake. Let them spread on butter and eat warm. Save another for a snack or freeze to pop in the toaster on another day. If you wish, the batter may be colored with food coloring. Make a "smiley face" on a pancake by allowing the child to put on whipped cream from the spray can after the pancake is done.

7. **Make vegetable soup.** Let each child choose one vegetable to wash and scrape. Have vegetables on hand such as carrots, onions, celery, potatoes, and tomatoes. Add tomato juice or meat, if desired. Season to taste and let the soup simmer all morning on a cold day so the children can smell the soup cooking. Eat for a snack or a lunch.

8. Make chicken noodle soup. The recipe for this dish is included in Appendix D. When children help prepare this recipe, two days of preparation are required. The chicken is cooked the first day; the vegetables are added and the soup simmers on the second day. The children can also help prepare the noodles and add them to the soup. Children who may not prefer soup will eat it if they helped prepare it.

9. Make jello. Making jello can teach the children the principles of how some things dissolve in water and how they congeal when cooled. Give each child a cup with some jello powder. Let children taste the jello powder (a solid). Then pour hot water into each child's cup. Have the child stir the jello mixture and taste the dissolved jello (a liquid).

Add an ice cube instead of cold water, and the jello will gel as children watch (a solid). Let the children eat the jello he has made in his cup. Children feel very important when they can say at mealtime, "I helped make this," even if you did most of the work!

10. Cook or bake together. In Appendix D, I have included several recipes my children and I enjoyed preparing together.

Trips

1. Take a walk outside to collect leaves, insects, etc. Small lunch sacks or empty half-pint milk cartons with string or wire handles make good individual collection boxes. After collecting, we all sat on the ground outside or at a child-sized table. I taught them the names of the items they had collected. If we had gathered leaves or needles from trees, I let them glue the leaves or needles on the paper. (If you do not know the name of a certain item, either go to the library or buy a leaf or flower book for proper identification.)

2. Visit a grocery store. Choose a time when the store is not extremely busy, usually early on a weekday morning. Occasionally I asked the manager if the children could see the large coolers, freezers, packaging of meats, and trucks unloading. Encourage the person who is showing you the store to speak on the child's level by asking questions. Make sure you take a thank-you letter or picture from the child the next time you go to the store.

3. Visit a home to see an animal, a tree, etc. Let the child take a small gift to show appreciation. The child can also draw a picture and tell you what he enjoyed so this can be mailed or given to the person.

4. Visit a park or a wooded area for a picnic. Even though you have play equipment in your yard, it is fun for the child to have variety. One summer when I was at the park in Oregon with our grandchildren, Derek and Karissa, they discovered wild blackberries. We picked them and made blackberry cobbler for dinner that night. Just walking around the block in a subdivision to smell flowers and look for dogs and cats can be exciting. We had a certain place where I would tell them stories.

5. Visit a post office. Let the child mail a letter to himself, to his parents, to his grandparents, or to a shut-in. Let the child put on the stamp and put his letter in the mail slot. Explain how the post office works. Sending mail is a way we can make others happy. "*As cold waters to a thirsty soul, so is good news from a far country.*" (Proverbs 25:25)

6. Visit a public library. Help your children obtain a library card for which he is responsible. Help them choose books which you approve. Make a book list because many books have wrong philosophies and language. Design a reading contest to encourage your child to listen to books to build his vocabulary, and to increase his attention span.

7. Have a policeman, fireman, or nurse meet the child and talk about what they do. A preschool child is more interested in the badge, the gun, and the uniform than the specifics of a job the child may not understand. Ask questions so the child will not become bored if the information is confusing.

Years ago, I found a preschool child stealing when he was at church under my supervision. The following week, I took the children on a field trip to the Hammond City Jail. When they returned, each child was asked to draw a picture of what he enjoyed most about the trip. My "thief" drew a picture of a boy behind bars looking sad and a happy boy on the outside of the bars. When I asked him to tell me about his picture, he said, "The happy boy is me because he is never going to be in jail for stealing."

8. Take a field trip to a fire department, a museum, an airport, a bakery, a bottling company, a pet shop, a greenhouse, or a dairy farm. Make sure the people in charge understand the age of the children and that they should present information on the level of the child. Make sure the children are under control during the visit so the people will welcome a future visit.

Books and Stories

If you can teach your children the alphabet before he goes to school and do so in a way the child considers "fun," it is good. However, if you try to "hammer the alphabet into the child's head" and he dislikes the lesson, you may do more harm than good. If the child has been read to and loves books, he will be excited about learning to read them himself. If the child has developed a long attention span, you can read lengthy books, a chapter at a time. I remember reading *Heidi, Charlie and the Chocolate Factory, Squanto, Wind in the Willows,* and many other books to our preschool age children. If you know well-written children's books and encourage your child to read these, they will be more interested in reading. A well-written children's book is as interesting for an adult to read as it is for a child. No video or video tape will ever take the place of reading.

In my opinion, one of the best things parents can do for their preschool children is read books to them and encourage the children to act out the stories. This requires time, but the benefits to the child are invaluable. This develops the relationship between the child and the parent or authority, and it builds the child's attention span so the child can learn when he goes to school. Regardless of how smart the child may be or how accomplished the teacher, a child who cannot sit and listen will not learn. Reading to the child will develop his vocabulary and his comprehension of the English language, as well as give the child a desire to learn to read himself. (A book list for preschool children is included in Appendix E.)

Flannel Board Stories

Some of our children's favorite flannel board stories are included in Appendix F.

Storytelling from Your Life

Every child will benefit from having at least one storyteller to enrich his life. This is a skill that must be developed, but children are a good audience because they appreciate any effort. My father was a storyteller, and I have so many wonderful memories of the stories he told. Two of our grandchildren's favorites are found in Appendix G. One of the stories my dad added to his repertoire was one my mother never learned to appreciate!

Telling a story at the party of grandson, Trent Cowling

Games

Choose games that are on the level of the child and those that can be played quickly. If the game lasts too long, the child will become bored. Sometimes if the child is losing, he wants to quit. However, the rule we followed was "You finish what you start whether you are winning or losing." Another rule was that no one was allowed to "cheat" when playing a game. Games that our children enjoyed as preschool children and games I played with them often are included in Appendix H.

Wondering

I wonder why the north winds blow—
    The tide flows in the sea.
I wonder why the bluebirds fly—
    And God can make a tree.

I wonder why the grass is green,
    I just can't understand.
I wonder how that God can hold
    The whole world in His hand.

I wonder about the deserts
    All filled with burning sand.
I wonder how that we can live
    As a part of His heavenly plan.

I wonder, I wonder, I wonder,
    Of the things that I don't see.
I'll search till I find the purpose
    That God created me.

                          – Frieda White Cowling

Grade School

Grade School
(Photos on page 113)

Top left: Trent Cowling at a baseball game
Top right: "Grandpa Bill" White with Kelly, Kevin, and Krysten
Center right: Kevin making a snow fort
Bottom: Grandpa with Sam and Stephen on a toboggan

Someone has said that a child's personality is formed by age three, and a child learns 60 percent of what he will know throughout his life by the time he starts school. God wants us to influence our children all our lives, but children usually spend more time in our homes during the first five years of their lives than at any other time. A trait that is often evident in firstborn children is the desire to please authority. We watched this play out in an incident with our grandson, David Cowling.

"I Always Wanted a Daddy Like You!"

My husband and I had gone to the home of our son Keith to help hang some decorative curtain rods in their living room. Their two sons, three-year-old David and one-year-old Peter, were enjoying the excitement of the moment as they played with the empty boxes after we had removed the curtain rods. One rod was up and Keith was looking for a small box of screws needed to put up the second rod. We all joined in a massive search for the missing box with no success.

Thinking David might have been playing with the box, Keith interrogated David, hoping to discover some clue leading to the recovery of the screws. Patience was wearing a little thin, and the fun atmosphere of the evening became somewhat strained. Keith climbed up the ladder, and David walked over to the foot of the ladder and looked up at his dad.

Suddenly, in a small, quiet voice, David said, "I always wanted a daddy like you."

"I love you, Buddy," Keith replied. "Don't worry about the screws."

The tension disappeared along with the screws (which were never found). Life is too short to cry over spilled milk or break a relationship over missing screws.

By the way, a simple trip back to the store produced more screws which are now in their places holding up the rod.

Incidents like this are necessary. The child should learn by the time he is grade school age that it is fun to work, to obey authority, and to live by schedule.

Schedule

Our four children went to bed at the same time every night unless we were at a church activity. I always told them I did not care if they went to sleep, but I did not want to see them or hear them until the next morning. (If you have not mastered this rule, please read the suggestions given in the pre-school section.)

Now that our children are grown with children of their own, they love to tell things they did that I never knew about! Our daughters shared a room with a blue rug. They had lots of stuffed animals on their bed. They tell how they would throw the stuffed animal on the blue rug, pretending it was water, and "swim" out to get it. My husband and I never heard them as they engaged in these "rescue" operations.

They also love to tell how they would get out of bed and crawl down the hall toward the den where my husband and I were talking. We didn't see them or hear them! I'm not sure how often they did this, but they have fun telling about it now. We followed the same bedtime ritual described in the preschool chapter.

When the children were in grade school, we let them stay up 30 minutes later than the other children. Usually my husband would tell them a story before they went to bed, we prayed with them, and kissed them good night.

Getting Up

By the time the children were grade-school age, they had learned that they had to be dressed, have their bed made, and have their room cleaned if they wanted to eat breakfast at 6:30 a.m. Since all our children loved to eat, very rarely did they miss breakfast. I checked their rooms after breakfast, and then we had our family altar. If two children shared a room, the bed and room were divided in half, and each child cleaned his half. I do not mind if an older child teaches a younger child, but I do not think a younger child should learn to be lazy while the older child does all the work.

If two children sharing a room were arguing over the cleaning, I washed both of their mouths with soap by rubbing the soap on their teeth. I had them hug one another and work together until they could get along. I taught them we lived together according to Ephesians 4:32, *"And be ye kind one to another, tenderhearted, forgiving one another, even as God for Christ's sake hath forgiven you."* All of our children memorized this verse and were asked to quote it when they were not getting along with their siblings.

Work

From the time our children were very small, they were taught the "If-you-don't-work, you-don't-eat" philosophy according to II Thessalonians 3:10, *"For even when we were with you, this we commanded you, that if any would not work, neither should he eat."* In addition to cleaning their rooms, they each had daily jobs. For the boys, such chores as feeding the animals, doing yard work, and taking out the trash were performed. The girls set the table, helped with the dishes, helped with the laundry, and so forth. I made sure they knew exactly what I wanted them to do, taught them how to do it, and checked to make sure the job was done to the best of their ability. *"And whatsoever ye do, do it heartily, as to the Lord, and not unto men."* (Colossians 3:23) If the job was not done correctly, I had them do it over until it was done to the best of their ability. The children soon learned that it was easier to do the job right the first time. I wanted them to realize work was enjoyable if done on schedule daily in the right way and in the time allotted for it. It is easier for the parents to do the work themselves, but it harms the child by encouraging him to be lazy.

I remember one summer when Kevin, our oldest son, was grade-school age. My husband told him to mow the yard before he got home from work at 5:00 p.m. When we had lunch, I reminded Kevin; and he assured me that the lawn would be mowed. However, at 5:00 p.m. when my husband came home, the yard was still unmowed. My husband did not call for Kevin to correct him; he walked into the kitchen and said, "Remove Kevin's place from the table"—which I did.

A few minutes later when I called everyone to eat, Kevin walked into the kitchen, noticed his plate was missing, and walked outside. In a few minutes, we heard the lawn mower. That was the last time I remember Kevin failing to mow the lawn when he was told to do so.

When a child is given a chore to do and fails to do it properly, it is a mistake to call him shiftless, lazy, and irresponsible. It is also unwise to compare one child unfavorably with another industrious child by making statements like, "Why can't you be like ___?" No one enjoys being "weighed in the balance and found wanting." II Corinthians 10:12, *"For we dare not make ourselves of the number, or compare ourselves with some that commend themselves; but they measuring themselves by themselves, and comparing themselves among themselves, are not wise."*

If we simply make the child redo the job, he will learn that it is easier and requires less effort to do the job right the first time. As I have already mentioned, if the authority sees work as "fun," so will the child. Work should be done because it is assigned to the child and should not be used as a punishment for wrongdoing. If the child's room is not cleaned daily and resembles a "pig sty," it is the fault of the authority and not the child. When a room is untidy, the child feels it is impossible to bring order from chaos and will tend to play around instead of cleaning the room.

Sometimes well-meaning parents feel they are saving time by doing all the work for the child, which will take less of the parent's time when the child is preschool age. However, if the child is taught to work, it will be beneficial to both the child and the parent by the time the child enters grade school.

In the summer when our children were out of school, they were not allowed to sleep until noon, doing nothing beneficial. We had breakfast at 7:30 a.m., family altar at 7:45 a.m., and all of us worked from 8:00 a.m. until noon. We "deep cleaned" one room at a time, and we all worked together. We would put on lively music and wash walls, windows, and floors. It is amazing how quickly things are accomplished if everyone works. After lunch, I would continue working, but the children were allowed to read, play, or do what they wanted to do.

I remember one day I decided we would clean the garage and surprise my husband when he came home from work. The children worked very hard, sweeping, organizing, and dusting. We were so proud of the job we had done, and we were sure Pete would be over-joyed when he got home from work. That afternoon we led him out to see our garage masterpiece. He was impressed until he walked over to the shelves holding the nails and screws. The one who organized that area had dumped out all the individual boxes and grouped them by size—which surprised him in a negative way. After this experience, we left cleaning the garage to my husband!

When our sons, Kevin and Keith, were grade-school age, Hyles-Anderson College had a work program whereby grade-school age boys worked on the college grounds for three hours a day at $1.00 an hour. It cost me more in gas to take them to work and pick them up than they made! However, my husband and I felt it was worth the price to have them work for an outstanding man, Mark Pfeifer, who is still in charge of the grounds at the college. They started weeding the iris beds; and if they worked hard, they were given more preferable jobs. I remember how excited Keith was when he was allowed to cut weeds from ditches instead of weeding the iris beds!

Every day when I picked them up, I looked at the work they had done. Teaching your school-age child to work requires time and effort but will be worth it as the child gets older. I have never known a person greatly used of God who doesn't know how to work hard and give his best.

Time

The most valuable gift you can give a child of any age is your time. When you give time, you are giving your life. As we voluntarily give time to a child, it makes them feel important and encourages them to see us as a fun person. In the activities section, several ideas are given for ways to spend time with children. Actually, what you do with a child (or children) is not as important as the fact that you are spending time with them. The following are ways I spent time with our school-age children.

1. **Work together.** When our son Kevin was in second grade, my husband offered to let him work to buy a gasoline-powered minibike. Kevin agreed to pay for the bike by working one hour a day for 50 cents until the bike was paid for in full. My husband bought Kevin a little account book to record the time he worked. Every afternoon after school, I had to think of an hour's worth of work for Kevin (in addition to his regular chores). This was difficult because there is a limit to what a second-grade boy can do, and I often felt sorry for him working while his brother and sisters were playing.

However, I did exactly what my husband had instructed, and it was a wonderful day when we, as a family, had a burning of the account book when Kevin had paid for the minibike. Kevin kept that minibike long after he was too big to ride it, and he enjoyed many hours of fun when the work was done. We value things that cost us effort and time.

2. Go to the park and take a picnic lunch. During the summer, we went to local parks at least once a week and took a picnic lunch. The same lunch tastes better at the park.

3. Make a time to spend individual time with each child. I gave each child a different morning of the week from 6:00 a.m. to 6:15 a.m. If the child wanted to get up, I made a special treat like hot chocolate, and we talked, played a game, or read a book. I woke them at 5:45 a.m. on their special morning, and they could decide if they wanted to get up. Most of the time, they got up. This idea works with grade school children, but do not try it with teenagers!

4. Read aloud to your children. I read books out loud to the children even after they could read. One summer when we were taking a trip together, I read *The Skinner Mill Fire* by Tom Grafton to Trevor Cowling who was in the second grade. I read *The Secret Garden* by Frances Hodgson Burnett to Ashley Cowling, who was in the fifth grade at the time. The previous year, I read *The Wolves of Willoughby Chase* by Joan Aiken to Ashley. I will never see any of these books without remembering the precious time we spent reading them together. For other books to read aloud, consult the index at the back of the book.

5. Play both indoor and outdoor games with children. Some are listed in the activity section. The summer of 2002, I bought a 4-Square ball and taught this game to our Arizona grandchildren, ten-year-old Ashley, eight-year-old Trent, six-year-old Trevor, and three-year-old Trey Cowling. Since Trey was only three, he played with me. To play the game, a six-foot square is drawn and then subdivided into four squares, numbered from one to four. Each person stands in a square with the leader in the number one square. The leader drops the 4-Square ball and hits it into one of the other squares. The person in that square must hit the ball once into another square or he goes out of the game or he would leave his

| 1 | 4 |
| 2 | 3 |

square and go to square 4. If more than four are playing, the child waiting in a line by the number 4 square enters it. All the children move up. This is a fast game which allows a large number of grade-school-age children to play. The game requires very little skill and is lots of fun.

6. **Listen when grade school age children talk.** If we are always busy and give our half-hearted attention, the child will not want to talk to us. If listening is impossible when the child wants to talk, set a specific time for listening later and keep your word.

7. **Check their homework.** On Mondays, Hammond Baptist Grade School always sends home a paper listing the grade schoolers' weekly assignments. I posted these on the side of my refrigerator and checked each sheet for every child every night to make sure the work was done. I did not just ask if the work was done; I looked to make sure. I reviewed spelling words and listened to Bible verses. Before the child went to bed, he put his book bag with his school work in it beside the front door. Sometimes I had our older children help the younger ones.

When Kevin was in the sixth grade, every child in his class had to write a five-minute speech. The best speech in each of the three sixth-grade classes was to be given in the Spring Meet when all the parents were invited to attend. Our daughter Kelly helped Kevin with his speech and checked it for grammatical errors. Kevin's speech was chosen as the winner in his class, but he told his teacher he did not want to give his speech. "Let someone else do it," he said.

His teacher called my husband and asked what should be done. My husband decided that since Kevin's speech was chosen, he was obligated to give it. Kevin explained that he would never be able to give a speech in front of so many people, but my husband reminded him that Philippians 4:13 was in the Bible and applied to him. *"I can do all things through Christ which strengtheneth me."* My husband said, "It is three weeks until the Spring Meet; and every night after we eat supper, you will practice giving the speech to the family."

We all quickly grew to dread this time of the day and viewed it as a preview of the Tribulation! We would finish eating and file to the living room where Kevin seemed to be creative in thinking of as many wrong ways to give this five-minute speech as he could! Sometimes he would speak so softly that we could not hear him—

even though we were in the same room. When my husband asked him to speak louder, he would shout. Sometimes he would speak very fast and when he was asked to slow down, he would speak so slowly no one could possibly follow the thought. Sometimes he would put his arms behind him and distract us with his gyrations. When corrected, he would put his arms by his side and look like a wooden Indian.

Kelly said, "That is a good speech, and Kevin ruins it every time he gives it."

Kevin never gave the speech well, and I grew to dread the night of the Spring Meet. The night finally came, and we rushed home so Kevin could put on his suit. On the way to the school, my husband asked, "Kevin, do you need to say your speech again?"

"No, sir," Kevin replied. We all breathed a sigh of relief!

As we walked into the grade-school auditorium, my husband said, "Let's sit in the back so we can make a quick getaway after Kevin's speech." We did not know which of his many unacceptable ways of giving the speech Kevin would choose to use. After all, he had never once given the speech in an acceptable way.

At last his turn came. Kevin walked to the microphone. What a surprise! We heard a mature voice giving the speech in an outstanding way with voice inflection and gestures. In fact, Kevin won first place. My husband looked at me and said, "Kids, who can understand them?" We were all in shock.

At this writing, Kevin is pastoring Valley Baptist Church in Mesa, Arizona. I believe my husband's insistence on Kevin's presenting his speech correctly was one of many factors that pointed him to becoming a successful pastor. If Kevin signs your Bible, he will sign Philippians 4:13, *"I can do all things through Christ which strengtheneth me,"* by his name.

Recently I asked our son Keith, who is now 30 years old but was in the first grade when Kevin gave that speech, if he remembered the episode. Keith replied, "I'll never forget that speech—'Never, never, never turn back....' We all had it memorized."

8. Ride bikes. When our children were grade-school age, we all had a bike and rode together. We found it was fun to ride our bikes together. If money is lacking to purchase bikes, check yard sales. During the fall of 2003, someone gave me a used mountain bike so I could ride with my grade-school age grandchildren.

9. **Take them out to eat.** This outing does not have to cost a lot of money because a meal with you at a fast-food restaurant is a treat for a grade school child. If I felt our children were getting a little careless in cleaning their rooms, I announced a contest for one week. Each of our four children would clean their room and make their bed as they always did; then I checked and decided which room was best for that week. The winner would go out for breakfast. Each child worked hard to win. At the end of the week, I chose a winner. I used this time to remind them of God's command in Ecclesiastes 9:10 which says, *"Whatsoever thy hand findeth to do, do it with thy might; for there is no work, nor device, nor knowledge, nor wisdom, in the grave, whither thou goest."* I reminded them that God always expects our best even if there is no contest. I used praise liberally because they all did a good job.

9. **Make birthdays special.** The birthday child could choose as many children to attend a party in his honor as the number of years he was old. He also chose the cake that I made. I planned lots of activities with a definite starting and ending time. I found two hours was usually enough. In addition to the party, I sent treats to their school class in grade school if the birthday fell within the school year. We also had a family birthday night when I made the birthday child's favorite meal, and he had his meal on the "special red plate." We also used the plate when the child was chosen as "Student of the Week," won an award, or received any other honor.

10. **Send notes and cards.** Children love to receive notes and letters. These can be sent to congratulate the child for doing well in a particular area, for his birthday, for a special occasion such as Thanksgiving, Valentine's Day, Easter, or for no reason except to tell him that you love him and are proud of him. In grade school when our children went to camp, I wrote to them and made them a bag of treats to eat on the bus. Sometimes I left a note at the school office to be delivered to the child.

11. **Encourage them to write notes to grandparents, shut-ins, the pastor, Sunday school teachers, and choir leaders.** Doing so teaches the principle that time spent making life fun for others results in true joy for us.

12. **Attend their sports- and school-related events.** Being there

when your child is involved in any event says to the child by your actions, "I love you, and you are important to me." God is looking for parents who will rear their children according to biblical principles. He is also looking for children who do not have to have all the attention in every situation. Giving a child everything he wants gives that child a wrong value system, encourages selfishness, and discourages his becoming a team player.

I Corinthians 3:9-11 says, "For we are laborers together with God: ye are God's husbandry, ye are God's building. According to the grace of God which is given unto me, as a wise masterbuilder, I have laid the foundation, and another buildeth thereon. But let every man take heed how he buildeth thereupon. For other foundation can no man lay than that is laid, which is Jesus Christ." As I stated before, God is looking for parents who will rear their children according to Bible principles. He is also looking for children who do not have to have the preeminence in every situation and are willing to yield their wills to the will of God.

Praising talent instead of character encourages a child to be a solo player—not a team player. Our sons loved sports because my husband loved sports. We moved to Indiana the summer before Kevin entered the fourth grade, and he excitedly signed up for the Hammond Baptist intramural sports program and was assigned to play for Gamma.

Keith practices for Gamma

Soccer was the first sport he played. Kevin practiced and practiced soccer until he became a good player and dreamed of being selected as a member of the all-star soccer team. His team Gamma won the championship in his fifth grade year, and he was named to the Hammond Baptist Grade School all-star soccer team. His sixth grade year, Gamma was undefeated during the regular season and, if the truth were known, he was more worried about being an all-star than winning the championship again.

When the championship game was over, the score was 1 to 0, with Gamma losing in overtime. Kevin made the all-star team. However, he realized he would gladly trade his all-star trophy for a team victory. Though his team lost, Kevin learned a valuable lesson. Now my husband and I are again cheering for Gamma as we cheer for our grandsons.

Church

The church was the center of our life and our children were taught that nothing was more important in our lives.

1. **Every activity planned for their age group was attended by the child.**

2. **No negative report of an authority placed over them was allowed.** Romans 13:1, 2 says, *"Let every soul be subject unto the higher powers. For there is no power but of God: the powers that be are ordained of God. Whosoever therefore resisteth the power, resisteth the ordinance of God: and they that resist shall receive to themselves damnation."* When we support the authority placed over our child, we build our own authority; and when we criticize authority, we tear down our own authority.

3. **Our family rode the church bus together.** Our children visited with us for about two hours, we took them to lunch, and then we went home. We did not reach as many people as we could have without them; however, we were most interested in letting them see that serving God was fun, was something He would bless, and was a way of life.

Our son Kevin was a leader in the First Baptist Church of Hammond "B" bus ministry before he and Dawn were married and had children. After they were married and had children, the children became a part of the bus ministry. When they moved to Mesa, Arizona, and he became pastor of the Valley Baptist Church, his daughter Ashley was five years old. The first Sunday in Arizona, Ashley asked, "What time will we get on the bus, Daddy?"

"Honey," Kevin answered, "I'm not sure I can pastor the church and run the bus right now."

"But Daddy, I **have** to ride a bus," Ashley explained. (She had never known anything else.)

Kevin contacted the bus captain, and the bus still comes by their house. Each of our grandchildren were allowed to ride the church bus when they reached four years of age. In 2003 Ashley entered the sixth grade and is still riding the bus. Last summer when I was visiting and riding the bus with her, she pointed to some teenagers who towered over her and said, "Grandma, these are my bus kids." Love for people makes them ride the bus in 120 degree Arizona weather in August!

4. **Our family sat in church together and listened to the preacher.** They were not allowed to draw pictures, write notes, read books, or talk during the service. They sang during the song service. If a child was breaking the rule, my husband looked at them and expected them to shape up. If the child's behavior did not improve, he got up and sat by the child. Our children were told to go to the bathroom before the service started and were not allowed to leave during the service. Today our married children and our grandchildren sit with us. I guess habits are hard to break, but we enjoy it!

5. **The pastor was our man of God.** We stressed to our children that God spoke to us each service through the pastor. Every time our children needed to make a decision that would affect their lives, we told them to ask the preacher. Then we prayed that God would speak to them through him. We were **never** disappointed. If we had criticized the pastor, they would not have wanted to listen to him.

Keith, our youngest son, asked Dr. Hyles everything including who he should take to the banquets. I remember thinking, "Dr. Hyles has the weight of the world on his shoulders, and Keith is at his door again." However, Keith was never made to feel that his questions were unimportant, and when major decisions arose in his life, he always consulted Dr. Hyles. Now he does the same with Dr. Schaap.

6. **We tried to teach our children it was more important to please God rather than men.** *"For do I now persuade men, or God? Or if I yet pleased men, I should not be the servant of Christ."* (Galatians 1:10)

My parents taught me that pleasing God brought blessing to my life and that displeasing God brought punishment. I clearly understood the philosophy because pleasing and obeying them brought joy and praise and disobeying them brought "the board of instruction to my seat of knowledge." However, the pain of physical punishment did not compare to the pain I felt when I disappointed my parents. The approval of God and my parents was more important than pleasing my friends. Our children were taught the same way.

We moved to Indiana from Tennessee the summer before our daughter Kelly was to enter the sixth grade. She had been in the same school system in Tennessee all of her life, and it was difficult to enter Hammond Baptist not knowing one person. Some of the girls in her class had formed a clique and would not accept her. Many times they would say things we had taught her were wrong, and this was confusing to her since it was Kelly's first experience in a Christian school. Dr. Phil Sallie was her teacher, and he helped her to stand for right. "Honey," he told Kelly, "don't let those girls destroy you. In ten years, you'll be serving God and they won't." I don't know where those girls are today, but Kelly and her husband and their three sons are serving God.

It is natural for us to desire man's approval and popularity with those we know. However, as much as we would want this approval, it is not always possible.

Activities for Grade-School Children

Many activities were given in the Preschool Section that may be enjoyed by grade-school children which will not be repeated. Refer to Appendixes A-H.

Music

Music should be a part of every child's life, and grade school-age children are not yet self-conscious about their abilities. God felt music was important, or He would not have caused the longest book in the Bible to be the book of Psalms, the songbook of God's people.

Finger Rhymes

Several finger rhymes are included in Appendix A for grade-school age children which my children enjoyed.

Crayon Activities

1. **Crayon Etching.** Cover paper by coloring with a light-colored crayon, then cover the light surface with dark crayon. Scratch through the light surface with the edge of blunt scissors or a tongue

depressor to create a picture or design.

2. **Crayon Leaf Prints.** Place leaf under newsprint or any other paper, and rub the entire surface with crayon on top of the paper to make the impression of the leaf. Prints can also be made with coins, string, pieces of paper, wire screening, burlap, etc. Use your imagination.

3. **Crayon and Paint.** Draw on paper with light-colored crayons, then cover with a tempera wash or dark paint. Paint will cover all but crayon markings. You can do the same with dark-colored crayons and light-colored paper.

4. **Colored Paper.** Using crayons on colored paper teaches children what happens when one color is applied to another. For instance, coloring with a red crayon on yellow paper will look orange. Coloring with a blue crayon on red paper looks purple. Coloring with a yellow crayon on blue paper looks green.

5. **Single Colors.** Choosing one color to use for an entire picture offers a change from having a variety of colors to use.

6. **Variety in Diameter.** Wide crayons can be used with younger children to stimulate more extensive drawing; narrow crayons can be used with older children to stimulate more detailed work.

7. **Crayon Stenciling.** Draw any design on a cloth with a firm, even weave of light, solid color using a crayon. The child should be encouraged to create the design with a pencil which will wash out, and use the crayon when the design pleases him. Place the material face down between two pieces of smooth paper and press with a hot iron. Do not rub the iron across the paper.

8. **Silhouettes.** Have the child lay on a piece of thick paper that is long enough and wide enough so you can trace around the child. Have him draw his face and clothes. Have him cut around the finished figure and hang it on the wall.

9. **Potato Printing.** Cut a potato in half and make a design by cutting down into the potato or cutting away the potato. Put liquid tempera on a Dream Whip container lid and dip the potato in paint, then stamp a paper with the created design. Carrots or turnips can also be used; potatoes are more ideal because they are softer and contain less liquid.

Chalk Activities

1. Dry Paper. Use colored or white chalk on colored or white construction paper. Spray with inexpensive hair spray to set the chalk and keep it from rubbing off the paper.

2. Wet Paper. Wet fingerpaint paper permits chalk to slide more easily, gives more fluid motion to drawing, and makes color more brilliant. Construction paper or paper towels may be used also. If the paper is too wet, it will tear and make a big mess.

3. Wet Chalk. Chalk is dipped in a bowl of water before being used on dry paper. The effects are similar to those mentioned with wet paper.

4. Buttermilk or Diluted Liquid Starch. This is used to the wet the paper. The chalk adheres to the paper after drying.

5. Fixative. One fixative is hair spray which may be sprayed on dried chalk drawing. Add a small amount of either Elmer's glue or liquid starch to water for wet paper drawing. Using a fixative prevents the chalk dust from rubbing off.

Paste Activities

1. Paper Scrap Pictures. (The only glue I like for pasting is Elmer's glue, but remember to twist down the top when finished using the glue.) Tear up scraps of colored paper or scraps of colored paper from magazines. Children will make a picture using these scraps by gluing them with Elmer's glue.

2. Collage Christmas Tree. During the Christmas holidays, cut a green triangle for each child and put collage materials on the table. (See the list of collage materials located in the preschool section.) Let the child create his own Christmas tree by selecting his own materials. Put the "trees" on the wall of the classroom. Each triangle tree is one section of a large tree. Some trees have the point of the triangle facing up; others are facing down.

3. Paper Chains. Cut one-inch to two-inch colored strips of paper and glue together. Encourage the child to make a chain, a paste activity that never seems to grow "old."

A collage tree made by Kelly with buttons, Easter grass, pieces of material, and ribbon

4. Mobiles. Mobiles are floating designs of interesting shapes and materials. Make mobiles from scrap materials—small boxes and scraps of wood, plastic pill boxes, pine cones, "scrunched" tin foil, tin cans, all sorts of bottle caps and corks, toothpicks, washers, and pipe cleaners. The list of items that can be used is endless.

Use one or two coat hangers and hang objects with string or yarn from the hangers. Glue torn paper pieces together to hang from the yarn or use packing pieces or cardboard for the base of the mobile. Punch holes with a paper punch and tie the strings through the holes.

5. Wood Collage. Collect scraps of wood for children to glue together with Elmer's glue. Add a bag of wood balls and knobs found in the craft section of Wal-Mart, and children will have a "ball."

6. Potpourri. When potpourri has lost its scent, let children create posters with it instead of throwing it away.

Karissa Vestal hangs Easter eggs on the "seasonal" tree.

7. Decorated Tree. Find a small tree about three to four feet in height with lots of twigs that is bare of leaves. Cut it down and bring it into the house or classroom. Place it in a container that will not tip over. To stabilize the tree in the container, use rocks, stone, sand, plaster of Paris, or drywall compound. Once the tree is stabilized, place it on the floor or on a table. In the fall, cut out colored leaves from construction paper and attach them to the tree or collect colored fall leaves, iron them between two pieces of waxed paper with a warm iron, cut out, and hang them on the tree. The tree can be used to display salt dough ornaments at Christmas or paper chains or old Christmas cards. Add decorated valentines on Valentine's Day, decorated shamrocks on St. Patrick's Day, and decorated eggs at Easter. (An easy recipe for salt dough is in Appendix C.)

8. Collage Hats. Give every child a paper plate and attach two pieces of string to the plate in order to tie the hat under the chin. Use art tissue or any scrap material to decorate the hat. Give a prize for the best hat.

9.   Decorated Glass Bottles. Cover a glass bottle with art tissue using a mixture of one-third Elmer's glue and two-thirds water. Tear paper using different colors and make designs on the bottle. Let dry and shellac or use a protective finish to keep the paper from "bleeding" if it gets wet.

10.   Papier Mâché. Soak old newspapers in water in a plastic container overnight. Reduce paper to pulp by mixing with hands. Stir in powder wallpaper paste until the mixture begins to feel like modeling clay. Add a few drops of oil of wintergreen* to prevent a sour odor. Use the mixture to make designs on cardboard, mold over objects for masks, bowls, or form elevations on flat surfaces by adding a succession of layers. (You can use a thick paste of flour, water, and salt instead of wallpaper paste.) When dry, paint and shellac. (*Oil of wintergreen may be purchased at a Wal-Mart pharmacy. It has to be ordered one day and picked up the next day.)

To make a bowl, choose a metal or plastic bowl without a ridge on the bottom of the bowl. Rub outside of the bowl with vegetable oil and pack on papier mâché at least one-half inch thick all over the bowl. If you want a handle, make two holes on the side of the bowl near the edge where a handle would go. Make sure you do not cover the bowl rim or you will not be able to remove your papier mache bowl. Let dry on the bowl and then remove. The papier mache bowl can be painted.

11.   Strip Papier Mâché. Crush or roll newspapers to the basic shape desired and tie with string. Wind with torn strips of newspaper dipped into a flour and water paste about the consistency of heavy cream. (You can also use wallpaper paste.) Shape as the strips are added. Strips of paper toweling may be added to the last layer to make a white surface for painting. When dry, paint or shellac.

12.   Balloon Papier Mâché. Blow up balloons and tie securely. Tear a single thickness paper towel into one-inch strips lengthwise. Use liquid starch and dip strips into starch. Wrap balloon until you cannot see the color of the balloon. Make sure the balloon is wrapped in both directions, or the paper will slide off the balloon as it is drying. Hang to dry.

Other Activities

Other activities that children enjoy include making and using sidewalk chalk, slime, silly putty, goop, and super bubbles. These recipes are included in Appendix C. If you blow bubbles outdoors on a sunny day, you can see a rainbow of colors in the bubbles. Dip a long, looped cord shaped in a circle into the bubble mixture on a windy day, and the wind will make the bubble for you!

Dramatic Play

Grade school children love to act out nursery rhymes, folk tales, Aesop's fables, and Bible stories—with or without props. (Some examples are given in Appendixes F and G as well as on the DVD.) If the teacher tells the story first and gets volunteers for the parts, children love acting. This is an easy program for a parents' meeting if the children practice in advance, and a few simple costumes are obtained.

Science

There is no limit to the amount of scientific information a school-age child can learn if it is taught on his level and with a visual aid to help him understand. The following are some scientific activities I have done with school-age children.

Year-Around Activities

1. **Smelling or tasting party.** Put vinegar, rubbing alcohol, lemon juice, vanilla, etc. in glasses and have the children identify by odor. Blindfold children and let them taste carrots, celery, grapes, etc., and identify them. Discuss how sight affects taste because identification is difficult when blindfolded.

2. **Keep an aquarium.** Washing sand and pebbles, helping arrange plants, helping to carry water, learning when to feed the fish (only three times a week), watching the fish, and observing their habits are all-important matters to consider when keeping an aquarium. Watching the development of tadpoles in a pond is a fascinating study. When our daughter Krysten was in grade school, she received some goldfish as a bus promotion on our bus. For over a year, she conscientiously fed them, cleaned the fish tank, and her fish

grew. One day I noticed her carrying the fish out the kitchen door, and I asked what she was doing. "I have taken care of these fish long enough," she replied. "Now I am putting them in the creek so they can care for themselves."

3. **Keep pets.** A child should learn how to treat animals. Some possible choices are cats, dogs, rabbits, turtles, guinea pigs, insects, white mice, salamanders, canaries, hens, and chickens. Making animal cages, feeding the animals, watching them, listening to them, observing

Keith and Amen

their habits, learning care in handling them, and collecting them from the country or buying them from the pet shop are all part of learning how to properly treat animals. Children can also learn to feed and clean up after the animal. Extra effort on the part of parents is required if the children are to learn.

4. **Care for house plants.** Watering plants each day, growing slips in a cutting pot in sand, caring for bulbs such as a paper-white narcissus or hyacinth in water so you can see root development, or keeping a chart to record the growth of bulbs are character-building activities for a child to do.

5. **Maintain a nature table.** Bring in interesting objects of nature such as acorns, seeds, flowers, leaves, rocks, and birds' nests. Watch the growth of plants. Provide ideal growing conditions for some plants, while depriving others of sun, water, or growing space. Observe the difference.

When I taught first grade in a low-income area, I tried to think of a project that would involve all the children in my class. We had a lesson on rocks, and I suggested that each child find one interesting rock to put on a table I named the "rock table." The children were so excited because this was something all of them could do.

The following day, the rocks started coming in. The children felt if one rock was good, many rocks were better! Soon the "rock table" was overflowing with rocks of every size and description. I announced the end of the rock study, but the children kept bringing them. Sometimes the rocks were so large I was amazed the child could pick it up—let alone carry it to school! This situation taught me how much children want to please you if you give them a way to do so.

6. Go on excursions. To find nuts, flowers or bouquets, or just to explore are three good reasons for taking excursions. (Two walks a week are considered a minimum!) Sit in the woods and listen to all the sounds. The children can learn to identify them.

7. Choose and watch a class tree. Watch it drop leaves and observe it under various conditions throughout the year. Teach children that every tree has seeds, fruits, and flowers.

8. Make a museum. Make exhibits of rocks, shells, nuts, insects, nests, plants, quills, bark, bones, cotton, wool, fungus growth, and gourds. Make sure the children do not just bring in items, but they understand the lesson to be learned from studying that item. A teacher can never take a child further than she has gone herself. No one is too old to keep learning, and this makes teaching exciting!

Seasonal Activities

FALL

1. Leaves. Collect and sort leaves according to size, shape, and color. Make leaf prints; mount the leaves; use them for room decorations; press them between two pieces of waxed paper with a warm iron and then paste them in a leaf book. Scuff through the leaves; and rake, pile, and jump in the leaves. Take up and store bulbs for winter protection. Get an amaryllis bulb and watch it bloom. Put the plant outdoors in the summer; store it in a dark place for at least two months in the winter, bring it out of the dark place, water it, and put it in the sunshine. The plant will bloom again, and it will multiply.

2. Flowers. Arrange bouquets for room decorations, make weed bouquets, harvest vegetables or flowers from a garden, have exhibits of vegetables grown in the garden, or arrange fall flowers that the children have picked. Talk about how some vegetables (green beans, peas, and corn) grow on top of the ground, and some (carrots, onions, turnips) grow under the ground.

When I taught first grade, a child brought me a flower, and I put it behind my ear in my hair. When the other children noticed the flower, I received flowers or weeds every day until the frost killed them. Every day when I got home from school, I removed a wilted flower from my hair and threw it away. However, I treasured the love of the child who had picked it and had given it to me.

3. **Fall insects.** Collect, feed, and observe crickets, grasshoppers, or ants. Putting a few grains of sugar or crumbs of bread near an anthill will provide a wonderful science lesson.

4. **Plant spring bulbs.** Choose bulbs from a catalog and prepare the soil properly.

5. **Seeds.** Watch how they "catch" rides—by blowing in the wind or clinging to a sleeve. Sort them and arrange a seed collection. Collect seeds as food for the winter birds. Make a poster showing seeds that "fly," such as milkweed or maple seeds.

6. **Gather nuts.** Make candy and cookies with nuts that have been gathered. Compare your gathering to animals who also gather nuts.

7. **Make general observations.** Watch the leaves fall. Notice how insects become less abundant in the cold weather. The robins leave. Watch the squirrels storing nuts for winter.

WINTER

1. **Feed winter birds.** Make a feeding tray. As the birds come to eat, watch the habits of the different birds as they come to the feeding station. Learn the names of the birds that come to eat, and find out what to feed them. Make a Christmas tree for the birds by wrapping a string around a pinecone so it will hang on a tree in your yard. Spread peanut butter on the pinecone and roll it through birdseed on waxed paper. Hang the finished product on your tree. Also, birds will enjoy stringed popcorn. Hang suet in a mesh bag. (Suet can be made using fat trimmed from a roast.) Make bird houses for spring. Plant trees and shrubs that will furnish food and shelter for the birds.

2. **Christmas greens.** Arrange mistletoe and holly. Observe the cones on Christmas trees. Smell the balsam. Make balsam pillows of needles from the Christmas tree. Notice the difference between evergreen and deciduous trees.

3. **Snow and ice.** Watch snow as it falls. Model snowmen. Catch snowflakes on a dark coat sleeve or mittens to see the form of

the flakes. Give each child a piece of black construction paper when it is snowing, and as the child "catches" the flakes, he can see the shape of the snowflakes. Play with sleds. Put dishes of water outside to freeze and see that ice expands when it freezes. Bring in ice to watch it melt. Teach that it takes heat to melt ice. Our children loved to put one-half inch of water in a pan, set it outside to freeze, then put the pan on a hot plate to see the three forms of water—liquid (water), solid (ice), and gas (steam).

4. **Thermometer readings.** Put a thermometer out of doors and compare it with indoor readings. Notice that the thermometer registers higher when it is warmer and lower when it is cooler. Learn to read the thermometer.

5. **Wind.** Watch what it does to smoke, leaves, and flags outdoors. Watch the wind move clouds in the sky. Fly kites. Listen to the sound of wind when it rustles leaves and grass.

SPRING

1. **Birds.** Watch for birds, especially robins, bluebirds, and the "early" birds that signify spring is coming. Keep a record of the date when the first robin or first bluebird is spotted. Put out short pieces of string or worsted yarn for birds to use in building nests. If a nest is nearby, let children watch eggs hatch and birds develop.

2. **A school garden.** Plant and care for a school garden. Prepare the ground, but let the children help with the hoeing or breaking up the dirt clumps. Select flowers or vegetables that are hardy. Children can weed, water, and dig around plants.

3. **May baskets.** Pick flowers to make May baskets. Learn to pick only plentiful flowers in an acceptable place—not from other people's yards. (Smelling is allowed but not picking.) Learn how to pick flowers properly.

4. **Plant experiments.** Plant lima beans or scarlet runner beans. From time to time, pull up one plant to see how it grows. Give each child a lima bean to plant in a cup or can. Each child is responsible to water his plant. The plant which reaches the greatest height wins. The child can measure his plant every day or two.

Watch sprouted potatoes grow in dark and light. Cut a potato "eye," plant it, and watch it grow. (These potatoes should be purchased from a farmer's market or farm because those in stores have been treated to prevent sprouting.) Bring twigs of flowering shrubs into the room in early spring, put the ends in a container of water, and watch them develop. Grow sweet potatoes and carrots in water. Again, sweet potatoes must be from the farm market. Push four toothpicks into the sides of the sweet potato. The toothpicks need to sit on the rim of a container. Fill the container with water so that the bottom of the sweet potato is covered with water. Put the cut top of a carrot in a small amount of water. Cut a stalk of celery in half lengthwise, leaving the top two-thirds of the stalk intact. Place one half of the cut stalk in red-colored water and the other half in blue-colored water. Watch how the plant draws the colored water into each half section of the stalk. Plants must have water to survive.

Activities Related to Physical Science

1. **Magnets.** Notice what items magnets will and will not attract. Fish with magnets. Catch a paper fish with a nail put through the fish so it will be attracted by the magnet.

2. **Sound.** Play on a drum. Play the treble and bass keys of a piano, noticing the vibrations of strings on the piano. Fill glasses with various amounts of water, tap them with a dinner knife, and listen to the different sounds. Have a band of boxes, using hat boxes, oatmeal boxes, etc., but letting the children use the boxes as drums. Listen to chimes and church bells. Fill a paper bag with air and make it burst. The loud noise is made by the air being compressed.

3. **Light.** Watch light reflected on the ceiling from an aquarium. Play with a prism hanging in a sunny window. (Inexpensive prisms may be obtained at the chandelier section in any home improvement store.) Look in a hand-held mirror and play with the mirror to see how it reflects sunshine. Observe variations of shadows at different times of the day. A good game to play outdoors on a sunny day is "Shadow Tag." Have the children try to step on your shadow.

4. **Chemistry.** Dissolve different items in water such as salt or paint. Watch salt and crystals form as water is evaporated from salt water. Make gelatin—observing the three forms gelatin can have (powder, liquid, and solid). As mentioned previously, do the same with water—solid, liquid, and gas.

5. **Electricity.** Ring a bell with a dry cell connected with a key,

discovering what makes the bell stop ringing. Make sparks by shuffling over carpet and touching another person. Turn an electric current off and on. Experiment with a flashlight. Watch the action of a hairbrush on hair.

6. **Mechanics.** Balance on a seesaw. Play with blocks, learning balance relationships between more than one block. Hammer nails and learn to make the nails go straight. Experiment with steam. Observe machines, such as steam shovels and cranes, in a construction area.

7. **Weather.** Observe weather—snow, clouds, sleet, frost, fog, and hail. Keep a record of the weather on a calendar.

8. **Astronomy.** Notice the phases of the moon, shadows, the beauty of the stars, and how they make pictures in the sky. Prick the outline of the big dipper in an oatmeal box so that it will show through when held up to the light. Look for the sun at various times of the day and note its position in the sky.

9. **Air.** Make whirligigs from paper. Cut a square piece of bond paper into an eight-inch square. Carefully cut diagonally from the four corner points to one-half inch from the center. Bring the opposite corner tips to the center to meet. **Do not fold!** Put a straight pin through each of the four tips through the center of the paper and push it into the eraser on a pencil. Let the children blow on their whirligigs. Show that air can move things, keep things out, be powerful, pick up objects, push up, and even hold up children on the inflated wheels of a bicycle.

Light a candle and put a jar over it. Why does the flame go out? (Because the oxygen supply is removed.)

10. **Water.** Discover what will float in water and what will sink. Catch steam on glass when water is boiled. Observe the differences between dew and rain. Watch rain make rivers in gutters. Boil water and watch it disappear from the pan. Put water in the sun and in the shade to see which will evaporate faster. Take two identical pieces of tinfoil and fold one into a boat and crush the other piece into a ball. Explain that the boat floats because it presents a greater surface area displacing little water. The crushed foil ball displaces more water and sinks. The ball sinks just as the boat would sink if a hole were punched in it.

Activities

Magnetic Attraction

PURPOSE: To learn more about the power of a magnet to attract different types of objects.

MATERIALS: Magnets, nails or tacks, sawdust, paper, salt

PROCEDURE: Use the magnet to separate the nails and tacks from the pile of sawdust. Try to pick up other objects from the sawdust and point out the magnet is not effective on the other objects.

RESULTS: When the magnet is close enough, the objects like the nails and tacks actually jump to meet the magnet. This attraction is due to the magnetic field present in the magnet ends and the fact that these are attracted by iron and steel. For this reason, the paper, sawdust, and salt will not be picked up.

CONCLUSIONS: Magnets have the interesting ability to attract objects made of iron or steel. They have no effect on paper and salt.

Children can learn about magnets from play. Recently, I purchased a child-sized plastic fishing pole and some colored plastic fish with magnets in their mouth because I thought our pre-school grandchildren would enjoy "catching" the fish in the laundry sink. Four-year-old David, two-year-old Peter, and five-year-old Simon enjoyed letting the magnets on the end of the fishing line attract the magnet in the fish's mouth so the fish could be caught. One of the magnets in one of the fish's mouth was reversed, and it repelled the fishing pole magnet. Peter was fishing alone and suddenly started to scream.

We ran to the laundry room thinking he had fallen off the stool and was hurt. Instead, he was angry and kept saying, "Catch fish! Catch fish!" He was frustrated because the fish with the reversed magnet could not be caught!

Try explaining how the magnet in the mouth of the fish was reversed to a two year old!

Experiments with Water

PURPOSE: To see what will or will not float. To see what will or will not mix with water. To experiment with water in different forms.

MATERIALS NEEDED: Water, rocks, wood, paper, capped and uncapped bottles, aluminum foil, crayons, leaves, sand, oil, sugar, salt, soda, food coloring, dirt, juice, and a pan

FLOATING OBJECTS: Lay out materials next to a pan and let children experiment with them. Observe that some objects float and others do not, explaining why.

MIXING SUBSTANCES: Put out some materials that mix with water (sugar, salt, food coloring, baking soda) and some that do not (dried beans, pebbles, uncooked pasta). Explain.

ICE: Place water in an ice tray in the freezer. Place water in juice glass full to the rim with waxed paper on top. Place the filled glass in the freezer and explain that water expands as it freezes and will push up the waxed paper. Water in the tray will freeze faster than the water in the glass due to the greater surface area exposed. Ice is another form of water and expands as it freezes. Surface areas affect freezing time.

STEAM: Put a small amount of water in kettle and heat. Boil rapidly so steam comes out the spout. Carefully let the children feel the steam. Let steam collect on the bottom of a glass until moisture (water) collects. Explain that steam is many droplets of water.

FROST: Place empty glasses in the freezer for a short period of time. Take out of the freezer and watch the glass turn "frosty" as the air hits it, explaining that air hitting a cold surface makes frost since there is moisture in the air. Let the glass sit at room temperature, and the frost turns to droplets of water.

EVAPORATION OF WATER: On a sunny day, put the same amount of water in two wide-mouthed jars. Mark the water line on each jar with adhesive tape. Place one jar in the sun and one in the shade. At the end of the day, see which one has the most water. Discuss the fact that the warmer the air, the faster the rate of evaporation. There should be more evaporation from the water in the jar placed in the sun because warm water helps water turn to vapor. The warmer and drier the air, the more rapidly the process of the evaporation.

MAKING FOG: Pour a glass of hot water into a clean glass bottle with a small opening, like a juice bottle. Rest an ice cube on top of the bottle and hold the bottle in front of a strong light. The warm damp air rises and meets the cool air under the ice, and the tiny drops of warm water in the damp air are cooled. When the warm, moist air meets the ice, real fog forms. What you see swirling up and down in the bottle is fog. The warm water in the bottle is like the water in the lakes and rivers which the sun warms. The ice is like the cooled air when the sun is not shining. The fog in the bottle is just like the fog on rivers, roads, and cities. When warm, moist air is cooled, fog forms. Fog is thick. Fog is similar to mist; mist is thinner than fog.

Experiments with Thunder

PROBLEM: What makes thunder?

MATERIALS NEEDED: A paper sack for each child

PROCEDURE: Discuss ideas that children have about thunder. The teacher should explain that lightning flashes are big sparks of electricity, that lightning is very hot, that air is suddenly made very hot and expands, and that sudden movement of expanded air makes thunder. Then give each child a paper bag and ask him to inflate it by blowing it up. Let each child pop his inflated bag.

RESULTS: 1) A loud noise results. 2) The teacher explains that the loud noise results from the sudden movement of air out of the bag. 3) Explain that lightning heats the air, causing it to expand with rapid movement, thus producing the loud, crashing sound known as thunder.

CONCLUSION: Rapid movement of air causes noise.

Language Development

When children do not say words clearly, you should say the word in the right way, but do not force the child to continually repeat it. Forced repetition makes him feel like a failure and may make his speech worse. This principle also applies to a stuttering child.

If you tell stories to your children, they will want to tell or read stories to each other. Stories can be used strictly for fun or to teach lessons to children. If they remember the story, they will remember the lesson. You are also building a relationship with the children as you spend time telling the stories.

I wanted to teach the lesson of honesty as found in Romans 12:17, *"Recompense to no man evil for evil. Provide things honest in the sight of all men."* When I was nine years old, we spent a week visiting my mother's parents, who lived on a small farm in Tennessee. They raised tobacco as their money crop, and one morning my grandfather said he was going to hoe the tobacco plants. This sounded like a very important and exciting job to me, so I begged to be allowed to do it. I could see that my grandfather was less than enthusiastic about my help, but he agreed to let me try. He gave me a hoe, and we walked to the field. The tobacco plants were only about six inches tall, and he showed me how to loosen the dirt around the plant without chopping the plant in half. I was given a row to hoe, and my grandfather said he would see me at the end of the long row. I quickly discovered that this job was not quite as exciting as I felt it would be. However, I was determined to make it to the end of the row. As I was hoeing, I would occasionally get too close to the plant and chop it in half. Afraid to tell my grandfather, I took the top of the plant and packed the dirt around it so it would look normal. When I reached the end, my grandfather praised me because I finished the job, and no plants were on the ground.

However, the next morning, it was a different story. All the plants I had chopped in half had fallen over and were now lying on the ground—never to grow again. I do not remember my grandfather giving me a lecture, but I remember his telling me that covering over sins instead of confessing them cuts us off from God's blessing. *"He that covereth his sins shall not prosper: but whoso confesseth and forsaketh them shall have mercy."* (Proverbs 28:13)

My tobacco-hoeing career started and ended with that one experience, but I never have forgotten the lesson I learned.

Teaching Children to Tell the Truth

As long as I can remember, my parents stressed Proverbs 12:22, *"Lying lips are abomination to the LORD: but they that deal truly are his delight."* They told me the stories of Achan and of Ananias and Sapphira, who died as a result of lying. I was not made to repeat, "I will not lie" every day, but I knew God hated and punished lying.

My parents practiced what they preached and taught me truth was absolute—not black, white, or gray. I never remember my parents lying to me, so I knew lying was taboo.

I remember the first time that as a child of nine, I was exposed to lying. Our next door neighbor was a doctor, and he had a daughter my age who was my friend. I was visiting at their house late one afternoon when the telephone rang. My friend answered and said, "No, my father is not here."

Looking into the den, I could see her father reading the newspaper. Thinking she was blind, I pulled on her arm and said, "Your father is in the next room."

Smugly, she shook her head and said to the person on the telephone, "No, I don't know when he will be home."

As she hung up, I said in horror, "You lied."

With a shake of her head, she casually said, "That's what my father told me to say."

I went straight home and told my mother the story. My mother made it clear that my main job was to make sure I always told the truth—that I was not to be a watchman of the world and correct others. This incident happened over 50 years ago, and I have never forgotten this lesson.

When our children were little, we used the Bible to teach the same lessons about God's hatred of lying such as Colossians 3:9, *"Lie not one to another, seeing that ye have put off the old man with his deeds."* Psalm 119:163, *"I hate and abhor lying: but thy law do I love."* Proverbs 6:16-19, *"These six things doth the LORD hate: yea, seven are an abomination unto him: A proud look, a lying tongue, and hands that shed innocent blood, An heart that deviseth wicked imaginations, feet that be swift in running to mischief, A false witness that speaketh lies, and he that soweth discord among the brethren."*

Lying was never a problem with our children. Before they were able to write, we explained how much God hated lying, required them to look us the eye and admit what they did wrong, and why it was wrong. We then washed out their mouths with soap to cleanse their dirty heart. I also asked them if they wanted to make God and me sad. Since young children want to please the authority, this also discourages lying.

When we lived in Tennessee, we would drive 40 miles to visit my parents, Mr. and Mrs. Bill White, once every week. We would eat together, and the children would usually take a bath and put on their pajamas because they would often fall asleep before we got home.

One night when Kelly was six years old, my mother, whom the children call "Mimi," started running the bath water and called Kelly to come and take her bath. Kelly was playing in the den and said, "I am busy, Mimi. I don't want to take a bath."

Hearing this response, I told Kelly to go to the bedroom where I planned to apply the "board of instruction" to her "seat of knowledge." Kelly was crying on her way to the bedroom because she knew the punishment for rebellion.

Mimi said, "Are you going to spank that poor little thing? Maybe she didn't hear me."

"Yes, Mother," I replied. "I am planning to spank this rebellious child because she heard you call and chose to ignore you. To delay is to disobey." Proverbs 22:15 says, *"Foolishness is bound in the heart of a child; but the rod of correction shall drive it far from him."*

Cooking

Children love to help with cooking. It is true that it takes longer when they help, but the time spent with your child is worth the effort. The following are some of the things our children enjoyed.

1. Apple caramel dip. Every fall we go to the apple orchard as a family and pick apples—first with our children and now with our grandchildren. We go home, slice the apples, and enjoy apple caramel dip. (This recipe is included in Appendix D.)

2. Macaroni and cheese. Every time we get together with our Cervantes grandchildren, Stephen, Sam, and Simon, we make box shells and cheese—their favorite kind. I have offered to make something else, but shells and cheese is always their choice. They stir it together and then eat it all—two boxes!

3. Frozen grapes. Have children wash and remove the seedless grapes from the stem. Spread on a cookie sheet covered with waxed paper. When frozen, store in Ziploc® bag. Eat frozen grapes instead of popsicles for a snack.

4. Frozen bananas. Peel the bananas and cut in half lengthwise. Insert a wooden ice cream stick into the cut end of the banana. Lay on baking sheet on waxed paper until frozen. On wax paper, spread crushed graham crackers or crushed peanuts. Roll banana in chocolate syrup, then in crumbs or nuts. Freeze. Serve frozen.

Recipes are also included in Appendix D for cookie flowers, rice krispy snacks, oatmeal cookies, dipped chocolate crackers, and fresh fruit dip.

Books

Several books lists for preschool through grade school are included in Appendix E in this book. Dr. Jack Hyles said the most important books a child could read are biographies that reflect Biblical values as opposed to modern biographies of movie stars, rock stars, and modern sports figures. Included in the book lists are biographies, historical books, and informational books. I want every book I read to pass the Philippians 4:8 test: *"Finally, brethren, whatsoever things are true, whatsoever things are honest, whatsoever things are just, whatsoever things are pure, whatsoever things are lovely, whatsoever things are of good report; if there be any virtue, and if there be any praise, think on these things."*

One of the most important things you can do for your child is to teach him to love books and reading. If a child does not learn to read well, he will never do well in school. It is important to provide books with the right philosophy because error stored in our minds can never be erased and will affect our thoughts and actions.

Story Recreation

Take any story and cross out key words in the story replacing it with that word's part of speech. Ask the children to give you the words to fill in the lines. For example, ask for a noun or a verb or an adjective and write the words they give you in place of the original words. Read the story back to the class when you are finished. Asking for unusual words will make a more interesting story.

Games

Games enjoyed by our family are included in Appendix H. Games are a quick and inexpensive way to spend time with your children.

Trips

A child can benefit from trips to common places if the teacher is prepared. The preparation of the leader will largely determine the success of the trip. Before a trip:

1.   Organize your materials so all supplies will be there. Be sure to take water and cups if the day is warm.

2.   Visit the place ahead of time and know what to mention to the children so they will receive the greatest benefit from the trip.

3.   Sing on the way or play simple games so children will not

become bored and misbehave.

4.   Try to help the authority where you are visiting speak on the level of the children by asking questions or telling him of the children's interests ahead of time. If information is given that is too complex for the children to understand, the children will become restless.

5.   Set limits and make sure the children are under control so the place you are visiting will welcome you back. If a child will not stay with you, hold his hand.

6.   Plan ahead so that the children can have firsthand experience at the places being visited. For instance, if the class is visiting a bakery, it would be nice if each child has the money to buy a cookie. The following are some of the places our children have enjoyed visiting:

- Greenhouse
- Grocery store
- Farm
- Museum
- Construction area
- Teacher's home
  (*Check ahead.*)
- Bakery
- Poultry farm
- Hospital or clinic
- Laundry
- Cleaners
- Car wash
- Produce market
- Seed store
- Pet store
- Park
- Flower garden
- Fish hatchery
- Dentist
- Fire department
- Truck terminal
- Bottling plant
- Police department
- Factory
- Railroad station
- Airport
- Aquarium
- Zoo
- Vegetable garden
- Post office
  (*Let child mail a letter.*)
- Candy store

After the trip, talk about what the child saw. Have them make a picture or write a story about what they remembered from the trip. If the child cannot write, have him draw a picture and ask him to tell you about the picture. Print what the child says on the picture. A child will enjoy the trip if the leader enjoys it and will learn as much as the leader is prepared to teach him. Thank-you notes or pictures for those who helped make the trip a reality help children learn to be appreciative of others.

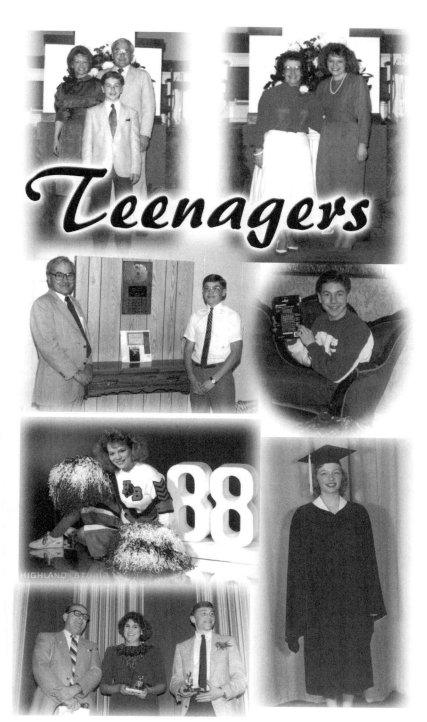

Teenagers

Teenagers
(Photos on page 147)

Top left: Pete, Frieda, and Keith Cowling at Keith's junior high graduation

Top right: Mrs. Elaine Colsten and Krysten Cowling

Center right: Keith

Bottom right: Frieda White's high school graduation

Bottom left: Kevin receives an award from Dr. Hyles

Middle left: Krysten the cheerleader

Middle left: Kevin and his dad with high school shop project

By the time a child becomes a teenager, he is more like an adult then a child and usually spends more time with his friends than with his parents. It is to be expected that he will build his life away from his parents because soon he will leave home and be on his own. A teenager does not want to be treated like a child and will resent being treated this way. This concept is difficult because you have known your child for 12 years as a child, and it is hard to shift gears to see him in any other way. One moment your teen will seem very grown up and the next regress to childlike behavior. This behavior is normal, and if you have a critical spirit, it will make the behavior of your teen worse. If you want your teenager to view you as a fun person, you must plan to do things with teens that they enjoy at a time that is convenient for them.

The following are some of the rules we established when our children became teenagers as a way of maintaining a close relationship with them. If the authority develops a close relationship with a child, as well as consistently enforcing the rules, teens will be a joy instead of a trial. The worst part of every punishment should be the broken relationship between the authority and the teen. It is a mistake for the authority to become the teen's "buddy" instead of his authority, and if this happens, the teen will lose respect for the authority.

1. Rules for our teenagers were not to be questioned or changed. When I was in high school, I was never allowed to ride alone with a date, and I had to be home by 11:00 p.m. or call to tell my father why I was going to be late. These rules were much stricter than those of my friends; but I knew if I questioned the rules, I would not be dating at all. If I rode in a car with a date, my brother David, who was four years my junior, rode with us. I accepted this rule because I loved my dad and wanted to please him.

One night after a high school football game, my brother and I waited for the guy I was dating, who was the captain of the team, to dress and take us home. We went by a restaurant after the game and I noticed it was getting close to 11:00 p.m. There was a pay phone and when I went to call my dad, someone else was using the phone. I should have waited, but I decided that we could probably make it to my house by 11:00 p.m. We started home and were almost to my house when I saw my dad's truck coming toward us. I realized I was in trouble. I quickly said good night to my date, and my brother and I walked inside the house. The clock said 11:05 p.m.

Instead of going to my room, I sat on the sofa in the den and waited for my dad to get home. In a few minutes I heard his truck come into the driveway. I thought he would be angry. I was a high school junior, and this was the first time I had broken the 11:00 curfew rule. However, my dad was calm as he asked, "What time did I tell you to be home?"

"Eleven," I replied.

"What time did you get here?" he wanted to know.

"11:05," I meekly replied.

I remember how disappointed my dad looked as he said, "I thought I could trust you."

I was 16 years old at the time, and my dad spanked me. I do not remember being hurt by the spanking, but my dad's words cut me to the heart because I knew I had disappointed him. I vowed that I would never be late again, and I wasn't, not because of the spanking but because of the broken relationship.

By the time a child becomes a teenager, he should be familiar with the rules the parents have established to guide his behavior. I always prayed that God would have the confidence in my husband and me that He had in Abraham in Genesis 18:19 which says, *"For I (God) know him, (Abraham) that he will command his children and his household after him, and they shall keep the way of the Lord, to do justice and judgment; that the Lord may bring upon Abraham that which he hath spoken of him."*

It has been my experience that there are no exceptions to God's rules. God intends for parents to establish rules for children to follow, to praise them when they obey the rules, to punish them when they disobey the rules, and to build a close relationship with children so the worst part of every punishment will be the broken relationship between the child and his parent. This relationship is a result of the child's knowing the parents love him unconditionally and love him enough to punish him when he breaks their rules. (Saying "I love my child too much to spank him" comes from Satan and contradicts biblical philosophy.) How Satan must enjoy it when we fall for his advise in rearing our children – hook, line, and sinker.

Proverbs 13:24: *"He that spareth his rod hateth his son: but he that loveth him chasteneth him betimes."*

Proverbs 19:18: *"Chasten thy son while there is hope, and let not thy soul spare for his crying."*

Proverbs 20:30: *"The blueness of a wound cleanseth away evil: so do stripes the inward parts of the belly."*

Proverbs 22:15: *"Foolishness is bound in the heart of a child; but the rod of correction shall drive it far from him."*

Spending time with the child builds the relationship. When you give time, you give the most valuable gift – yourself. This responsibility of rearing teenagers is not given to the pastor, the youth leader, the Sunday school teacher, or to the Christian school. Their role is simply to reinforce what the parents have taught the child.

Colossians 3:20: *"Children, obey your parents in all things: for this is well pleasing unto the Lord."*

Ephesians 6:1-3: *"Children, obey your parents in the Lord: for this is right. Honour thy father and mother; which is the first commandment with promise; That it may be well with thee, and thou mayest live long on the earth."*

When my children would want to disobey my husband's rules, I would look them squarely in the eyes and ask them if they wanted to shorten their life, and then I waited for an answer. This sobering thought was effective in changing their behavior. If their behavior did not change, the penalty for breaking that rule was administered.

From a very young age, our children were told by my husband that if they did not want to obey the rules he had set, he would bring in their suitcases from the garage, help them pack, kiss them goodbye, and allow them to provide food, shelter, and clothing for themselves. Allowing a child or teenager to do what he chooses to do instead of obeying God and his parents gives him the impression that the parents are condoning the child's rebellious behavior.

Proverbs 29:15: *"The rod and reproof give wisdom: but a child left to himself bringeth his mother to shame."*

God's cure for this rebellious behavior is given in Deuteronomy 21:18-21 which says, "*If a man have a stubborn and rebellious son, which will not obey the voice of his father, or the voice of his mother, and that, when they have chastened him, will not hearken unto them: Then shall his father and his mother lay hold on him, and bring him out unto the elders of his city, and unto the gate of his place; And they shall say unto the elders of his city, This our son is stubborn and rebellious, he will not obey our voice; he is a glutton, and a drunkard. And all the men of his city shall stone him with stones, that he die: so shalt thou put evil away from among you; and all Israel shall hear, and fear.*"

By the time a child becomes a teenager, he should have learned to obey the rules the parents have set or have to pay a price that is worse than the pleasure of having his own way when the rule is broken. Since teens are more like adults than children, they should be allowed to make decisions that do not contradict the Bible. This is difficult for parents because they have known them longer as children. Treating a teen like a child and making all the decisions for them is something they hate and creates resentment towards parents. Rules give security to a teenager who is teetering between childhood and adulthood.

Our Rules for Wearing Makeup

Our two girls were allowed to wear makeup when they entered the seventh grade. However, they did not go from no makeup to an excessive amount of makeup. My husband told them makeup should enhance their appearance, not call attention to them in a worldly or garish way. I don't remember either of them deciding to wear black lipstick or dark fingernail polish. If they had, my husband would have drawn a line forbidding it. My husband always made it clear that there should be a clear difference in the way we look and the way the world looks. They did not rebel because my husband and I lived the same way and followed the same rules.

We made sure we were in a church with a pastor who preached that women should be modest and chaste and dressed according to the Biblical standard for women in Deuteronomy 22:5, "*The woman shall not wear that which pertaineth unto a man, neither shall a man put on a woman's garment; for all that do so are abomination unto the LORD thy God.*" I believe women should never wear trousers of any kind for any reason. We made no provision for a double standard at home, church, or school. We did not allow our children to watch movies or television programs that glorified immodest dress. We did not allow them to dress improperly or wear worldly makeup. We tried to emphasize the benefit of rules instead of dwelling on the negative.

Praise is so important when the teenager follows the rules the parents have set. When correction needs to be given, the parents should administer it lovingly, privately, and without anger. If the parent is angry, he should wait to give correction. Proverbs 15:1 says, *"A soft answer turneth away wrath: but grievous words stir up anger."* Proverbs 25:15, *"By long forbearing is a prince persuaded, and a soft tongue breaketh the bone."*

Our Rules for Church Attire

One word my husband stressed was "appropriate." Our daughters were not allowed to wear sloppy, ragged clothes to church. My husband required our daughters to wear hosiery for church and for special occasions when they entered the seventh grade. On Sundays our sons wore dress shirts, ties, and sport coats to church when they entered junior high. On Wednesday nights, he allowed them to wear only a dress shirt and tie. They were not allowed to wear tennis shoes. When they said, "Our friends are wearing such and such," and what their friends were wearing did not agree with my husband's rules, he said, "What is your last name?"

"Cowling," our sons would reply in unison.

"Those who live under the Cowling roof will following the Cowling rules." End of discussion! He gave them a hearing as long as they were respectful, but my husband had the final word. Our children did not want to be different from their friends, but because our children loved and respected their dad, they complied with the rules—sometimes happily and sometimes grudgingly. The only way you can make these kinds of rules and enforce them is to start building a close relationship from infancy. *"Children, obey your parents in the Lord: for this is right. Honour thy father and mother (which is the first commandment with promise;) That it may be well with thee, and thou mayest live long on the earth."* (Ephesians 6:1-3) *"Children, obey your parents in all things: for this is well pleasing unto the Lord."* (Colossians 3:20)

Our Rules for Dating

My husband encouraged our children to participate in all the youth activities sponsored by the church. Attraction to a member of the opposite gender is natural from the sixth grade on for girls and from junior high school on for guys. We tried to make it easy for our children to talk about those whom they liked, but my husband always told them they should graduate from college before they married. He stressed that marriage was the second most important decision they would make after salvation and one that should last "until death do you part."

None of our children dated seriously in high school even though they had friends of the opposite gender, and they went to all of the banquets sponsored by the church and the Youth Department. If a special activity came, and they did not have a date, we encouraged them to go with a friend of the same gender so they would benefit from all the activities of their high school years. My husband made our sons get a date for the Valentine's Banquet each year. He said the experience was a part of their education.

One year when Kevin was a high school senior and Keith was in the seventh grade, they had dates with sisters for the Sweetheart Banquet. Keith was "Mr. Organization." He got a swatch of material from the dress his date was having made, took it to the florist, and ordered a rose corsage to match. That night as we sat around the dinner table, Keith shared what he had done. Kevin replied, "Oh, no! How could you do that? I can't give her sister the carnations I ordered. You rat!" (Both girls received roses.)

My husband established and followed these dating rules for our children:

- *A girl was not allowed to call either of our sons on the telephone.* Our girls were not allowed to call young men. A few times one of our daughters wanted to call a young man to ask a question about a class assignment. My husband said, "Have Kevin call so-and-so for you and get your answer."

- *Our children were not allowed to sit with a date for every church service.* When they did sit with a date, it was with our family or with the parents of the date. If they objected to this rule, they were not allowed to sit with a date in church.

- *Our children were not allowed to have any physical contact with a member of the opposite gender.* We tried to eliminate the opportunity for this to happen.

• *Our children were never allowed to ride in a car with a date without a chaperon.* A younger brother or sister could ride with the dating couple, or my husband and I would accompany them. I have many special memories of chaperoning our children on dates during their college years.

• *College graduation should come before marriage.* Our four children all graduated from Hyles-Anderson College, met his or her future mate at Hyles-Anderson College, but had their college diploma in hand before their wedding. Our youngest son Keith finished college in three years so he could get married. After marriage, he worked and paid the bills so his wife could receive her college degree one year later. My husband felt it was Keith's responsibility to see that his wife Michelle graduated from college since her parents had sacrificed to send her there. My husband and I, as well as Michelle's parents, are glad that Keith followed his dad's advice and paid the price to see that she graduated. She did not work to pay her way; Keith worked to pay her way. Michelle did not have to give up her dreams or her degree to marry our son.

• *Any dating rule mentioned by Dr. Hyles, our pastor during our children's teen years, was followed without question.*

• *We encouraged our children to ask Brother Hyles for his approval on those whom they wished to date.* We stressed that if a person is lazy, unfaithful, and has a bad attitude, he will not be the right kind of marriage partner. My husband always told our daughters, "No man is handsome when you are looking at him with two eyes he has just blackened for you." He told our sons, "True beauty in a girl doesn't wash off at night. If she spends a massive amount of time painting on her beauty, you will spend a large portion of your life waiting for her outside the bathroom door."

Prayer is vital as you allow God to direct you to the one He has chosen to complete you. I prayed for years that God would make our children all they should be for their future mates and that His will would direct them to the right person at the right time. God could not have given me four more wonderful people than the spouse of each of our children. I kept my big mouth shut, and God answered my prayer!

2. When your teen is not at home, know with whom and where he is. When I was in high school, my parents gave me permission to go out with a group of my friends with the mother of one of them as the driver. I was told what time to be home and was told not to go beyond the city limits of our little town in Tennessee. We drove around Madisonville and then the group decided they wanted to go to Sweetwater, a town nine miles away. Everyone agreed, so I did not want to be the "wet blanket" of the group. I thought, "My parents will never find out we went to Sweetwater."

The very next afternoon when I got home from school, my mother casually asked, "Did you go to Sweetwater last night?"

"Yes, ma'am."

"If your dad and I cannot trust you to follow the rules we set, you can stay at home," explained my mother.

I believe that is the last time I went somewhere without my parents' approval because I loved my parents and wanted to please them. *"Children, obey your parents in all things: for this is well pleasing unto the Lord."* (Colossians 3:20)

3. Know your teenager's friends. *"He that walketh with wise men shall be wise: but a companion of fools shall be destroyed."* (Proverbs 13:20) From the time our children were very young, we tried to stress that their friends should not determine their behavior. We did not allow them to visit in the home of a friend we did not know well; instead, we preferred to have their friends in our home.

When Kevin was in high school, I thought of one of his friends, who had been to our house on several occasions, but I had not seen him in quite a while. When I asked Kevin about him, Kevin said, "Mom, if you knew what he was doing now, you would be glad I am not spending time with him any more." Shortly after this incident, this boy was expelled from our school. I felt sad about the boy but glad that Kevin had enough wisdom to have the right kind of friends.

4. Ask your teens to give you "veto power" in the people they date. *"Hear counsel, and receive instruction, that thou mayest be wise in thy latter end."* (Proverbs 19:20) We did not encourage our children to date in high school, but if our sons were interested in a girl, we told them to talk to the girl's father first. We expected the same from young men who were interested in dating our daughters.

Our daughter Krysten was receiving calls from a young man in high school when they were both seniors. He sat with her in church for a few times with our family. One day the calls stopped and I asked Krysten about the young man. "He's too serious," she replied and that was the end of the relationship.

5. **Go to ball games and share that experience with your teenager.** However, don't expect them to sit with you when they can sit with their friends! If you want a teenager to talk to you, you must talk about the things in which he is interested and enter his world. We went to every game we could possibly attend when our children were playing or cheering. Doing so required time and money, but the shared experiences were worth it.

When I was in high school, I played basketball as well as faithfully attended church every time the doors were open. One year my basketball coach announced a practice on Thanksgiving morning and said if a player did not attend the practice, she would not play in the next game. Our church was the only church in town that had a Thursday morning Thanksgiving service, and we always went to that service. I told my coach of my problem, and he informed me the rule applied to everyone. I told my dad of the problem, and he informed me that church was more important than basketball and I would be going to church. He did not say one negative word about my coach. However, when I returned to school, I was allowed to play in the next game. That particular rule was never mentioned again during my high school career. This experience increased my respect for my dad and his desire to make Matthew 6:33 real to me. *"But seek ye first the kingdom of God, and his righteousness; and all these things shall be added unto you."*

6. **Take your teens to the mall if they need to go.** Never send them to the mall alone because of the worldly influence. Our teenagers liked shopping and wanted to be in style, which is fine unless the dress violated Bible rules which we had already set for them. I took them shopping at the mall one at a time and was willing to look as long as they wanted to look. I did not tell them what to buy because often they were spending money they had earned, but I gave my opinion when they asked for it. I helped them look for the sales and to buy wisely. It is amazing how frugal a teen will be if he is buying anything with money he has worked to earn. Sometimes I would help them buy something they could not afford, and I would

always buy food for them. It can be fun shopping with your teens if they know you will not treat them like children. I went to the mall with our sons because my husband hates shopping, but I did not tell them what to buy.

My daughters and I went to the mall, but we also loved shopping at resale stores. My daughter Krysten and I were at Village Discount in Chicago Heights one afternoon in the winter, and a lady walked in who was wearing a beautiful, full-length fur coat. We were admiring the coat when she took it off and began trying on blouses. The only problem was the only thing she had on underneath the coat were undergarments. We stood gaping at her, but she did not seem to notice! Another afternoon we were shopping at the same thrift store when a man about 40 years old walked up to my daughter, pulled up his pants legs, and asked, "What do you think of these?"

Krysten looked at a pair of white socks with lace around the top and a pair of black heels. We gasped and ran the other way, but I have to admit, we all took turns peering around the clothes racks to see what he would try on next!

7. Stand for authority. Respect for authority is necessary if a teenager has fun doing anything. If a parent tries to be a buddy, that is, having no rules for the teen, they will not have a good relationship. When a parent tears down the authority God has placed over their teenagers, he tears down his own authority. *"Let every soul be subject unto the higher powers. For there is no power but of God: the powers that be are ordained of God. Whosoever therefore resisteth the power, resisteth the ordinance of God: and they that resist shall receive to themselves damnation."* (Romans 13:1, 2)

When our son Keith was in the seventh grade, he didn't care much for singing, but my husband informed him that singing was a part of his education and he would be singing in the junior high choir. One Wednesday night, I passed by Keith's choir teacher, and she informed me that Keith was 15 minutes late to choir that night.

I knew we had arrived at church in plenty of time for Keith to go to choir on time. I assured her we had gotten to church on time, that I felt my husband would take care of the problem, but asked her to let me know if this ever happened again.

My husband said nothing to Keith until we got home that night. However, shortly after he arrived home, my husband told Keith to go to his bedroom. Upon being questioned about his late arrival at choir practice, Keith said he was helping one of his friends find his parents. My husband informed Keith that the right kind of friends would be in choir instead of running around the church. He also informed Keith that he never intended to receive another report of a late or missing appearance at junior high choir. He gave Keith the following two choices:

A. You will do whatever it takes to get to choir on time every Wednesday, realizing I will tell your choir teacher to let me know anytime you are late or absent.

B. Your mother and I will go to choir with you each week if you cannot get there on time.

No one needs to be told which one he chose, and we never received another call from his choir leader. My husband did not yell at Keith and call him rebellious, but Keith knew my husband meant everything he said and did not make idle threats. We never received another call during his junior high choir career.

8. Create special times with your teenager. In the previous chapters I mentioned that I gave each of my children 30 minutes to spend extra time with me when they were in grade school. This type of offer is not appealing to a teenager, but the following ideas worked for us.

A. *Teens love to eat, especially if the adult is paying!* Treat them and talk while you are eating. You can take your teen shopping, but don't be guilty of criticizing everything they like if it is not sinful. The "wrinkled look" was popular when one of our daughters was in high school, and I did not care for it. She wore it because it was my preference, not a conviction. Treat your teen like a child, and he will not care to do anything with you. I always took our children shopping and tried to give my opinion only when they asked for it. If a teen knows you value his opinions, he will be more likely to ask for yours. When you give your opinion, remember they do not have to follow it if it is not an established rule.

B. *Use every available moment wisely to build relationships.* We spent a lot of time driving our children to activities, and this traveling together can be used as a time to get close and talk to your teen. Turn off the radio and enter their world.

C. *We rode bikes around our neighborhood together.* I remember riding my bike with Kevin when one day when he "disappeared." A few minutes later he rode out of the woods with his hand behind his back. I stopped to wait for him, and he handed me a bunch of wild flowers he had picked. I needed the love the flowers represented more than the flowers. Accept any expression of love a teenager is willing to give—even if it is a five-pound box of chocolates and you have just gone on a diet.

D. *Make memories with your children.* Several years ago, I spoke at our son Kevin's church, Valley Baptist Church in Mesa, Arizona, for their annual Mother-Daughter Banquet. Our daughter Krysten, who lives in Oregon, flew to Arizona so we could share this time together. Before I spoke Kevin asked, "Krysten, what is your best memory of doing something with Mom as a teenager?" I was curious to hear what she would say. "When Mom would go the store, she would buy two containers of Dannon strawberry yogurt; after the other kids were in bed, we would sit on my bed, eat the yogurt, and talk," Krysten answered. I had forgotten about these times until she answered his question. We never know what will make a lasting impression on our children.

9. Serve God as a family. Since our children grew up helping on the bus route, they continued to do so when they were teenagers. The year Kevin was a senior in high school, we started our second bus route just off Ridge Road in Gary, Indiana. Kevin was the captain, and the other kids and I ran the bus. We poured our lives into this route, but at the end of the first year, we had a high day of 19 on the bus. The driver and the other workers quit in discouragement at the end of the year. However, we reached two brothers, nine-year-old Tony and ten-year-old Johnny. The brothers lived in a rundown house at the end of a dead-end street. They both were saved and baptized and rode the bus faithfully until they moved to Portage, Indiana. We did not see or hear from them for ten years.

One summer while my husband and I were on tour for Hyles-Anderson College, their mother called the only "Cowling" she could find listed in the telephone book (our son Keith) and wanted to know if Johnny had accepted Christ while going to church with us. Keith could remember their being saved and baptized. The mother said that Johnny, who was now 20, had been killed; she was hoping he had gone to Heaven. That one call made that hard year in the bus ministry worthwhile. (We now run eight buses in the area where we started that one bus route because God blesses faithfulness.)

That year we needed a song leader on that bus, so my husband told Krysten she would do it. "But Dad," she pleaded, "I'd be embarrassed to stand up and lead the songs on the bus."

"Then you will lead songs while you are embarrassed. I have taken you to singing group practices for the last four years. I have watched you lead cheers for the last six years in front of people, and you have lived through it. You can claim Philippians 4:13, '*I can do all things through Christ which strengtheneth me,*' and lead the singing on the bus." She did, and she did an excellent job. My husband could tell our children things like this because he had built a close relationship with all of our children when they were younger.

10. Our teenagers sat with us during all of the church services. This way we knew they were listening to the preaching and not "hanging out" in the hallways of the church. They were allowed to walk around between services and talk to their friends as long as they were in their places by the time the choir came out. They were not allowed to leave the service for a bathroom break, and they were responsible to plan ahead to make this possible.

It works better with teenagers to set the rules and let them decide how to keep them. Constantly reminding them causes resentment because they feel you are treating them like children. They were not allowed to sell things at church. If one of our teens was not singing during the song service or if he was talking during the service, their dad would send a note down the row as a way of correcting the teen. If the note did not correct the problem, he moved down the row and sat between the two "talkers." Occasionally, a friend would sit with our family as long as the friend followed our rules.

Our children were occasionally allowed to sit with a friend as long as the friend sat with his parents. This was not a regular occurrence. When Dr. Hyles would say, "The ushers will be taking names of teens in the hallways and their parents will be called," we didn't fear receiving a call because we could look down the row and see them.

11. Give your teen a variety of opportunities to serve God. Our two sons, Kevin and Keith, loved sports of all kinds. However, they were not as excited about music and auditioning for a singing group. Kevin wasn't excited about going to tryouts, but my husband told him he would use music longer than the sports he enjoyed. Kevin went to try out, was chosen for the singing group, and now leads the choir in his church in Arizona.

However, Keith took a little more persuading. Keith mentioned every reason he could think of for not auditioning, but his dad told him, "You are going to audition, and that is that." The Sunday afternoon before he was to audition, his dad said, "Keith, do you have your song picked out you will be singing tonight?"

"Yes, Sir," he replied.

"Krysten, go to the living room and let Keith practice while you play the piano." In a few minutes, a frustrated Krysten reappeared and said, "I think Keith is intentionally singing off key so he won't have to be in a singing group. His singing is so bad, I hate for anyone to know he's my brother."

Keith said, "See, Dad, I told you I couldn't sing, and that's why I shouldn't audition."

"You will audition if every word you sing is wrong," his dad assured him.

Keith did audition, and he did not make the group. The following year, tryouts were announced, and Keith announced that he could not sing, so he did not need to try out. His dad said, "You will be auditioning every year whether or not you can sing. Go pick out a song." Keith auditioned this time and made the group. (I don't know if it was because he tried to sing or because his brother and sisters had made the groups, and Mrs. Colsten and Brother Eddie felt sorry for him!)

12. **Teach them that work is fun.** For eight years I was in charge of a corn detasseling bus because I wanted our teenagers to learn the value of money. We got on the bus at 4:15 a.m. and to the cornfield between 5:00 and 5:15 a.m. It was wet and cold at this time of morning which required us to wear plastic garbage bags until 9:00 a.m. Then we started to swelter. We worked in the sun and in the mud; at times, the mud was ankle deep and even ripped the soles off our tennis shoes. However, I tried to make it fun for the 50 teenagers who rode my bus.

Our first field supervisor was a man named Darwin who was shy. The first day I asked him if he could explain why we were pulling the tassels from some plants and leaving them on others. I'm sure he knew the answer, but he seemed frustrated with 50 teens staring at him. He pulled up a short corn stalk and said in a country drawl, "Wal, this is a little one." (I never did decide what this answer had to do with my question.)

Our son Kevin soon learned to imitate his drawl (not in front of Darwin though). Darwin was very good to us because the teens worked hard and often, if he had a field he was worried about, he would call our crew to do it and add an hour's pay to all of our crew members. One of his jobs was to check behind our crew to determine if we were doing a good job. One day I noticed him walking with a crew, and I was worried that Darwin was not pleased. I walked over and asked if we were doing something wrong.

Darwin replied, "I just lack bein' 'round good young'uns onct in a while." At the end of the season the team took up some money and bought him a pocketknife. When they gave it to him, he cried and said, "Wal, no one ever done such a nice thing for me before." I also had the opportunity to lead Darwin to the Lord by the end of the season.

Our girls had many opportunities to babysit, and I set the following guidelines to help them do a good job.

A. *Learn how to control children in a positive way.*
- Set rules and decide how to dispense punishment for broken rules. For example, the child could sit in a chair or write Bible verses.
- The first time a rule is broken, enforce the punishment.
- Never get angry with children.
- Keep children busy doing fun things.

B. *Take a pen and paper to write numbers where parents can be reached in case of an emergency as well as to write down instructions for the children.* Ask questions before the parents leave, such as: Can the children leave the yard? Can the children play with the neighbor children or go to a neighbor's house? Can the children make telephone calls? Are the children to take a bath before bed?

C. Ask about the snacks the children should or should not be given.

D. Ask at what time the children should go to bed.

E. Plan activities the children can do that will help keep them busy and occupied. If the children like you and look forward to having fun when you stay with them, you will not have as many discipline problems .

F. Wait until you get home to talk on the telephone unless it is an emergency. When you are occupied with other things, children will misbehave.

G. Help the children straighten the house before they go to bed or before the parents come home. Praise them as they work and be willing to help.

H. Always leave the house neat and clean when you leave, regardless of how it looked when you came.

Having these rules in mind usually worked quite well, but sometimes people would take advantage of our teenagers. I remember one lady who would call them to babysit when every dish in the kitchen was dirty—an accumulation of several days. When they complained, I told them to boil water, let the dishes soak, and clean up the mess. I told them washing dishes was something they would do the rest of their lives, and it would be good experience for them, but they should learn to wash dishes as they cooked and after they had their meals.

I remember another time they had babysat for several hours when the lady came home, and instead of paying them, she gave them two pictures they did not want. They came home wanting to complain, but I explained that God put us here to be "used," and they could learn a lesson in being fair to baby-sitters from the experience.

13. Teach your child to stand alone for right even though it is difficult. Any person with a desire to please God instead of man will have times in his life when this desire requires him to stand alone, paying a price to be different. *"Yea, and all that will live godly in Christ Jesus shall suffer persecution."* (II Timothy 3:12) No one likes to be different, but it is an important lesson to learn. My father taught me to stand alone for right in three ways.

A. Stand alone for right by being the right example. *"Be ye followers of me, even as I also am of Christ."* (I Corinthians 11:1) My father was the chairman of the deacon board at our church, and he was respected by everyone in our church and community because he stood for right and kept his word. He believed drinking alcohol was wrong in any situation. In fact, while growing up, he would not let me visit or spend the night with a friend if either parent drank.

When I was in the seventh grade, I faithfully attended BYPU (Baptist Young People's Union). The teacher was a respected lawyer in our town, and I had known him all my life. One Sunday night he was teaching on alcohol and drinking. In the lesson he said, "The Bible teaches that being drunk is wrong, but there is nothing wrong with an occasional social drink in pleasant company."

At the time I did not question the statement, but his words bothered me greatly. That night on the way home from church I asked my dad if an occasional social drink in pleasant company was acceptable to God.

My dad replied, "Of course not. Drinking alcohol is always wrong. Where did you get such a foolish idea?"

I explained that I thought my teacher had taught that in class, but I might have misunderstood. My dad dropped the subject and never brought it up again, but the next Sunday night when I went to BYPU, our teacher was gone and a new teacher had taken his place. This lawyer remained in our

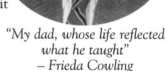

"My dad, whose life reflected what he taught"
– Frieda Cowling

church, and my dad never said a critical word about him; but I learned the importance of being the right example at all times. In later years, this lawyer became an alcoholic.

B. Stand alone for right by choosing the right friends. *"He that walketh with wise men shall be wise: but a companion of fools shall be destroyed."* (Proverbs 13:20) Friends will influence your behavior.

My father was very strict in determining what I would do and where I would go. However, I never doubted my father's love for me and knew he set the rules to protect me. I could not ride alone in a car with a member of the opposite gender, could not visit a friend in a home where either parent drank, and had to be home by a set curfew. None of my friends followed such strict rules, but none of them had a home like mine. My dad was a fun person and attracted young people. In warm weather, we would build a fire outdoors, sing, roast marshmallows, and listen to my dad tell stories. In cold weather we popped popcorn, pulled taffy, sang, and talked. My friends loved my dad, but his presence definitely encouraged right behavior. If any of my friends were uncomfortable around my dad, I was nice to them; however, I did not cultivate a close friendship. I brought every boy I dated to our house to see my father's reaction to him. If I sensed disapproval, I did not date him any more. My parents were my best friends.

When a teenager is allowed to be in the wrong place, doing what he wants to do instead of what has been planned for him, he will find himself in the wrong crowd, making it easy for him to get into trouble. Fun results when a teenager is in the right place, doing the right thing with the right people.

C. Stand alone for right by pleasing God rather than men. *"For do I now persuade men, or God? or do I seek to please men? For if I yet pleased men, I should not be the servant of Christ."* (Galatians 1:10)

My parents taught me that pleasing God brought blessing to my life and displeasing God brought punishment. I clearly understood the philosophy because pleasing and obeying them brought joy and praise and disobeying them brought "the board of instruction to my seat of knowledge." However, the pain of physical punishment did not compare to the pain I felt when I disappointed my parents. The approval of God and my parents was more important than pleasing my friends. Our children were taught the same way.

We moved to Indiana from Tennessee the summer before our daughter Kelly was to enter the sixth grade. She had been in the same school system in Tennessee all of her life, and it was difficult to enter Hammond Baptist not knowing one person. Some of the girls in her class had formed a clique and would not accept her. Many times they would say things we had taught her were wrong, and this was confusing to her since it was Kelly's first experience in a Christian school. Dr. Phil Sallie was her teacher, and he helped her to stand for right. "Honey," he told Kelly, "don't let those girls destroy you. In ten years, you'll be serving God and they won't." I don't know where those girls are today, but Kelly and her husband and their three sons are serving God.

It is natural for us to desire man's approval and popularity with those we know. However, as much as we would want this approval, it is not always possible. We must learn to take a stand if we would say, "*I have fought a good fight, I have finished my course, I have kept the faith.*" (II Timothy 4:7)

14. Make vacations fun. We went to visit our children's grandparents in Tennessee and North Carolina, but we planned activities to do while we were there so the teenagers would not get bored. They loved to go to "Sliding Rock" in North Carolina where on two occasions Krysten didn't remove her watch before sliding down the rock, and it was history. We went across Canada and down the East coast to the Outer Banks in North Carolina, and to Charlestown, South Carolina. If you and your husband are having fun and getting along, your children will do the same.

I remember going on a vacation out west when I was a teenager. We were cooking breakfast in Yellowstone National Park when a bear came to breakfast! We hurriedly started packing our supplies. My dad was throwing him slices of bread and just as we got into the car, the bear arrived. This experience wasn't much fun when it was happening, but it provided a great memory and lots of conversation.

15. Refuse to be moody and try to be the right kind of example. "*All the days of the afflicted* (moody) *are evil: but he that is of a merry heart hath a continual feast.*" (Proverbs 15:15)

"*A merry heart maketh a cheerful countenance: but by sorrow of the heart the spirit is broken.*" (Proverbs 15:13)

Satan is the author of defeat, depression, and discouragement. No one is exempt from Satan's wiles, and he tries to take joy and the abundant life away from every child of God. Since Satan knows he can never take away our gift of eternal life, he initiates negative thinking; and we become moody. Jesus is our example. Our lives should be joyful and not moody. "*Jesus Christ the same, yesterday, and to day, and for ever.*" (Hebrews 13:8)

Every Christian's goal should be to live a joyful life that will make the world see the difference Christ can make in our lives and want what we have. God promises that we will all face problems in life, but the saved person has Christ, Who will go through the problem with us. James 1:2 and 3 says, "*My brethren, count it all joy when ye fall into divers temptations; Knowing this, that the trying of your faith worketh patience.*" I Corinthians 10:13 says, *"There hath no temptation taken you but such as is common to man: but God is faithful, who will not suffer you to be tempted above that ye are able; but will with the temptation also make a way to escape, that ye may be able to bear it."*

The potential to be moody is always there. It is determined by whether we think positively or negatively on any person or situation. Basically a moody person is a selfish person who thinks about himself more than about others.

The bus ministry helped our family in this area. A moody parent will help create a moody child or teenager. Since our children were small, they visited on the bus route and rode the bus on Sunday. This participation allowed them to see the

Brother Cowling's bus—Route 72 Keith is helping his dad. •

heartache and suffering sin brings to people firsthand— whether it was a result of alcohol, drugs, immorality, broken homes, or abuse. It is difficult to come home and complain about your problems when you have seen others suffer more—all without depending upon a Saviour to help them. The bus ministry helped drive away our tendency to be selfish and moody.

When our daughter Krysten was a freshman at Hyles-Anderson College, she visited on a Chicago bus route for the first time. She had been on the bus route since she was three years old, but our route was a middle-class route; and she had not experienced ghetto life for the children in Chicago. She came home for dinner that night and found our son Keith, who was a high school student, was in a bad mood because he did not care for the food I had prepared for dinner that night. He didn't verbally complain, but his displeasure was obvious. Krysten looked at his sullen face and empty plate and said, "If you had seen what I saw today, you would be happy about anything Mom fixes for us to eat." Keith did not eat, but his mood changed.

The cure for a bad mood is to get our eyes off of ourselves and do something for someone else. There is never a shortage of children, teens, and adults whose lives can be changed by a smile, a kind word, or the love of Christ which flows through us to them.

16. Failure to have fun with teens may drive them toward the "temporary" fun the world offers. Learn to listen to your teen when they feel like talking and refrain from lecturing. Take them shopping, play action games like kick ball or volleyball as well as board games, and take them out to eat. The key is to discover what your teen enjoys and learn to enjoy those activities yourself.

On page 175 is a letter my husband and I received from a teen who decided to have fun—the world's way. The name has been withheld to protect the family.

17. Teach your child to refuse to quit. My parents reared me with the philosophy that God would help me to do anything He wanted me to do—regardless of whether or not I wanted to do it, felt like doing it, or knew how to do it. The basis for this teaching was Philippians 4:13, "*I can do all things through Christ which strengtheneth me.*" This philosophy helped build my self- confidence as we tried to rear our four children in the same way. Success in our lives is not determined by our talent or intelligence but by our willingness to allow God to give the victory because of our faith. I can think of many times in the lives of our children when this was true.

Kelly worked on a Chicago bus route for eight years. She had no formal instruction in speaking Spanish, but she had a desire to get the many Spanish people on her route to ride the bus to church and to receive Christ. Each week she would learn more Spanish from the Spanish children who rode the bus. She now speaks Spanish fluently.

When Kevin went to Hyles-Anderson College, he became a bus captain on a route located on the north side of Chicago during his second year of college. His bus route reached many for Christ, but his father and I did not realize why until years later when Krysten, our younger daughter, went into college and decided to work on Kevin's bus route.

After her first Saturday in Chicago, she came home and said, "Kevin speaks Spanish." Later when my husband asked Kevin about this, Kevin said, "It was either learn to speak Spanish or come to church with an empty bus." One of the Spanish adults Kevin reached was a man named Rafael Cervantes, who several years later became our son-in-law. Rafael is now `a bus captain of one of the buses on our route and a deacon at First Baptist Church in Hammond. Kelly is on staff at First Baptist Church.

Kevin, our oldest son, played basketball in grade school, but as one of the shortest boys in junior high and high school, he spent most of his time sitting on the bench. In Kevin's sophomore year, every boy trying out had to survive three cuts to make the team. He had survived the first two cuts, and we were all praying he would make the last cut—not because I wanted him to play but making the team was something he desperately wanted. The day of the last cut came, and Kevin woke up with a sore throat and fever. Our children rarely missed school, but I said, "Kevin, you are too sick to go to school today."

"Mom," he replied, "if I don't go to practice today, I know I will be cut. If I go, maybe I'll have a chance." He went.

The list of the team was posted on the locker door after school. One look at Kevin as he walked to the car told the story, and no one spoke (at least not audibly).

In my mind, I was giving God a piece of my mind. "God, how can You do this to him? He has given his best, had his heart set on making the team, and You let him down."

However, the next day Kevin came home excited because the coach had asked him to be the manager. Personally, I feel this experience was much better than sitting on the bench because he learned to be a servant—to clean the floor, wash the uniforms, and take care of the equipment. (It also meant I had to apologize to God!) *And whosoever will be chief among you, let him be your servant.* (Matthew 20:27)

Krysten wanted to be a cheerleader from the day she entered second grade at Hammond Baptist Grade School. It was a good day when she reached fourth grade, received her "Gamma" sweater, and cheered for her brother Kevin. She cheered for nine years at home, at school, and at games. We drove her to

Krysten with Dawn Boyd Moncado and Trina Boyd Reynolds

Tennessee to attend a cheerleading camp because she was determined to be a good cheerleader. Our house resounded with bumps and thumps, but I am glad she wanted to be the best cheerleader she could be.

18. Praise character instead of talent. God is looking for parents who will rear their children according to Bible principles. He is also looking for children who do not have to have the preeminence in every situation and children who are willing to yield their wills to the will of God. Giving a child everything he wants gives that a child a wrong value system, encourages selfishness, and discourages his becoming a team player. Praising talent instead of character encourages a child to be a solo player—not a team player. I Corinthians 3:9-11 says, *"For we are laborers together with God: ye are God's husbandry, ye are God's building. According to the grace of God which is given unto me, as a wise masterbuilder, I have laid the foundation, and another buildeth thereon. But let every man take heed how he buildeth thereupon. For other foundation can no man lay than that is laid, which is Jesus Christ."*

Our sons loved sports because my husband loved sports. We moved to Indiana the summer before Kevin entered the fourth grade, and he eagerly signed up to play in the Hammond Baptist sports program for one of the six intramural teams. He was assigned to Gamma. Kevin practiced and practiced soccer until he became a good player and dreamed of being selected as a member of the all-star team. His team Gamma won the championship in his fifth grade year, and he was named to the all-star team. His sixth grade year, Gamma was undefeated during the regular season, and if the truth were known, he was more worried about being an all-star than winning the championship again. When the championship game was over, the score was 1 to 0 with Gamma losing in overtime. Kevin made the all-star team. However, he realized he would gladly trade his all-star trophy for a team victory. Though his team lost, Kevin learned a valuable lesson.

God's way of living goes against our human nature. *"Be kindly affectioned one to another with brotherly love; in honour preferring one another."* (Romans 12:10) We should yield our will to others instead of demanding our own way. Children will learn this lesson by watching our lives. The way to get what we want is to give it away. *"Give, and it shall be given unto you: good measure, pressed down, and shaken together, and running over, shall men give into your bosom. For with the same measure that ye mete withal it shall be measured to you again."* (Luke 6:38) If there are three toys and two children, they will generally fight for the same one. Giving up your way is a sign you are growing in Christ and in Christian maturity.

19. Teach your child the value of determination. Keith, our youngest son, loved basketball and dreamed of being tall. Every day, we measured to see if he had gained in height, but it did not happen. My husband said, "Keith, you can play ball and be short, but you will have to work harder to do it." They decided on a plan of action to accomplish this goal. Keith jumped rope, ran every day, lifted weights, squeezed balls, practiced in special shoes, and spent hours practicing his shots in our driveway. When Keith saw his taller teammates dunking the basketball, he dreamed of doing it, too. This was a problem because he was only five feet, eleven inches in height. However, after hours of jumping, a broken ankle, and many failures, he could dunk the basketball.

God commands us to give our heart in everything we do in Ecclesiastes 9:10, *"Whatsoever thy hand findeth to do, do it with thy might; for there is no work, nor device, nor knowledge, nor wisdom, in the grave, whither thou goest."* Colossians 3:23 says, *"And whatsoever ye do, do it heartily, as to the Lord, and not unto men."* In addition to giving their best, we wanted to teach our children to set goals and refuse to quit before achieving these goals. Proverbs 24:10, *"If thou faint in the day of adversity, thy strength is small."*

A child or teenager who lacks determination to reach a goal will become an adult who lacks determination to reach a goal. Dr. Hyles said, "That person is a success who gets up one more time than he falls down." That is what determination is all about and brings joy to our lives.

20. A teen's success in his Christian life and usefulness to God is determined largely by his attitude. God has promised that if a person is in His will, everything that happens is for his good and God's glory. Proverbs 16:18, *"Pride goeth before destruction, and an haughty spirit before a fall."*

Proverbs 16:32, *"He that is slow to anger is better than the mighty; and he that ruleth his spirit than he that taketh a city."*

Proverbs 18:14, *"The spirit of a man will sustain his infirmity; but a wounded spirit who can bear?"*

Proverbs 25:28, *"He that hath no rule over his own spirit is like a city that is broken down, and without walls."*

Children and teenagers learn to have the right attitude and rule their spirits by observing their parents. When parents have the wrong attitude, children and teenagers can learn to have a bad attitude. Allow me to illustrate. This example is found in the section for teenagers because the term children refers to both children and teenagers when it is used in the Bible. The term "teenager" was coined in the 1950's. In II Kings 2, Elijah had just been taken to Heaven by God, and his mantle has fallen upon Elisha. *"And he (Elisha) went up from thence unto Bethel; and as he was going up by the way, there came forth little children out of the city, and mocked him, and said unto him, Go up, thou bald head; go up, thou bald head. And he turned back, and looked on them, and cursed them in the name of the LORD. And there came forth two she bears out of the wood, and tare forty and two children of them."* (II Kings 2:23, 24)

In this sad story, 42 children died because of irreverence for the man of God. Elijah and Elisha are walking together, and Elijah is taken to Heaven just as God had said in II Kings 2:11, *"And it came to pass, as they still went on, and talked, that behold, there appeared a chariot of fire, and horses of fire, and parted them both asunder; and Elijah went up by a whirlwind into heaven."* I believe these children heard the mocking from someone else—possibly their parents. I also believe if the parents had had the proper respect for the man of God, the children would not have mocked him. Elijah was a man of God who preached about specific sins, making it impossible for someone to listen to his preaching and not be under conviction—exactly like a fundamental preacher today. Apparently Elijah had been stepping on the parents' toes while preaching, and probably they were glad he was gone. However, Elisha was still around and preaching the same irritating, convicting messages and stepping on the same toes. More than likely, these same parents were wishing to be rid of Elisha and were hoping that God would take him to Heaven in the same way Elijah had gone. Evidently the children heard these parents voice their opinions, and when they repeated their criticisms, it cost 42 of them their lives. The attitude displayed in our homes will be reflected by our children in public. Man's nature is the same. I believe when these parents were informed of their children's deaths, they wanted to take back their critical words; but the children were gone and the words could not be recalled. *"Whoso keepeth his mouth and his tongue keepeth his soul from trouble."* (Proverbs 21:23)

When our children were little, we were visiting some friends at Christmas. Our children were excited because their friends had received new bicycles for Christmas, and they were anxiously awaiting a turn to ride. I had started to walk outside when the mother (not realizing I could hear her words) said to our children, "They don't want to share their bikes with you. When we come to your house to visit, you don't have to share with them."

That mother's words contradicted everything we had tried to teach our children; and even though they looked disappointed, they found something else to do. I was furious, but I backed around the corner, making sure I was not seen by our children or the mother. Revealing my bad attitude would cause our children to feel the same way instead of obeying authority. *"A fool's mouth is his destruction, and his lips are the snare of his soul."* (Proverbs 11:7)

Whether or not a child gets a turn on the bicycle will not have a lasting effect on the life of the child. However, when I stand against any authority, it destroys my own authority in the eyes of my child. According to Romans 13:1, 2, God always supports authority. *"Let every soul be subject unto the higher power; For there is no power but of God: the powers that be are ordained by God. Whosoever therefore resisteth the power, resisteth the ordinance of God: and they that resist shall receive to themselves damnation."*

When the authority exhibits a critical attitude, it is like a cancer that spreads from the authority to the followers. A critical attitude is a disease for which there is no cure. This critical attitude will destroy the influence of the person criticized in the life of your child as well as the parents' authority. The word "critic" or "criticism" is not found in the Bible, but the word "scorner" is.

Proverbs 9:8, *"Reprove not a scorner, lest he hate thee: rebuke a wise man, and he will love thee."*

Proverbs 13:1, *"A wise son heareth his father's instruction: but a scorner heareth not rebuke."*

Proverbs 21:11, *"When the scorner is punished, the simple is made wise: and when the wise is instructed, he receiveth knowledge."*

Proverbs 22:10, *"Cast out the scorner, and contention shall go out; yea, strife and reproach shall cease."*

Ignoring God's instruction for rearing children and teenagers will bring heartache to parents and teenagers. The rules we established when our children became teenagers helped us maintain a close relationship with them. By developing close relationships with teenagers as well as consistently enforcing the established rules will produce teens who are a joy instead of a trial. I realize that there is never a guarantee any of us will resist the attack of Satan on our journey to Heaven. Only when we reach Heaven have we won the victory.

In ending this section on teenagers, I want to share a letter from a choice young man who had all the opportunities and advantages to live a life that counted for God. I trust this letter might make a difference in the life of a teenager who might be considering making the same wrong choices this young man made. Life is a series of choices, and every individual must decide whether or not to let God direct his path.

Rebellion Will Cost You

Rebellion is something that everyone will face at some time in life, and not just teens, but younger kids and adults as well. Still, the problem of rebellion seems to be most common in teenagers. You may ask, "Who are you to tell me about rebellion and what I should do with my life?" Or you might say, "You just don't understand me. My parents are too strict, and they don't want me to have any fun."

Well, I just so happen to have gone down a long road of rebellion, thinking my parents were too strict. I started rejecting the Lord's will for my life and went the way of the world. I found what the world and the Devil had to offer me, and I wasn't happy with what I found. At the age of 17, I left home to attend a Bible college, but soon found the "worldly" crowd, started doing the wrong things, and going to the wrong places. I dropped out of college, jumped from job to job, and went from house to house until I was at the bottom of the world, or so I thought. I then decided to move back home with my mom and dad, but I brought my rebellious attitude and lifestyle with me. It wasn't long before I was back on the streets and into more trouble.

I tried premarital sex, not caring whether or not the woman I was with was married. I started smoking and drinking, but neither made me happy. I tried smoking marijuana. I went to the places where the worldly crowd went, smoked what they smoked, drank what they drank, and dressed like they dressed. Man, was I cool! I was so-called "hanging out." Something was missing though—my joy. I thought doing what the world did would make me happy, but it only made me bitter and unhappy. I went as far as trying to kill myself because I was so unhappy.

I started going to a mental health facility, and the doctors prescribed a lot of medicine to make me happy; but deep down inside, I still was not happy. I felt lonely and empty inside and thought everyone was out to get me. I spent two months in jail, but it did not stop there. I was placed on five years probation, which I violated by getting into a fight. I went to court and was sentenced to ten years of labor. God knows exactly what it will take to get your attention, and He knows what buttons to push on each and every person—even you. The sad part about it all is you hurt not only yourself but others around you as well. For me, it took prison to get my attention.

Look at the story of Jonah. He ran from God, and God prepared a great fish to swallow Jonah. What will be the great fish in your life that will swallow you? Will God have to place you in prison where you are cut off from your family, friends, and society to get your attention? Maybe cancer from smoking or a liver disorder from drinking or maybe fried brain cells from doing drugs to the point of becoming a vegetable will get your attention. Maybe He will have to take home a loved one to get your attention. What will it take for you? How far will you go?

I now know one thing for sure: 1) Sin will take you further than you want to go, 2) Sin will keep you longer than you want to stay, and 3) Sin will cost you more than you want to pay. All of your friends who think it is cool to smoke, drink, do drugs, steal, sleep around, and live for the world are not really your friends. You may think they are, but when you need them, they will not be there for you.

During my time of incarceration, I gave my life back to Christ and through the Lord, I have found a joy and peace that the world could never offer. I once thought that my parents were too strict, but I found out they were just trying to protect me from the harm that the Devil and the world had to offer me. God gave me a special gift to play the piano, but I did not use that gift for Him. Now that I am in prison, I play the piano for the church services held in prison.

I can promise that if you do not live for God, He will put you in a place where you will. You may say, "Nothing like this will ever happen to me." Well, look out, because I said the same thing and look at where I am now. Serve the Lord while you have a choice because if you do not, one day you will regret it and wish you had served Him.

Just a thought...

Dear Santa Claus,

Don't leave anything at our house this year unless it's a good stick to spank with. Peter and Peggy don't pick up any of their things, and they all get broken.

Peter grumbles constantly and is never satisfied with anything and doesn't mind worth two hoops.

They tease each other and fight all the time and teach Joan to be naughty and sassy—just like they are.

Give all your toys and gifts to some other little boys and girls who will appreciate them.

I hope I can write you a nicer letter next year.

Goodbye now,
Peter, Peggy, and Joan's
Mother

Unmarried Children

Unmarried Children
(Photos on page 179)

Top left: Krysten earned her master's degree the same time Keith earned his bachelor's degree.

Top right: Kelly with Kevin at Kevin's college graduation

Center: Krysten, Kevin, and Kelly at our twenty-fifth wedding anniversary which was planned by our four children

Center: Kelly when she was teaching at Hyles-Anderson College

Bottom left: Dr. Hyles praying for Kevin at Kevin's ordination

Bottom center: The Cowling family with Amen

Bottom right: Kevin

P salm 127:1-4 says, "*Except the LORD build the house, they labour in vain that build it: except the LORD keep the city, the watchman waketh but in vain. It is vain for you to rise up early, to sit up late, to eat the bread of sorrows: for so he giveth his beloved sleep. Lo, children are an heritage of the LORD: and the fruit of the womb is his reward. As arrows are in the hand of a mighty man; so are children of the youth.*"

No relationship can be happy without at least one person who is yielded to the Holy Spirit of God, who is willing to die to self, and who prefers the other person. When we have problems with a relationship, it is usually with a person who is much like ourselves. That is why mothers and daughters often have conflicts. If the one who is more spiritually mature will decide to cultivate a good relationship, it is possible for two very different people to be close.

When my husband and I married, his mother and I had some of the same personality traits—strong, determined, organized—and we had definite opinions about everything. Ginnie, his mother, was very thoughtful and loving to me, but I could see a potential for problems. She was unsaved, a faithful member of a very liberal church, and she had a different value system from mine. I made the following decisions to help prevent alienating my mother-in-law because she was a good mother to my husband, the man I knew God had chosen for me and the grandmother of the children God would give to us in the future.

1. I majored on our similar tastes and minored on our differences. Pete's mother was a shopper, and so am I. We spent many happy hours shopping together for bargains. There was a small restaurant in the shopping mall that carried delicious vegetables that I enjoyed. She took me there and bought lunch for me every time I visited. When we were at their house, she prepared the favorite food of everyone. I remember having "Hello Dollies," boiled shrimp, homemade bread, flank steak, and many other foods. The flank steak was marinated and grilled by Pete's dad. Our children would eat so much that I was embarrassed. I remember one visit when we were feasting on flank steak and Keith asked, "Why don't you ever fix this, Mom?"

I didn't reply, but the reason was because of the price of the meat. He continued, "If there is some left, can we take it to eat on the way home?" After this incident, we never left without flank steak sandwiches to eat on the way home.

2. I was appreciative of her and all that she did for me. When she bought lunch or sent me an article of clothing she felt I would enjoy, I always sent a handwritten thank-you note as well as a verbal thank you.

3. I kept in touch. Every week, I wrote a letter to both my mother-in-law and my mother. In fact, I tried to be as thoughtful to one as I was to the other. One time I put the letters in the wrong envelopes, and Ginnie called saying, "I think you are trying to do too many things."

I felt like saying, "Maybe one of the things I should eliminate is my weekly letter to you"; however, I knew Satan would be delighted if I responded in that way, and Ginnie might never accept Christ. I kept writing and tried to be more careful.

4. I wanted to build a relationship between our children and their grandparents. When the children were small, they often made a cassette tape with speaking and singing to send their grandparents. These were fun for the children to make and fun for the grandparents to hear. We taped over them, but now I wish we had saved them for our grandchildren to hear the southern drawls that have disappeared after living 27 years in the north.

5. Develop simple ways of expressing love. The Bible says that "love never fails." Many times at Christmas I would have the children draw four pictures of things they remembered doing with their grandparents. We would make a book and give the book as a present. The books were kept on the coffee table in their den. One year I had the children write six memories of things they had done with their grandparents. I folded them and put them on a calendar with a folded card on four different days each month. Every time Pete's parents opened a note, they called us. We gave my mother a similar calendar, and she called to say she couldn't wait and opened them all! (She did put them back on the calendar so she could open them again when the day came.) At the end of the year, my mother made a scrapbook of the notes and pictures she had of each event the children described.

6. Do not react to criticism. I decided that I would not respond to criticism or negative remarks—even if I felt they were ridiculous. When my husband left his tenured position teaching engineering at the University of Tennessee, it was very upsetting to my mother-in-law—not because she wanted to run our lives but because she felt we were in a cult that would destroy us. Even though she had grown up wearing dresses as a girl, she called our daughters "old ladies," and she gave them beautiful pants outfits that they did not wear. We thanked her for buying them.

I remember one day Ginnie said to Kelly, "What kind of a nut is this Dr. Hyles who wants you to be so old-fashioned?"

Kelly was horrified and replied, "Oh, Grandma, if you just knew Dr. Hyles you wouldn't say such mean things about him."

Later Kelly said, "Mom, why didn't you help me when Grandma was saying those awful things?"

I replied, "If I said anything, it would cause an argument; and I will not argue with Grandma Ginnie."

In order to accomplish this goal, I sometimes felt like biting off my tongue. It was very difficult, and I often wanted to slap her face instead of keeping my mouth shut. Over 50 years later, I am glad I chose to keep my mouth shut. In the beginning we created some of these problems because of wanting so badly for Pete's parents to receive Christ we were guilty of "shoving the Gospel down their throats." This was a great mistake. It was a good day when we realized that love was the greatest weapon available to us as a means of reaching Pete's parents, who are both in Heaven today.

Genesis 13:8, "And Abram said unto Lot, Let there be no strife, I pray thee, between me and thee, and between my herdsmen and thy herdsmen; for we be brethren." When there was not enough water and grass for both Abraham's and Lot's cattle, strife developed between their herdsmen. The Canaanite and Perizzite (the world) were watching this strife, and it was a poor testimony. Lot chose the well-watered plain and pitched his tent toward Sodom. Abraham preferred Lot and God blessed him.

Psalm 133:1 says, "Behold, how good and how pleasant it is for *brethren to dwell together in unity!*" God's plan is for parents to avoid conflicts with adult children. When parents do not get along with their children, it is a poor testimony to their grandchildren as well as a poor testimony to the unsaved world. There should be a difference in the lives of Christians—not because of who we are, but because of who Christ is and the fact that He indwells every believer. The decision to get along is a choice we make. When we fail to prefer the other person, our choice should be to apologize and restore the relationship.

7. **Love your adult children unconditionally.** I Corinthians 13:8 says, "*Charity* (love) *never faileth: but whether there be prophecies they shall fail; whether there be tongues, they shall cease; whether there be knowledge, it shall vanish away.*"

I John 4:7 and 8 says, "*Beloved, let us love one another: for love is of God; and every one that loveth is born of God, and knoweth God. He that loveth not knoweth not God; for God is love.*" Love your daughter-in-law as much as you love your son and love your son-in-law as much as you love your daughter. A good policy is keeping our big mouths shut!

When all of our children married, we began our "Family Mondays." Some families choose to eat Sunday dinner together, but since our family is in the bus ministry, there was not enough time on Sundays. It doesn't really matter when families spend time together, but it is important that they do in order to maintain a close relationship.

Sometimes holidays can present problems for family gatherings. For instance, rarely have we had Christmas on December 25. We select a day during Christmas vacation that is convenient for all and designate that day "Christmas." That way the other parents can have the "real" day, and everyone is happy. Hurt feelings have a way of wrecking relationships and destroying the Christmas spirit.

My parents loved me, and that is a fact I never doubted. However, when Pete and I married, my dad said, "This is no longer your home. Your home is with your husband. After you are married, coming home to Mama is not an option." I never forgot his advice, and I never came home to Mama (even though I mentioned it a few times to my husband).

In 1962, the first year we were married, I was upset about something so important I cannot remember the incident. I threatened my husband, "I'm leaving." He opened his wallet and handed me our fortune—$5.00. "Go as far as you can go," he said. Even in those days, I realized that I could not get to Tennessee on that amount. In a short time, I realized that hugging and kissing is better than winning an argument.

8. **Adopt the policy of preferring others.** *"Be kindly affectioned one to another with brotherly love; in honour preferring one another."* (Romans 12:10) Adopting this policy is difficult because we all prefer to be selfish and have it our way. We need to decide to yield our way to others. (Of course, this is easier said than done.)

Two of our married children lived with us after they were married. Krysten and Chris Vestal lived with us for two months while they were saving money for a down payment on a house. Before they moved into our house, I realized it would be difficult for two women to coexist in the same house. I decided there would never be a conflict between us, and I honestly do not remember any. Just in the area of doing dishes, conflict could have occurred.

I always washed dishes as I cooked when I grew up and dried them all before I left the kitchen so the kitchen would look neat. Krysten feels if you dry dishes with a dish towel, you put germs back on the dishes from the cloth. She prefers to air dry the dishes. Since I could see a potential problem over drying dishes, I decided to adopt Krysten's method as long as they lived with us.

Our son Keith and his wife Michelle lived with us for over a year. Brother Hyles told them to be ready to take a church at a moment's notice. Again, I do not remember having any conflicts. In fact, I remember Michelle cooking many meals and cleaning every week which was a help and a blessing for me. However, I remember being taught to clean by a mother who thought "cleanliness is next to godliness" was the gospel. I remember noticing after Michelle cleaned that dust was still on the chair rungs. My mother had taught me to dust the chair rungs. I thought about mentioning it, but I decided I would rather have dust on the chair rungs and a good relationship with my daughter-in-law than demand my own way.

9. **Give no unsolicited advice!** Remember the old and true saying, "Unsolicited advice is seldom heeded and never appreciated." *"Only by pride cometh contention: but with the well advised is wisdom."* (Proverbs 13:10) It seems the older we get, the greater the desire we

have to give our opinion about everything—and believe we are right. The price of being right and destroying the relationship is never worth it. One of the prayers I pray daily is, "Lord, help me keep my big mouth shut!"

At this writing, I have 16 grandchildren, and it would seem that my children would appreciate my help in rearing their children— WRONG! If I practiced this philosophy, I probably would see very little of my children and grandchildren.

10. Treat adult children as adults—not as children. Realize their decisions will not always meet with your approval. Avoid strife.

"The beginning of strife is as when one letteth out water: therefore leave off contention, before it be meddled with." (Proverbs 17:14)

"It is an honour for a man to cease from strife: but every fool will be meddling." (Proverbs 20:3)

"He that passeth by, and meddleth with strife belonging not to him, is like one that taketh a dog by the ears." (Proverbs 26:17)

No matter how difficult it is, we must let our adult children go to live their own lives. It is difficult to view adult children as adults because we have known them so much longer as children. If we treat them as children, they will rebel against us, try to avoid us, and the relationship will always suffer.

We have always been a close family, and when our daughter Kelly started to like a man she met on her bus route and at college, we were concerned. She tried to talk to my husband and me about him, but my husband felt he could not be the man for her (even though we did not know him). To make a long story short, Kelly and Rafael eloped and moved 70 miles away to live on the north side of Chicago where he worked. Immediately, we realized we had made a drastic mistake in refusing to try to know Rafael and decided to do what we could to restore the relationship. Since we had driven them away, we took the initiative in accepting Rafael as a son-in-law and making it clear that we loved them. We drove to visit them and helped them decorate their apartment. We never brought up anything negative from the past, and as time went by, we realized how wrong we had been.

Today, everyone should have a son-in-law exactly like Rafael. He is a wonderful husband, father, and provider. When he is around, he looks for things he can do to serve others. I don't know anyone who works harder. He is a deacon at First Baptist Church of Hammond and a bus captain of 72D on our route. No one could have made a greater mistake then we made in trying to discourage Kelly from marrying Rafael. We have spent the last 12 years trying to make up for our mistake and hopefully there are no hard feelings on their part toward us.

   11. Never give up on an adult child when trials come. Luke 6:36 and 37 say, *"Be ye therefore merciful, as your Father also is merciful. Judge not, and ye shall not be judged: condemn not, and ye shall not be condemned: forgive, and ye shall be forgiven."*

   Romans 12:9, *"Let love be without dissimulation* (hypocrisy). *Abhor that which is evil; cleave to that which is good."*

   I John 4:7, 8, *"Beloved, let us love one another: for love is of God; and every one that loveth is born of God, and knoweth God. He that loveth not knoweth not God; for God is love."*

   No matter how young or old, it is heartbreaking to see our children suffer. However, when they disappoint us or go away from the Lord, that may be the time they need our prayers and encouragement the most. We should not condone sin, but we can love the sinner. We would all be in trouble if God didn't feel that way about us.

   Dr. Hyles repeatedly said that no young person would go into sin if one person truly believed in him and loved him. If the person is our child, it is difficult because we always see our children as part of ourselves. When our children make mistakes, we feel responsible and our embarrassment makes us want to distance ourselves from them at a time when they need us the most. When my heart is breaking, I get up, get dressed, drink coffee, and follow my schedule for the day, begging God to help me deal with the trial in His strength and not my own.

   This kind of consistency will give stability and hope to your adult child. Do not discuss the situation or answer any questions about the situation. If counsel is needed, refer your adult child to the pastor. If you have not criticized the pastor and destroyed his authority over the years, they will be willing to go to him for help.

   When Rafael found their eight-month-old daughter Sara not breathing one night in her crib, it was heartbreaking for all of us. Sara lived with the help of machines for 24 hours. During the long night in the Pediatric Intensive Care, I sat by Kelly or we sat by our precious Sara with our hearts breaking. Kelly said, "Why did God let this happen to our child when so many people don't even want their children—murdering them and abusing them? We wanted Sara. We loved her. We would have reared her to serve the Lord."

Tearfully I said, "I don't know the answer, but one day in Heaven we will know. Until then we have to trust and believe by faith that all things work together for our good and God's glory." Sara went to Heaven 24 hours later.

I told Kelly, "You can get bitter over this or let this make you a better person."

Kelly and Rafael walked on by faith and eight months later, Stephen was born. Two years later, Scott was born, and 12 days after that, he also went to Heaven, also a victim of crib death, even though we were told that SIDS never happened twice in one family. Scott went to Heaven early on a Saturday morning; and Kelly, Rafael, and Stephen rode their bus to Sunday school the next day. Some criticized their actions, but they answered, "We can't bring Scott back to life, but we can love children on the bus." God blessed them with three living children: Stephen, Samuel, and Simon.

12. Admit mistakes. When we make mistakes and break any or all of the "rules," we can't allow Satan to defeat us and cause us to feel there is no hope of restoring the relationship. Ask forgiveness of God and your adult child and try again. God will give us as many chances as we need to build the right kind of relationship with our adult children—even if the relationship is "one-sided." Philippians 4:13 says, *"I can do all things through Christ which strengtheneth me."*

God wants us to dwell together in unity with our adult children The recipe is avoiding conflicts by keeping our big mouths shut, loving unconditionally, preferring others, never giving unsolicited advice, and never giving up on a relationship. The world is looking for something real that will help them through heartaches and trials they face. If our lives are no different from theirs, why should they want a relationship with Christ? God will give us as many chances as we need to live our lives for Him.

Unmarried, College-Age Children

I believe the relationship you have with your unmarried adult children and college-age children is largely determined by the fun you have had and the relationship you have built with them as children. If you wait until this age in life to be close, they may reject your efforts. The following are rules I tried to remember when our children were in this stage of life.

1. **As long as they were living at home, they were expected to abide by the rules of our house regarding church attendance, music, dress, and so forth.** *"The eye that mocketh at his father, and despiseth to obey his mother, the ravens of the valley shall pick it out, and the young eagles shall eat it."* (Proverbs 30:17) I do not remember the rules being a problem, but my husband made it clear that we would not argue about them. Any time our college-age children felt they could not live with our rules which had been established in their childhood, we would kiss them goodbye and wish them well as they found their own place to live.

My husband made it clear that our preference was for them to attend Hyles-Anderson College. We encouraged them to make an appointment with their preacher, Dr. Hyles, and follow his advice concerning the college they would attend. My husband and I begged God that He would speak through our preacher to direct our children to His will. I believe if we had been critical of Dr. Hyles during their childhood they would not have been willing to follow his advice. My husband named two other Christian colleges he would help them attend, but he told them if they chose a secular college, we would love them but they would pay for their own education.

Why I Would Not Recommend
a State or Secular University Education Today
"Blessed is the man that walketh not in the counsel of the ungodly, nor standeth in the way of sinners, nor sitteth in the seat of the scornful."

(Psalm 1:1) As I read this verse, I believe God is making it clear that we should not be taught by unsaved people. I believe I have heard all of the arguments to the contrary, but a rule with exceptions ceases to be a rule. If I were a young person today, I would give a godly person veto power in my life. This choice could be parents or a godly pastor. It does not mean asking people until you find one who agrees with you and deciding that is God's will.

God loves us and wants to direct our paths according to Proverbs 3:5 and 6 which says, *"Trust in the LORD with all thine heart; and lean not unto thine own understanding. In all thy ways acknowledge him, and he shall direct thy paths."* When I graduated from the University of Tennessee in 1961, no authority in my life had advised me not to attend such a school, However at that time, every girl at the university was required to wear dresses to class, curfews were observed in the girls' dorms, and finding a guy in the girls' dorms was unthinkable. These rules are no longer true.

In 1977 my husband left his tenured teaching position in the College of Mechanical Engineering at the University of Tennessee when he decided he could no longer advise our four children to attend school there. This was a difficult decision because both my husband and I were graduates of UT. He had taught there for 11 years, and when cut, our blood "runs orange." (University of Tennessee's colors!)

When we left the University of Tennessee, drugs, alcohol, sex, and rock music were a way of life for many students at the university. I agree that if a young person can maintain a Christian testimony for four years in this type of worldly atmosphere, he will be a stronger Christian as a result. However, I watched many university students succumb to peer pressure, waste the life savings of their parents, and break their parents' hearts. My husband and I were not willing to take a chance with our own children.

In 1977 my husband left the University of Tennessee, taking a 60 percent pay cut, and leaving his profession to teach at Hyles-Anderson College. Was it worth it? YES—with no reservations! All of our children have graduated from Hyles-Anderson College. Our sons and daughters met their spouses at the college. All are serving God. Our dream is for our grandchildren to do the same.

One example of negative influence a state university can have on a young person is my brother. He was reared in a godly Christian home, taken to church every time the doors were open, and made a profession of faith as a young child. Today, he is a moral person with a genuine concern for people, but he does not serve God. After receiving a master's degree under a personable professor who hated God and church, his beliefs now reflect those of his professor rather than those of his godly parents.

I would not and could not recommend a state university for anyone today because I am not willing to take a chance in allowing an ungodly person to win his respect, destroy his faith, and warp his mind. Are you willing to take a chance with your children?

My brother David has been very generous with our four children. I believe when my father died 26 years ago, he decided to do for our children what my dad would have done if he were alive. The Christmas after my father went to Heaven, David set up a $10,000 trust fund for each of our children for their college education. Often, David would say to me, "You are sheltering your children from the real world."

My reply was that no child is sheltered who grows up riding a bus to church; instead, they see firsthand what alcohol, drugs, divorce, and immorality do to people they love. He felt as soon as they were "of age," they would choose to leave a life filled with biblical rules that he felt were unreasonable. In the spring when each of our four children graduated from Hammond Baptist High School, David called and offered to fly them anywhere in the country to visit a college they might want to attend so they could pursue a career of their choice. Since David is on the Board of Regents in Tennessee, he offered to meet them and conduct them over any campus in Tennessee. He told them if the $10,000 he had set aside for their education was not enough, he was willing to provide further assistance.

Each of our children said, "Thanks, Uncle David, but we plan to attend Hyles-Anderson College." When Kevin and Keith went to college, they preferred to work their way through college. When they graduated, David gave them the money. A few years ago, David told my husband and me, "I hate to admit it, but I have watched the way my friends reared their children and the way you reared yours, and your way seems to have worked better than theirs."

We were quick to respond, "It wasn't our way; it was God's way." Our youngest son Keith named his son David after my brother.

2. **Keep your mouth shut and never give advice unless your adult child asks for it.** *"He that hath knowledge spareth his world: and a man of understanding is of an excellent spirit. Even a fool, when he holdeth his peace, is counted wise: and he that shutteth his lips is esteemed a man of understanding."* (Proverbs 17:27, 28) This point is much easier said than done. It seems that the older we get, the more we see ourselves as an authority on every issue and believe our adult children are just waiting for our advice. Nothing is farther from the truth. I try to remember this admonition: "Unsolicited advice is seldom heeded and never appreciated." Constantly trying to give advice to your adult child of any age will drive them from you and harm the relationship. If you love them and have a close relationship, they are more likely to ask for your advice. Until then, I follow my own advice and try to keep my big mouth shut.

3. **Share experiences and invest in the people whom your adult children love.** *"When a man's ways please the LORD, he maketh even his enemies to be at peace with him."* (Proverbs 16:7) I have many memories of chaperoning dates with our children. If you believe dates should be chaperoned and your adult child should not ride alone in a car with a date, you must invest time and money to see that your children date according to the rules you have set.

When our four children went to college, they chose to leave the "A" bus route where they could have continued to work and go to the "B" Chicago bus routes. We enjoyed getting to know some of their "bus kids" because it was a way to be close to them often. I made bus bags of giveaway items for their buses.

From the time our children were very young, I always put "I love you" on a scrap of paper and put it in every lunch I packed for them. I included these notes from kindergarten through college, and they never even mentioned the notes. After our daughter Kelly had graduated from Hyles-Anderson and was a faculty member, she had an eight-year-old girl on her bus named Barbie. This girl had an unstable mother, and on several occasions, the state had removed Barbie from the home and placed her in foster care. Barbie had been returned to her apartment and was able to ride the bus again. Kelly asked if she could bring her to our house on a Saturday night, let her spend the night at our house, and take her back to the bus on Sunday morning. We agreed and planned how we could make Barbie's visit special. Saturday evening was fun, but Kelly and Barbie had to leave our house at 6:15 a.m. to go to the college to catch the bus to Chicago and to go pick up the bus riders to bring them to church. I thought I would let Barbie know she was important by making her a lunch when I made Kelly's lunch. I wrote down the kind of sandwich she wanted, the chips, the dessert, and the drink telling her I would bring the lunch to her at 11:00 a.m. when she arrived at junior church.

When she got to junior church, Barbie rushed into the room and said, "May I have my lunch now?" I explained that I would give it to her after junior church because if she had food there, it would be taken away. With a pleading face and voice, Barbie asked again, "May I please see my lunch now?"

I said, "Okay," thinking to myself that Barbie had been lied to so often she wanted to see that I really had made a lunch according to her specifications. I handed Barbie the small lunch sack and waited for her to see that I had given her everything she had ordered. However, I noticed she did not look at the sandwich or the chips or the drink or the dessert. Instead, she was scratching around in the bottom of the bag. In a moment a beautiful smile covered her face and she said, "I knew it would be here. I knew it would be here!" In her hand, she grasped a small scrap of paper from a person she hardly knew on which was written, "I love you." Tears filled my eyes as I thought of the many people who cross our paths on a daily basis who are starving for love. Kelly and I will never forget that experience or Barbie. Wherever she is today, I hope she remembers there are two people who love her because of Jesus.

Occasionally, my husband and I visited on our children's church bus routes when they were in college so we could know those they loved and were giving their lives to help. When our son Kevin was a division leader, his division sat in the section where we sat during the church services. I remember a junior high girl from Kevin's route named Christina who frequently wanted to go to City Baptist Schools, a school designed specifically for Chicago bus kids. Kevin raised the money for her tuition and her ride, but the first week of classes, Christina sat in the hall because of a problem with lice. Her home situation was such that even though Kevin bought the shampoo to take care of the lice, Christina always failed the head check. After a week of sitting in the hallway, Kevin said to Christina, "We've tried everything, and nothing seems to be working. You can't go to City Baptist unless we get rid of the lice, so next week I guess you will have to go back to the public school." The next morning when the bus came by to pick up Christina, she had shaved her head. She had gotten a horrible looking wig from a resale store to wear that kept sliding around on her head. Her friends made fun of her and pulled off her wig, but she went to City Baptist.

My husband asked Dawn, Kevin's wife, to take Christina and buy a wig that looked decent. One hundred dollars is a small investment if it draws you close to your adult children.

4. Discover the interests of your adult children and learn to enjoy them together. Psalm 133:1, *"Behold, how good and how pleasant it is for brethren to dwell together in unity!"* My daughters and daughters-in- law all love shopping at garage sales and resale stores.

Several years ago, a friend of mine introduced me to secondhand shopping. In our area, these shops are known as Village Discount and Unique, but the names change in different parts of the country. I have been a bargain hunter for as long as I can remember—visiting yard sales, garage sales, clearance racks, and junque (with a "que") shops, looking for bargains. When I started teaching full time, I found my time was limited. Secondhand shops put a lot of items in one place—a gold mine in one location! I enjoy secondhand shopping for the following reasons:

A. *Secondhand shopping is fun!* I'll have to admit that my memory of secondhand shops as a child was that of dingy rooms where dirty clothes were piled on tables in a jumbled mess. One look told me there was nothing that I could possibly want. The secondhand shops that I frequent today are clean, with organized clothing that is hanging so shoppers can see it clearly. If we have at least two hours, my daughter and I love looking for treasures. I have never been prospecting for gold nor hunting for wild animals, but the feeling must be similar when you find a dress you love for only $3.00.

It is fun to put clothes in your buggy that you might like and then go to the back of the store to try on your finds. At Village Discount, since there is no dressing room, we put them on over our street clothes. We giggle like school girls as we model our treasures. If you are thinking, "I would never do that," secondhand shopping is not for you. However, just remember that you can buy an entire new wardrobe for $20, and you can discard clothing when you tire of it without feeling guilty.

    B. *Secondhand shopping is inexpensive!* Most of my grandchildren's clothing comes from secondhand shops. It helps to know brand-name labels from nice shops so you can recognize quality clothing. Karen Scott, Liz Claiborne, Talbots, Heart Strings, Old Navy, Levi, Baby Beluga, Polly Flinders, and Baby Togs are just a few of the names for which to watch. How can you know which labels to look for? Go to a nice shop, find what you like, check the labels, write down the names, and take your list to the resale shop. After all, looking is free.

    After you find something in which you are interested at the secondhand shop, look at it carefully to see if it is worn-looking, faded, torn, or stained. Make sure the snaps and zippers work, and the buttons are all there. When I first started going to secondhand shops, I bought a lot of items just because they were inexpensive. However, nothing is a good buy if it will not be worn. I have become more and more selective in my secondhand shopping. Once I bought a nice dress for $1.25. When I got home and tried it on, I found a dollar bill in the pocket! I enjoyed my 25 cent bargain dress!

    Some clothes in the secondhand thrift store are new. I look year around and buy some of my Christmas gifts there. My goal is to have all of my presents by the first week of December; and at secondhand prices, the price is always right!

    C. *Secondhand shopping makes it possible to be well-dressed on any budget.* I carry a list of the sizes of my grandchildren in my purse so I will not buy something that does not fit. I carry a tape measure to check the waist size of trousers. If I need a belt or scarf to match an outfit, I either wear the outfit to the store or take a paint chip of the right color. I make a list of what I need before I go. Some secondhand shops staple a tag in a skirt or jacket so you can match it in the store. Ask as soon as you enter the store.

    D. *Secondhand shopping can be helpful in many ways.* I frequent secondhand stores to 1) buy clothes for bus kids who are entering a Christian school, 2) provide a dress for a woman who says she cannot go to church because she has nothing to wear, 3) buy stuffed animals to give away on the bus route or in a Sunday school class, 4) buy greeting cards of all kinds for ten cents each, 5) buy pie plates for cooking class or your own kitchen, 6) buy jewelry, 7) pick up flower vases to take to hospitals, and 8) get household items such as lamps and furniture for bargain prices. When I buy clothing, I launder it or have it cleaned. I clean the stuffed animals so they do not look secondhand when they are given away. I clean the vases I have purchased, buy a flower, a fern, and some baby's breath and make my own "gift" vases.

I have two lamps in a spare bedroom, a chandelier in my daughter's dining room, a fireplace set for the den, and sheers for my dining room window all from a thrift shop. When my daughter moved, we bought blankets from the secondhand store to protect the furniture.

Years ago, on one of my first trips to a secondhand store, I met a girl I knew who was also shopping there. Acting embarrassed, she said, "I won't tell anyone I saw you here if you'll do the same for me."

At that moment, I decided that secondhand shopping is wise to do if you are on a limited budget, and who isn't? Secondhand shopping is nothing of which to be ashamed! I decided that when someone complimented me on an item I bought at the secondhand store, I would tell that person where I bought it. Before Mrs. Marlene Evans went to Heaven, every time I passed her in the hall at Hyles-Anderson College, she wouldn't say, "Hello!" She asked, "How much for that?!"

By the way just in case you are thinking, "I would never buy all my clothing at used clothing shops," present me with a gift certificate to a nice store, and I promise that I will have no trouble spending it! However, I also promise I will check the clearance rack first!

5.   Realize that God gave you your children to give back to Him. It is natural for them to leave you to establish a home of their own. *"Except the LORD build the house, they labour in vain that build it: except the Lord keep the city, the watchmen worketh but in vain."* (Psalm 127:1)

When our four children were born, we gave them back to the Lord. I prayed not only for our children, but that at the right time, God would provide a mate for each of them. When our youngest son Keith was a freshman at Hyles-Anderson College, he met Michelle Miller from Hannibal, Missouri. He felt she was the one with whom

God would have him spend his life. However, we had always encouraged our children to graduate from college before marriage. In order to get married sooner, he graduated in three years. During this time of preparing for Keith's marriage, people often made remarks like: "Aren't you sad that your 'baby' is getting married and leaving home?" and "Do you feel depressed when you think of all your children being gone?"

At first I wondered why I didn't feel sad or depressed and if something was wrong with me. However, as I thought about this, the following thoughts came to mind.

- Children are given to us on loan by God—not to own. We train them to be used by God.
- God's will for our children does not come through the parents. Each child will learn the will of God for his life through his own personal walk with God.
- I must accept God's will for our children. If God's will takes them far from me, I must accept it.
- I will keep my mouth shut. I will give my opinions only when they are requested.
- Long before it was time for each child to choose his/her mate, we stressed that his/her choice was the second-most important decision he/she would ever make. The most important decision was, of course, their salvation. However, we stressed that they needed to make the decision with God's help.
- Marriage is a commitment "till death do you part." When you make your decision, make no allowance for divorce.
- The time to spend lots of time with your children is when they are young. This will create wonderful memories as well as nurture close relationships between you and your adult children.
- Accept your child's choice of a mate as part of the family. Never take your child's side against his spouse or criticize his mate even if you feel it is justified.
- Be willing to help your married children. Of course, they must first want your help. However, always keep your opinions to yourself.
- A wish from my husband or children is a "royal command." That wish is not to be resented.
- Make holidays special. However, do not get your feelings hurt if your married children decide to make plans that do not

include you or if they decide to spend a certain holiday with the family of their mate instead of with you.

- Let your married children rear their children (your grandchildren) in the way God leads them. If they want your advice, they will ask for it.
- Don't build your life around your children and grandchildren. This means you will not feel like your world is falling apart if they move.
- Enjoy every minute you spend with your children and grandchildren. You will have wonderful memories instead of regrets when this is no longer possible.

On August 13, 1994, Michelle Miller became Mrs. Keith Cowling. It was a day I had anticipated for 21 years. I did not lose a son; I gained a lovely daughter! The same is true of our other three children: Kelly and Rafael Cervantes, Kevin and Dawn Cowling, and Krysten and Chris Vestal. I am so glad I prayed that God would direct each one to the right mate. God's choices are always better than my choices.

6. Be willing to share some of the mistakes you made when you were their age if it will help them avoid making the same mistakes. *"There hath no temptation taken you but such as is common to man: but God is faithful, who will not suffer you to be tempted above that ye are able; but will with the temptation also make a way to escape, that ye may be able to bear it."* (I Corinthians 10:13) When I was in the seventh grade, I promised the Lord that I would marry the person He had planned for my life if He would direct my path. I also promised God that I would be pure when I came to the marriage altar. I never lost sight of this goal throughout junior high, high school, and two years of college. The summer after my sophomore year at college, I got a job as a summer trainee in Tennessee, working with the 4-H Club program.

The first week I was there, I went to a Farm Bureau picnic where I met many people—one of whom was a clean-cut young man about my age. I also met his parents who seemed like very nice people. The young man asked if he could call me sometime. The following week he called and asked if he could take me out for a Coke. It was lonely at night in my rented room, and I felt it would be okay. We went to a restaurant where we enjoyed talking and eating. I thought he would take me home when we left the restaurant, but he started driving in the opposite direction. In a joking way, I asked if he remembered where I lived.

"I have to show you the town," he replied.

I told him the town was tiny, and I had already seen it.

"Not the town I want to show you," he said.

He drove away from the small town to a dark road.

I said, "It is dark here, and I can't see a thing. Just take me home." (By this time I wasn't sure if I should be angry or afraid, but I was becoming angrier by the minute.)

He drove on and turned on a narrow, gravel road that was dark with no lights in sight. "I want you to see the lake," he explained.

"I'll look at it in the daylight," I said. "Please take me home now."

He stopped the car and tried to pull me across the seat to him. I was holding to the door handle with all my might, determined not to move. In this struggle, the door opened and I half fell out of the car. Somehow he lost his grip on my arm, and I found myself walking in my high heels in the mud. By this time, I was furious. As I walked back the way we had come, he was slowly driving beside me with the car door opened on my side. "Where are you going?" he asked.

"Home," I said.

"How will you find it?" he wanted to know.

"I'll find it if I have to walk all night," I told him.

"I believe you would," he answered. I walked on and he said, "Get in, and I'll take you home."

"I don't trust you," I told him and kept walking.

"I'm sorry. Get in, and I'll take you home," he replied.

I got in and kept my hand on the door handle. He took me home and had the nerve to say, "I'll call you again." I did not respond; instead, I opened the car door and ran inside.

When I was safely inside my apartment door, I started trembling so much I could not stand. I realized my vow to God to be pure at the marriage altar could have been made impossible by my foolish decision to trust a guy I had just met. I promised God that I would learn a lesson from this experience and asked Him to protect me until I met the man he had prepared for me. If sharing this experience will help anyone avoid a situation that could destroy their purity, it will be worth the sorrow and fear it brings back to my heart every time I remember it.

My Rules

If you want to marry me, here's what you'll have to do:
    You must learn how to make a perfect chicken-dumpling stew,
And you must sew my holey socks,
    And soothe my troubled mind,
And develop the knack of scratching my back,
    And keep my shoes spotlessly shined.
And while I rest, you must rake up the leaves,
    And when it is hailing and snowing
You must shovel the walk...and be still when I talk,
    And—hey—where are you going?!

Married Children

Married Children

(Photos on page 201)

Background: Krysten on her wedding day with us
Top left: Keith and Michelle on their wedding day
Center: Kevin and Dawn on their wedding day
Bottom right Chris and Krysten on their wedding day
Bottom left: Rafael and Kelly

When our children were little, I was always there to kiss away tears and apply a band-aid— the universal cure for all cuts and scratches. Now that they are grown, they have problems that only God can handle. I love them, listen to them, weep when they weep, and mourn when they mourn. I remember holding my oldest daughter and crying at her feet as she faced the loss of two children. No words were spoken, but we gave our heartache and grief to God and looked to Him for strength. *"The righteous cry, and the LORD heareth, and delivereth them out of all their troubles. The LORD is nigh unto them that are of a broken heart; and saveth such as be of a contrite spirit. Many are the afflictions of the righteous: but the LORD delivereth him out of them all."* (Psalm 34:17-19)

I remember crying with my married younger daughter when she was facing a problem neither of us could solve. As we wept together, I was reminded that God never gives us more than we can bear—as long as we rely upon Him and not ourselves. *"There hath no temptation taken you but such as is common to man: but God is faithful, who will not suffer you to be tempted above that ye are able; but will with the temptation also make a way to escape that ye may be able to bear it."* (I Corinthians 10:13)

Daily as I pray for my children and grandchildren, I trust God to take care of them. When death or health problems arise, I try to keep my mouth shut and by faith trust God—whether or not I feel like it. God's grace is always sufficient if we want it to be. *"And he (God) said unto me, My grace is sufficient for thee: for my strength is made perfect in weakness. Most gladly therefore will I rather glory in my infirmities, that the power of Christ may rest upon me."* (II Corinthians 12:9)

God has promised that trials, heartaches, and persecution are guaranteed in the life of a saved person if we have a desire to serve God. II Timothy 3:12 says, *"Yea, and all that will live godly in Christ Jesus shall suffer persecution."* If Jesus was criticized, beaten, and hung on the cross in spite of living a perfect life, how can we hope to escape trials? It is tragic that we lose this philosophy of life when we reach adulthood. God puts it this way: *"And we know that all things work together for good to them that love God, to them who are the called according to his purpose."* (Romans 8:28)

"Not that I speak in respect of want: for I have learned, in whatsoever state I am, therewith to be content." (Philippians 4:11)

"In every thing give thanks: for this is the will of God in Christ Jesus concerning you." (I Thessalonians 5:18)

If your life has been relatively free of heartache, frustration, and sickness to date, they may be on the way. God never gives us more than we can bear in His strength, but He sends these trials to help us become mature Christians. *"It is good for me that I have been afflicted; that I might learn thy statutes."* (Psalm 119:71)

"For he (God) does not afflict willingly nor grieve the children of men." (Lamentations 3:33)

"I had fainted, unless I had believed to see the goodness of the LORD in the land of the living." (Psalm 27:13)

When things are going well, human nature makes us feel there is no real need for God—inaccurate as this attitude may be. However, when trials and problems arise that are impossible for us to solve, we are faced with our inadequacy and have a choice to struggle along in our strength or turn to God Who has all the answers and Who can solve all our problems. *"Hast thou not known? hast thou not heard, that the everlasting God, the Lord, the Creator of the ends of the earth, fainteth not, neither is weary? there is no searching of his understanding. He giveth power to the faint; and to them that have no might he increaseth strength."* (Isaiah 40:28, 29)

If we are in God's will, all things that happen in our lives are for our good and God's glory.

I Refuse to Become Bitter

If I had my way, everyone I know would enjoy good health and live forever. (On second thought, that is exactly what will happen if we are saved!) However, we must wait for Heaven to make these desires a reality. I find I have peace in time of heartache when I accept God's will in every circumstance.

• I would not choose to see two of our grandchildren go to Heaven of SIDS (Sudden Infant Death Syndrome). Sara died at 8 months of age, and Scott at 12 days old. Doctors say this never happens twice in one family, but God allowed it to happen twice in ours.

• I would not choose to have had four of our grandchildren on infant apnea monitors. One child's monitor went off frequently, so the doctor told my son and daughter-in-law to keep him on the monitor at all times. When readings were taken from the monitor, they were told he would have died twice without it.

• I would not choose for my grandson to weigh eleven pounds at seven months which doctors term "failure to thrive" and have no explanation for this problem. (This condition miraculously improved after his first birthday.)

• I would not choose to have my daughter-in-law, Michelle Cowling, almost bleed to death and be placed on the critical list after giving birth to their first child.

• I would not give our daughter a skin condition that causes her hands and fingers to split and bleed. The doctor told he to keep her hands out of water, but try following that advice with four children under the age of six!

• I would take away the eye problems with which our son who pastors in Arizona struggles and refuses to discuss.

• I would take away the health problem of a wonderful daughter-in- law who keeps going in the face of pain.

• I would not allow a drunken driver to strike my son's car and break his neck five days before his wedding.

• I would not allow our son to black out coming home early on a Monday morning after spending the weekend in Chicago on the bus route, totaling his car one week before his marriage. (Our insurance agent suggested that if we had any more sons not to allow them to drive the week of their weddings!)

• I would not allow one of our grandsons to have poor hearing, requiring tubes to be placed in his ears.

• I would not allow our daughter to go in for a routine eye exam and be told she might have a tumor. After many anxious moments and trips to two specialists, now it looks as if it is a pseudo tumor that can be treated with medication.

• I would not allow our son-in-law to break his leg while taking teenagers on a trip they had won three weeks before their fourth child was due.

I would not allow any of these things to happen to those I love if I could choose. I would rather suffer myself than watch those I love suffer. However, my job is not to become bitter and resentful toward God—asking Him to explain circumstances we cannot understand. We see today, but God sees the future. He does not want us to suffer, but He sends trials to help us grow to maturity in Christ. "*My brethren, count it all joy when ye fall into divers temptations; Knowing this, that the trying of your faith worketh patience. But let patience have her perfect work, that ye may be perfect and entire, wanting nothing.*" (James 1:2-4)

The following thoughts have helped me when faced with frustrations and trials I did not understand:

1. I thank God for what has happened and ask Him to use it for His glory. I pray this by faith because there are times when I really don't want to thank Him for the trials. If I could choose to have heartaches come into my life instead of the lives of our children and grandchildren, I have made the choice. However, God doesn't always give us the right to choose.

In 1977 when God called my husband to leave his chosen profession of teaching engineering at the University of Tennessee, we received much criticism from those we loved. We knew that my dad, who was a wonderful Christian man, had cancer and was willing himself alive for our four children—his only grandchildren. We delayed moving for a year. I will never forget the day I told him. It was a beautiful day in Tennessee with leaves turning many colors, sunshine, and a crisp feel of fall in the air. We had built our house outside of Knoxville on 32 wooded acres overlooking the Tennessee River in one direction and the Smoky Mountains in the other.

No one came up our driveway by accident so I was surprised to see a pickup drive in front of our house. Two men got out of the truck. One of the men was walking with a cane, and I recognized my dad. I ran out to meet him, and he introduced me to the other man, who was a contractor. "Honey," he said, "you have so many people at your house, I want to add more bedrooms to your four-bedroom home. If you tell him what you want, he will build it. I will pay for it."

With a breaking heart I said, "Dad, Pete feels that God wants us to move to Indiana."

"Well, Honey," he replied, "if that is God's will, that settles it. I guess you won't need any more rooms in your house if you are leaving." He turned and slowly walked back to the truck. I wanted to die.

Shortly after that day, my dad's cancer came out of remission, and he spent much of the next seven months in the hospital. On a Sunday in June after the bus route, we drove to the hospital where I saw my dad on the earth for the last time. He was on morphine, and my mother said, "His pain is intense and he probably won't know you, but you can see him." As soon as Daddy heard the children's voices, he was alert and said, "I am giving you $5,000 because when you move, I want my grandchildren to have carpet on their bedroom floors."

That day he met Jesus, and we moved after the funeral. It was a difficult time in my life, but I know my dad is in Heaven and is suffering no longer. He has also witnessed every good thing that has happened in our lives—without pain.

2. I tell Satan I hate him, and I refuse to give him the victory by being defeated, critical, or discouraged. I promise Satan I will do more for God and make him regret that a hurtful situation occurred. When our eight-month-old granddaughter Sara went to Heaven due to crib death, I did not understand then, but I believe one day in Heaven I will understand. It was a shock because she was so full of life and had never been sick. I remember feeling numb the day after she went to Heaven. Since it was a Saturday, I visited our bus route. A father of one of our bus kids answered the door when I knocked. He had never before let me witness to him, but this day he looked at me and said, "Is something wrong?"

"Our granddaughter went to Heaven yesterday," I replied. "I'm still having a hard time, thinking I won't see her again until I go to Heaven."

"Why are you here then?"

"I can't do anything more for my granddaughter," I answered, "but I can love other children like yours."

For the first time he allowed me to lead him down the Romans' road, and he accepted Christ. If you are wondering if I would have sacrificed my granddaughter to see this man saved, the answer is, "No." (However, I am not going to give Satan the victory by feeling so sorry for myself that I am oblivious to the needs of people around me.)

3. I ask God to teach me every lesson He wants me to learn from the trial. I want to learn the lesson so that I will not have to face the same trial again. After our granddaughter Sara died, my husband would lay on her grave every Saturday morning and ask God to teach him every lesson He wanted us to learn from her death, so we wouldn't have to go through it again. However, our 12-day-old grandson Scott went to Heaven of SIDS three years later. Obviously, God still had some more lessons for us to learn. God's ways are not my ways, but I know God's ways are best. *"For my thoughts are not your thoughts, neither are your ways my ways, saith the LORD. For as the heavens are higher than the earth, so are my ways higher than your ways, and my thoughts than your thoughts."* (Isaiah 55:8, 9)

4. When I feel like hibernating and avoiding people I know, I force myself to get up, dress, and follow my regular schedule. This reclusive behavior causes me to dwell on my heartache, making it difficult to get the victory God can give me in every hard time. I try to remember that "A person wrapped up in himself is a very small package."

Our second grandchild went to Heaven early on a Saturday. My son-in-law and our daughter rode their bus to church on Sunday. When well-meaning friends asked how they could do this, they said, "Scott is in Heaven, and sitting at home would cause us to dwell on our heartbreak and loss. Using our time to love and help other children will take our minds off our loss."

5. I avoid negative, critical people who want to review each tragic event and savor it. I make a game of meeting a negative comment with a positive thought. For example, when Kevin's neck was broken, people made comments like, "What a shame their honeymoon was canceled." or "What a shame his tuxedo would not fit because of the halo and the rods attached to his back."

I answered, "I'm just glad God spared his life so he is able to be married on time."

When our granddaughter Sara died, people would say, "What a shame she lived only eight months."

I responded, "God was so good to give us eight months to love her. I hope I can bring as much joy to people I meet daily as she did in her short life."

6. I live one day at a time. The Lord might return or I could go to Heaven, and I would have worried needlessly. God reinforced this lesson one year when I was supervising a corn-detasseling bus of 50 teenagers. Early in the season, I sprained my ankle; and every step I took was agony. I had to determine to keep walking the five or six miles a day through the fields in pain or quit the job. I prayed a lot and kept taking one more step until I reached the end of the row. Each afternoon my ankle would double in size in spite of the ankle wrap. The high school kids kept saying, "Mrs. Cowling, why don't you go to the doctor?"

I replied, "Why should I go to a doctor and pay him to tell me to stay off my ankle when I don't plan to quit this job?"

God helped me finish the season without missing a day, but it took determination. It also took two months for the swelling to leave the ankle. The point is not whether I should have stayed in the fields, but that life should be lived one step at a time.

7. **I keep my mouth shut if I am tempted to complain, or at least, this is my goal!** It is impossible to have a negative and positive thought at the same time. I wish I could say I always follow this advice, but when I do, it certainly saves me from defeat and helps me have the mind of Christ. *"Let this mind be in you, which was also in Christ Jesus."* (Philippians 2:5)

8. **Read and memorize the Word of God. I believe the Bible has the answer to every problem we face in life.** However, if I don't read it, I will be ignorant of those answers. This ignorance is not God's fault. My husband and I travel each summer with a tour group from Hyles-Anderson College, and we memorize a verse every day on tour. Some chapters we have memorized are Romans 12, Psalm 37, Psalm 91, Psalm 103, James 4, I Corinthians 13, Titus 2, and I John 2. There are nine of us in the van, and we drive 10,000 to 15,000 miles in nine weeks. We have seven services a week, and it would be easy to complain and get on one another's nerves. We avoid this by reading the Bible together daily, memorizing the Bible, and telling people about Jesus everywhere we go. This could work for families as well as a tour group.

9. **I trust God to bring triumph through tragedy.** One Monday morning while we were on tour, my husband and I received a call from our youngest son Keith, who was 20 at the time. He was driving home after completing his work with the Sunday night

church bus and fell asleep at the wheel of his car. He woke up going down an embankment off the interstate. The car stopped abruptly in a sea of mud. Uninjured, he waded through the mud back to the road. The next morning as the wrecker pulled his car from the mud, the men noticed an amazing phenomenon. The tire tracks went to the guard rail, leaving no dent, traveled along the top of the guard rail, tearing out the gas tank, and flew down the embankment into the mud. The mud acted as a damp cushion to stop the car and prevent the ruptured gas tank from exploding. The man said, "It's almost as if someone lifted your car over the guard rail. You're lucky."

I don't call it luck. I call it the hand of God. I immediately thought of Psalm 91:1, 10, 12, "*He that dwelleth in the secret place of the most High shall abide under the shadow of the Almighty. There shall no evil befall thee, neither shall any plague come nigh thy dwelling. For he shall give his angels charge over thee, to keep thee in all thy ways. They shall bear thee up in their hands, lest thou dash thy foot against a stone.*"

If all of these nine suggestions fail, don't wallow in defeat. Most of us know what to do in any situation, but doing it is difficult. Swallow your pride, say, "I'm sorry," and start over asking God to teach you a lesson from defeat. I always keep in mind that to be truly successful, you must get up one more time every time you fall. "*A just man falleth seven times, and riseth up again: but the wicked shall fall into mischief.*" (Proverbs 24:16)

Grandchildren

Grandchildren
(Photos on page 211)

Background: Pete and Frieda Cowling
Top center: Rafael and Kelly Cervantes with Stephen, Sam, and Simon
Top right: Kevin and Dawn Cowling with Ashley, Trent, Trevor, and Trey
Right   Chris and Krysten Vestal with Derek, Karissa, Wesley, and Ryan
Bottom center: Keith and Michelle Cowling with David, Peter, and Joseph

If we follow God's guidelines as we rear our children and live our lives, we can claim God's promises found in Psalm 128:1-6, "*Blessed is every one that feareth the LORD; that walketh in his ways. For thou shalt eat the labour of thine hands: happy shalt thou be, and it shall be well with thee. Thy wife shall be as a fruitful vine by the sides of the thine house: thy children like olive plants round thy table. Behold, that thus shall the man be blessed that feareth the LORD. The LORD shall bless thee out of Zion: and thou shalt see the good of Jerusalem all the days of thy life. Yea, thou shalt see thy children's children, and peace upon Israel.*"

There is nothing I need or want in life as far as worldly goods are concerned. However, I greatly desire to see our children, grandchildren, and great-grandchildren experience the joy and peace I have found serving the Lord. I pray daily that they will always choose the will of God for their lives. I pray that our children will follow the same principles from the Word of God in rearing their children that we used in rearing them. I pray that we will always share a closeness and bond as we follow Christ and seek to tell a lost world about the Saviour.

The following are gifts my husband and I hope to leave our grandchildren:

1. A good heritage. Psalm 16:6, "*The lines are fallen unto me in pleasant places; yea, I have a goodly heritage.*" I grew up in a home where we were not rich in earthly goods, but we were rich in our love for God and for each other. My parents did not argue, fight, and call each other names, so my brother and I did not do these things (unless our parents were not around). We were in church as a family every time the church doors were open. I never remember feeling that I did not want to go to church—even though I would not have been allowed to stay home if I had wanted to stay home! The year after I graduated from college, and the year before I was married, I worked for the Extension Service in a mountain county in

Tennessee. One Wednesday we had a heavy snowfall, and I decided to walk the four blocks to church for the evening service. When I got to church, I was surprised to find no one else had bothered to come. I came, not because I loved God so much, but because of my heritage. The importance of being in church every time the doors were open had become a part of my life.

Without the gift of a good heritage from my parents, I could experience the judgment given in Exodus 34:6 and 7 which says, *"And the Lord passed by before him, and proclaimed, "The Lord, The Lord God, merciful and gracious, longsuffering, and abundant in goodness and truth, Keeping mercy for thousands, forgiving iniquity and transgression and sin, and that will by no means clear the guilty; visiting the iniquity of the fathers upon the children, and upon the children's children, unto the third and to the fourth generation."*

2. A good name. *"A good name is rather to be chosen than great riches, and loving favour rather than silver and gold."* (Proverbs 22:1) When a name is mentioned in the Bible, it is frequently used to designate the entire person, his individuality, and his power. A good name cannot be purchased; rather, it must be earned. My father gave me a name that was respected in the community where I lived as a child, and I was strongly encouraged never to dishonor this name. This was an incentive to obey the rules of the school and to respect all authority.

My dad was a strong man who never compromised his beliefs, but he was friendly, causing people to be drawn to him and to trust him. I only saw him upset one time. My dad owned an appliance store, and I would often walk to the store after school and ride home with him. One day I entered the store and heard my dad yelling, "Get out! You are fired!" The man who worked for my dad was trying to say something, but my dad handed him some money and told him to leave. I discovered that this man had been overcharging people who came into the store to buy parts and putting the extra money in his own pocket.

After he had left, my dad said, "I have worked hard to have the reputation of being a honest man, and no one will work for me who is a thief." It was a lesson I have never forgotten.

When our four children were young, my husband would tell them we had worked hard to give them a name that was respected.

If one of our children was exhibiting undesirable behavior or a bad attitude, my husband would say, "Change your ways or change your name."

3. Unconditional love. *"Beloved, if God so loved us, we ought also to love one another. No man hath seen God at any time. If we love one another, God dwelleth in us, and his love is perfected in us."* (I John 4:11, 12)

When our children were growing up, we tried to make it clear that we always loved them whether their activities pleased or displeased us. We loved them enough to correct them when they broke our rules, even though they did not welcome the correction. *"Now no chastening for the present seemeth to be joyous, but grievous; nevertheless afterward it yieldeth the peaceable fruit of righteousness unto them which are exercised thereby."* (Hebrews 12:11) Our son Keith learned this lesson with his son Petey.

"To Rejoice Is a Choice... *Even When All Drains Are Clogged"*

Our youngest grandson, Peter Cowling, has had a fascination for flushing toilets ever since he was tall enough to reach the handle. At first the problem was solved by keeping all the bathroom doors closed which was effective until Petey learned to opened doors. Each time Michelle, Petey's mother, heard a flushing noise, she corrected him; but the problem was not solved.

It was not long until a crisis arose. The septic system at Petey's house stopped working. Several home remedies were tried with no success. Finally, a professional company was called, and the drains began to work again—after three pacifiers and a jar of Vicks were removed from the drain outside the house under the deck which was removed and then replaced.

Did you ever try to explain to a one-year-old the expense and time required to repair the damage caused by flushing items down the toilet? Our frustration is probably similar to God's frustration as

He watches us do foolish things He has told us not to do because they are "fun" for a moment.

P.S. The cost of this lesson was $2,000. Keith said, "Petey will not receive an allowance for the rest of his life," but time may dim this resolve!

4. Prayer Offered to God on Their Behalf. I see some of our grandchildren on a regular basis because they live near me, but I see eight of them no more than once or twice a year. However, every day I have a set time when I pray for them, begging God to direct their paths and help them follow His will for their lives.

My husband was praying for our son Kevin when his parked car was struck by a drunk driver, and Kevin's neck was broken. A police-woman heard the crash, came to the scene, and prevented Kevin from moving which could have resulted in paralysis. Prayer is a supernatural power available to us if we take advantage of it. *"Confess your faults one to another, and pray one for another, that ye may be healed. The effectual fervent prayer of a righteous man availeth much."* (James 5:16)

5. The Mercy of God. *"But the mercy of the LORD is from ever-lasting to everlasting upon them that fear him, and his righteousness unto children's children; To such, as keep his covenant, and to those that remember his commandments to do them."* (Psalm 103:17, 18) We teach our children and grandchildren by our own example—what we say and what we do. I believe God is telling me that if I try to keep God first in my life and treat others as myself, God will bless our children and grandchildren.

God has said that we should go into the highways and hedges compelling people to come to Christ. We have tried to do this through the bus ministry for the past 30 years. We stayed on the route when many came and few came, in heat, in cold, when were encouraged or discouraged. Reaching one boy like Johnny, who is in Heaven today, murdered at age 20, but saved and baptized at age 9, makes the struggle worthwhile.

6. An Inheritance. Proverbs 13:22 says, *"A good man leaveth an inheritance to his children's children: and the wealth of the sinner is laid up for the just."* When God led my husband to take a 60 percent pay cut and leave his tenured position as a professor at the University of Tennessee, some people told us we would never be able to educate our children on the salary he would be making. They were forgetting the promise of Proverbs 13:22.

The Christmas we moved from Tennessee to Indiana, my brother set up a $10,000 trust fund for each of our four children for their education. I believe God led him to do this to silence the critics and because he wanted to do for our children what my father would have done if he were alive. At this date, all four children have college degrees and are serving the Lord. God has allowed us to help each of them make a down payment on a house, and we are asking God to help us do the same for our grandchildren.

7. **Food in the Time of Famine.** All of my life in America, I never remember a time when I did not have more food than I needed to eat. However, there is no guarantee this fact will always be true. Recently while talking to the Kevin Bakers, who returned from working on the China Mission Project sponsored by our church, he said, "One thing I will never forget were children holding the legs of people walking down the streets in China, hoping to receive a penny or food." (The average man in China works a ten-hour day and earns 25 cents.) I want to live so our children and grandchildren would not be in this position as I claim the promise of Psalm 37:25-28, "*I have been young, and now am old; yet have I not seen the righteous forsaken, nor his seed begging bread. He is ever merciful, and lendeth; and his seed his blessed. Depart from evil, and do good; and dwell for evermore. For the* LORD *loveth judgment, and forsaketh not his saints; they are preserved for ever: but the seed of the wicked shall be cut off.*"

8. **Support of the Grandchildren's Parents.** I have observed that many people become more lenient as they get older, failing to be as strict with grandchildren as they were with their children. (This is one reason why it is better for parents to rear children.) When I feel one of our children is too strict with our grandchildren, I try to remember that "unsolicited advice is seldom heeded and never appreciated." My policy is total support for the parents. My job is to love the grandchildren, play with them, and present a united front with the parent in every area.

It has been a tremendous blessing to see our children rear our grandchildren the way we reared them. Proverbs 23:24 says, "*The father of the righteous shall greatly rejoice: and he that begetteth a wise child shall have joy of him.*"

9. Time. Time is the greatest gift we can give anyone; when we give time, we give ourselves. I made many mistakes in rearing our four children, and I have regrets regarding the times I lost my temper and corrected our children in anger. However, I have no regrets regarding the amount of time I spent with our children, playing with them, teaching them to work, reading to them, or correcting them. The following are some special memories of time spent with our grandchildren.

"Hold You, Grandma..."

"The steps of a good man are ordered by the LORD: and he delighteth in his way. Though he fall, he shall not be utterly cast down: for the LORD upholdeth him with his hand." (Psalm 37:23, 24) Every morning I remind God of this verse and ask Him to make it a reality in my life. Satan loves for us to be so busy doing good things that we miss His best for our lives. For example, God is a God of order, and He expects us to have a clean house. (Lady reading this book, if your home is a pigsty, you are not right with God.) However, we can become so obsessed with cleaning that shoes must be removed at the door; the dishes are whisked from the table and washed immediately, leaving no time for conversation. We can become so preoccupied with cleaning that we fail to spend time with friends, children, grandchildren, and extended family members.

God has given me four wonderful children and sixteen precious grandchildren. As I have already mentioned, two of our grandchildren, Sara and Scott Cervantes, went to Heaven as a result of crib death. I treasure each minute spent with each family member, and I try never to take them for granted.

When Ashley Cowling, our second grandchild, was two years of age, she would run up to me with her arms outstretched and say, "Hold you, Grandma." No matter how busy I was, I would hold her and find things she would enjoy that we could do together. We would sing songs, read stories, feed the ducks, blow bubbles, cook, swing, play games, or walk outside in every kind of weather. Five minutes spent with a child can build a wonderful relationship. As Ashley grows older, I want her to remember a grandmother who always had time to "hold you."

Two Holes in One

One Friday afternoon our son Keith called and asked if my husband and I would like to go miniature golfing with him, his wife, and their two sons David, who was three, and Peter, who was seven months old. Actually, Peter went along for the ride!

I remember wondering if David would enjoy golfing at his age, but we went. I had forgotten that Keith occasionally plays regular golf and had sawed off one of his clubs for David to use. When we reached the miniature golf course, David was given a child's club which was too large for him, but nothing could dim David's excitement. He placed his ball on the starting point like the adults; and on the fourth hole, he made a hole-in-one. We were amazed! Michelle, David's mother, had brought a camera, so she took his picture holding his club and ball beside the hole in a "victory" pose.

In case you get the wrong impression, David is not a master golfer. We always let him go first; and if his ball would get behind an obstacle, he would pick up the ball, place it closer to the hole, and shoot it. (We did not give him a lecture on cheating. We felt he could learn that later when he mastered the game.) We wanted him to have fun and learn to enjoy the game.

A few holes later when David made his second hole-in-one, we cheered and clapped again. Michelle made another picture of him beside the hole, holding up his golf club and ball. It wasn't too surprising that David played all 18 holes. We felt he would get tired before he finished all of them and planned to stop when he got tired. However, if you make two holes in one and are being praised, you keep playing. We had a memorable time, and David was the "Golfer of the Day"!

"The Candy Is for My Three Friends— Kimberly, Kenna, and Grandma"

It is my desire to be close to all of my children and grandchildren—the ones who live nearby that I see often as well as the ones who live 2,000 miles away. Every week we have a family Monday for our six Indiana grandchildren where we play games, work puzzles, tell stories, and go the park. However, it takes a greater effort to be close to grandchildren I see only two or three times a year. I do the following to promote closeness:

1. **Send cards on special days like birthdays, Halloween, Thanksgiving, Valentine's Day, and Easter.**

2. **Talk to them often on the telephone.** I have given the grandchildren telephone calling cards, hoping they will want to use them to call me.

3. **Send packages through the mail with treats and clothes.** They may not need these things, but I need to give them. *"A gift is as a precious stone in the eyes of him that hath it: whithersoever it turneth, it prospereth."* (Proverbs 17:8)

4. **Plan activities.** When I see them, I tell them stories, and we also play games, sing songs, or go to the park. I want them to store up positive memories until the next time I see them.

I once went to a ladies' meeting in Marysville, Washington, so my daughter and son-in-law, who live in Oregon, drove there with their three children, Derek, Karissa, and Wesley. I took them several items, but they most enjoyed the playdough I had made for them. Three weeks later, Karissa who dearly loves candy, had been given three pieces of candy at church. When Karissa got home, she said to her mother, "I am going to give this candy to my three friends—Kimberly, Kenna, and Grandma." Karissa placed the candy on the kitchen counter.

Krysten said, "You won't see Grandma for two months."

"That's okay," Karissa replied, "I'll save it until I see her."

I don't need candy, but I need the love of a granddaughter who calls me her friend.

By the way, Krysten reported that my piece of candy mysteriously disappeared a day or so later.

More Ways to Be Close to Your Grandchildren

I was thankful every day that my children and grandchildren lived close to me because I realized there could be a day when God would take them to serve in another part of the country. I am glad I decided to let God direct the paths of our children because God did move two of our children and eight of our grandchildren 2,000 miles away and 2,000 miles apart.

I cannot say that I was glad to see them go, but I am glad they are following God. It is possible to be close to children who live far away if you pray for them daily, attempt to bear some of their burdens, and use visits to make memories that will not dim until the next visit. Some ideas I have used to maintain a close relationship are:

1. Mail a story book with a stuffed animal that complements the story, such as *Winnie the Pooh* with a Tigger.

2. Write a letter or send a postcard to them often. Include a stick of gum or an Andes mint as a treat. Use stickers on the outside of the envelope.

3. Use a tape recorder to talk to them or read a book to them and send a copy of the book. We mailed tapes to our parents when our children were young and could not yet write. My only regret is that we taped over them. The few we have kept my adult children still enjoy hearing.

4. Tape a song or finger rhyme. At Christmas this year, we made a DVD, not professionally, but it was fun.

5. Send money so the parent can take out the child for ice cream or a meal. Have the child dictate a letter or make a tape to mail to his grandparents telling about the special outing after you return home.

6. Have the child mail the grandparents some pictures often. A scrapbook for Christmas could be made from these pictures.

7. Have a time each week or month to call on the telephone. Check your finances and call when the rates are low or the call is free. Use a speaker phone if possible so everyone can hear.

8. Go to the store to find a game your grandchildren would enjoy or let them select one they like. Play the game with them.

9. Make a videotape to send back and forth. Some computers are equipped to do this.

10. Make holidays or vacations special and build memories you can talk about later.

11. Have your grandchildren visit and plan activities they would enjoy. Remember, a busy child is a happy child and one who will not get on your nerves.

I am determined with God's help to be close to my grandchildren—no matter where they live.

Correction from a Mother's Viewpoint when Visiting Grandparents

When our children were younger, we lived close enough to visit my parents once a week. I wanted these visits to be pleasant ones, but we also wanted our children to be well behaved at home or away from home. We wanted to avoid friction so we lived by the following guidelines:

1. **We made it clear to our children that obedience was required everywhere—at home or away from home.** Inconsistency on the part of the authority always causes disobedience on the part of children. It is unwise and dangerous to correct the child in public; however, you can take the child to your car or a bedroom in a private home, or wait until you get home if the child is old enough to remember the infraction for which he will be disciplined. If you promise the child a correction, do not overlook the correction because to do so encourages disobedience.

2. **Set the rules of behavior before you leave home so the children will know what is expected of them.** Children should know they will be praised if they obey the rules and punished if they disobey.

3. **If the children are visiting grandparents, allow the grandparents to "spoil" the children.** When I say "spoil," I am referring to the children having special treats, attention, and varying bedtime rules. If this were an everyday occurrence, it would not be good for the child. My parents gave treats such as candy, chips, and pop to our children anytime they wanted them. (We didn't.) They were allowed to drink from baby bottles long past the "baby stage" and were allowed to stay up past their normal bedtimes in order to hear stories or sing songs. However, my husband and I reminded them on the way home that we would return to the established rules my husband had

set as soon as we got home. We were consistent with these rules, and this arrangement worked well for us.

4. Draw the line at disobedience and rebellion on the part of children. God's feelings about rebellion are stated in I Samuel 15:23a, *"For rebellion is as the sin of witchcraft, and stubbornness is as iniquity and idolatry…."*

5. Decide before the visit what kind of television programs and videos your child will be allowed to watch. Our guide in this matter was Philippians 4:8 which says, *"Finally, brethren, whatsoever things are true, whatsoever things are honest, whatsoever things are just, whatsoever things are pure, whatsoever things are lovely, whatsoever things are of good report; if there be any virtue, and if there be any praise, think on these things."*

If grandparents are saved and have the same standards you have, this will probably not present a problem. However, if grandparents are unsaved and follow different standards, different convictions, and a life style different from yours, it can cause friction during every visit. Broken relationships and miserable visits result when arguments arise concerning standards and convictions. After some stormy visits, we decided on the following plan to make our visits pleasant:

A. Our visits never lasted more than three days. We did not tell loved ones this rule; we merely made the policy and followed it.

B. We made it clear to our children what they were and were not allowed to watch on television.

C. If they were in the room and either a grandparent or relative was watching a program we did not approve, they were not to say anything. They were to simply leave the room.

D. We told them to go to the bedroom where they were sleeping and read a book which we brought from home. When the offensive program was finished, they could come back into the room.

E. We made it clear that they were never to correct the grandparents for anything in word or action.

6. Provide an alternative to wrong influences. My husband got maps of the area and planned interesting trips that would take us away from the television that was on constantly in every part of the house. Advance planning made it possible to build good relationship and memories without clashes over standards and convictions.

My parents were saved, but my husband's parents were unsaved. His mother was saved after eight years of prayer; his father was saved after twenty-two years of prayer. Our relatives need to see the difference Christ makes in our lives and the love we have for them, regardless of whether they are saved or lost.

Correction of Grandchildren from a Grandmother's Point of View

Before I had grandchildren of my own, I observed many incidents of friction between parents and grandparents over the correction of children. The following are just a few of the situations I have witnessed:

* Parents corrected their children, and the grandparents thought they were too strict and too hard on the children, feeling free to express this displeasure.
* Parents did not correct their children, and the grandparents became upset because the children needed correction that was not given.
* Parents threatened to correct the children, but they never followed through; the grandparents felt that correction should be given and said so.
* Parents permitted their children to be incorrigible; the grandparents gave looks of disapproval.
* Parents permitted bratty behavior from the children so the grandparents corrected the children which caused resentment on the part of the parents who felt the grandparents were correcting the parents when they corrected their children.
* Grandparents corrected their grandchildren in front of their parents which caused resentment and encouraged the children to play one authority against the other.
* Grandparents avoided spending time with grandchildren because they disapproved of their grandchildren's behavior.
* Grandparents told their children how to correct their children by making statements like "I never let you get away with that!" which damages the relationship.

I am sure I could go on and on, but I wanted a different type of relationship with our four children, their mates, and our 16 grand-children. I have made some of the previously listed mistakes, but I try not to make the same mistake over and over again. I decided to apol-ogize to the child's parent who is present when I make the mistake. When I am the authority over the grandchildren in the absence of the parents, I correct them the way I feel they need to be corrected with parental approval. I set the following guidelines for myself when God gave us grandchildren:

1. **Build a close relationship with grandchildren.** Talk to them, write notes, mail small presents addressed to them, and play with them. After one Christmas our then three-year-old grand-daughter, Karissa Vestal, who lives in Oregon, told her mother, "If Grandma were here, she would play with me." (She was right!)

2. **Spend time with them.** I only see eight of our grandchildren once or twice a year so I work hard to make sure they remember the time we spend together. We read books together. One summer I read *Anne of Green Gables* to nine-year-old Ashley Cowling, who lives in Arizona. She can read as well as I can, but I enjoyed reading to her. My grandchildren and I go to the park, play games, make tents by covering the dining room table with blankets, and then crawl under them. I tell stories I can remember about their parents and folk tales as we sit under the tent.

3. **Remember that busy, occupied children are happy.** They are not as tempted to disobey and require correction when they are content.

4. **Make your house "child friendly."** I do not have priceless heirlooms in my house, but if I did, I would move them so children would not need to be corrected continuously when they visited my house. I have books and toys at my house so our grandchildren have something to do they enjoy. We work puzzles, read books, play games, and act out the stories we read. I do not want to be the kind of grand-mother who gasps every time a child gets near an object that is breakable.

5. **If a grandchild's parents are present, keep your big mouth shut and let them do the correcting.** If you do not agree with the method of correction, keep your big mouth shut! If you cannot keep your mouth shut without help, tape it shut. It would be better to do this than ruin the relationship with your children.

6. **Never take the child's side against the parents.** In so doing,

you are tearing down their authority, your authority, and encouraging rebellion in the grandchildren. Remember the rule of keeping your big mouth shut. (I have broken this rule on occasion and can speak from experience.)

7. **When parents are not present, correct your grandchildren using the method of punishment the parents recommend.**

8. **Realize there is a tendency to become more lenient as you get older.** If Bible principles are followed, you will not change in correcting your grandchildren. *"Jesus Christ the same yesterday, and to day, and for ever."* (Hebrews 13:8)

9. **Grandparents are not the "fount of all wisdom" in the correction of children.** I try to follow this principle: "Unsolicited advice is seldom heeded and never appreciated."

10. **Grandparents who always have to be right in correcting grandchildren will tear down the relationship between their children and grandchildren.**

For me true joy in life comes from having the right relationship with those we love. You may say, "I wish I had children and grandchildren that never caused a conflict, and I could have joy." Our family is tempted to disagree just like yours according to I Corinthians 10:14, *"There hath no temptation taken you but such as is common to man: but God is faithful, who will not suffer you to be tempted above that ye are able: but will with the temptation also make a way to escape, that ye may be able to bear it."*

I would prefer to demand my own way because I feel my way is always the best way, but I must learn to prefer others if I desire a good relationship. *"Be kindly affectioned one to another with brotherly love; in honour preferring one another."* (Romans 12:10)

If I demand my way, I will get it because everyone will leave, and there will be no relationship to build. I remind myself that it takes two people to disagree, and if I "give in," the issue will be resolved. I remind myself often of Proverbs 13:10, *"Only by pride cometh contention: but with the well advised is wisdom."* Is being right and having my own way more important than having a good relationship with those I love? I remind myself that "A person wrapped up in himself is a very small package." When I fail to follow these guidelines, I apologize to the one I have offended and try again. There is no price too high to have a good relationship with those I love.

Appendix A
Finger Rhymes

Keith

Peek-a-Boo
Pat-a-Cake
This Little Piggy
Where is Thumbkin?
Open, Shut Them
I Have a Little Turtle
Here Is the Church
Two Little Blackbirds
Five Little Monkeys
Here's a Ball
Grandma's Glasses
Teddy Bear
Here Is a Bunny
Five Little Squirrels
Put Your Hands Up in the Air
Five Little Pumpkins
My Book
Shape Rhymes and Figures
Snowmen
Cookie Jar
Bear Hunt
I Know an Old Lady

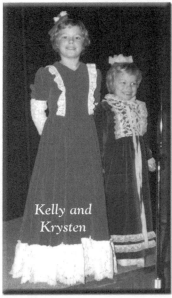

Kelly and
Krysten

Keith and Krysten with Mimi

Keith

Peek-a-Boo
Peek-a-boo, I see you! (*Cover face with hands, then remove them so infant can see you and laugh.*)

Pat-a-Cake
Pat a cake, pat a cake, baker's man. (*Help infant clap hands together.*)
Bake me a cake as fast as you can. (*Clap hands.*)
Roll it and roll it and put it in the pan. (*Help infant roll hands in circle*)
Pat a cake, pat a cake, baker's man. (*Help infant clap hands together.*)

This Little Piggy
This little piggy went to market. (*Pull infant's big toe.*)
This little piggy stayed home. (*Pull infant's second toe.*)
This little piggy had roast beef. (*Pull infant's third toe.*)
This little piggy had none. (*Pull infant's fourth toe.*)
This little piggy cried, "Wee, wee, wee" all the way home! (*Pull small toe.*)

Where Is Thumbkin?
Where is Thumbkin? Where is Thumbkin?
Here I am! (*Bring out right thumb in front of you.*)
Here I am! (*Bring out left thumb in front of you.*)
How are you today, Sir? (*Wriggle right thumb.*)
Very well, I thank you. (*Wriggle left thumb.*)
Run away! (*Put right thumb behind you.*)
Run away! (*Put left thumb behind you.*)

Repeat with same words and motions using:
  Pointer (*second finger beside thumb*)
  Tall Man (*middle finger*)
  Ring Man (*ring finger*)
  Baby (*small finger*)

Open, Shut Them
Open, shut them! (*Open and close fingers on both hands.*)
Open, shut them! (*Open and close fingers on both hands.*)
Let your hands go clap! (*Clap hands together.*)

Open, shut them! (*Open and close fingers on both hands.*)
Open, shut them! (*Open and close fingers on both hands.*)
Place them in your lap! (*Put hands in lap.*)

Creep them, creep them! (*Move fingers in front of you, chest high.*)
Creep them, creep them! (*Move fingers in front of you, chest high.*)
Right up to your chin! (*Stop fingers at chin.*)

Open wide your little mouth! *(Open mouth.)*
But do not let them in! *(Shake head from side to side.)*

I Have a Little Turtle

I have a little turtle who lives in a box.
   (Hold left hand with open hand to represent box.)
He swims in a puddle and climbs upon the rock.
   *(Use right hand as if it were turtle and "swim" in palm of left hand and
"climb" on the fingers.)*
He snapped at a minnow. *(Snap at body with fingers of right hand.)*
He snapped at a flea. *(Snap at body with fingers of right hand.)*
He snapped at a mosquito. *(Snap at body with fingers of right hand.)*
And he snapped at me! *(Repeat)*
He caught the minnow. *(Repeat the motion.)*
He caught the flea. *(Repeat the motion.)*
He caught the mosquito. *(Repeat the motion.)*
But he didn't catch me! *(Repeat motion, but shake head from side to side.)*

Here Is the Church

Here is the church. *(Lace hands together with the fingers on the inside of both
   hands to resemble a ball.)*
Here is the steeple. *(Lift two pointer fingers and put them together
   to make a steeple.)*
Open the door, *(Move both thumbs away from laced hands so it
   resembles a door.)*
And meet all the people. *(Turn hands over so fingers can be the people.)*

Two Little Blackbirds

*I remember my dad doing this rhyme with me when I was very young.
Sometimes he would paint faces for Jack and Jill on his fingers with a pen.*

Two little blackbirds sitting on a hill, *(Put pointer fingers of both the right
   hand and the left hand in front of you.)*
One named Jack
   (Make a circle with right pointer finger and return to position.)
And one named Jill.
   (Make a circle with left pointer finger and return to original position.)
Fly away, Jack! *(Put right pointer finger behind your back .)*
Fly away, Jill! *(Put left pointer finger behind your back.)*
Come back, Jack! *(Return right pointer finger to original position.)*
Come back, Jill! *(Return left pointer finger to original position.)*

Five Little Monkeys

Children can act out this rhyme by putting five of them in a line and having them jump up and down. Use the child's name and say, "David fell off and bumped his head." Let him walk to the doctor (another child) who says, "That's what you get for jumping on the bed." The child then sits on the floor or in a chair.

Five little monkeys jumping on the bed.
   (Jump five fingers of right hand on open palm of left hand.)
One fell off and bumped his head!
   (Hold up the pointer finger, tap head.)
He went to the doctor, and the doctor said, "That's what you get for
   jumping on the bed!"
   (Shake pointer finger in front of you as though you are giving instructions.)

   Repeat with "Four little monkeys..., Three little monkeys..., Two little monkeys..., One little monkey..."

Here's a Ball

Here's a ball,
   (Make a ball by putting your thumb and pointer finger together.)
And here's a ball.
   (Make a ball by putting your thumb and fingers of both hands together.)
And here's a great big ball.
   (Touch the fingers of both hands and make a ball in front of you.)
Now let's count the balls we've made...
One, two, three.
   (Repeat the three balls you made.)

Grandma's Glasses

Here are Grandma's glasses.
   *(Put your thumb and pointer finger together with both hands. Put in front
      of eyes like glasses.)*
Here is Grandma's hat.
   (Put both hands on top of head like a hat.)
This is the way she folds her hands
   (Fold both hands together on lap.)
And puts them in her lap.

   Do the same for Grandpa in deeper voice. On last line say: "This is the
way he folds his arms and puts them in his lap." *(Cross arms over chest.)*

Teddy Bear, Teddy Bear

Teddy Bear, Teddy Bear, turn around.
(Put finger on top of head and turn around.)
Teddy Bear, Teddy Bear, touch the ground.
(Touch the floor with both hands.)
Teddy Bear, Teddy Bear, show your stuff.
(Make a fist with both hands and shake.)
Teddy Bear, Teddy Bear, that's enough.
(Shake pointer finger like you are teaching.)

Here Is a Bunny

Here is a bunny with ears so funny. *(Two fingers on right hand, bent over.)*
And here is a hole in the ground.
(Make a hole with left hand by touching fingers and thumb.)
A noise he hears, he pricks up his ears, *(Two fingers on left hand, upright.)*
And jumps in the hole in the ground.
(Put two fingers on right hand in hole between thumb and pointer finger on left hand.)

Five Little Squirrels

Use names of children instead of numbers to make the children feel special.

Five little squirrels up in a tree. *(Hold up five fingers on right hand.)*
The first one says, "What do I see?"
(Hold up pointer finger and put hand above eyes as if looking for something.)
The second one says, "Let's hide in the shade."
(Hold up two fingers and cross over chest as if hugging yourself.)
The third one says, "I'm not afraid."
(Hold up three fingers and hook thumbs under armpits.)
The fourth one says, "I see a gun."
(Hold up four fingers and hook right pointer finger around left thumb with left pointer finger extended, snapping fingers of right hand.)
The fifth one says, "I've never run."
(Hold up five fingers and move pointer finger in front as if you are saying, "No.")
Then bang went the gun,
(Clap both hands together.)
And the five squirrel quickly did run!
(Move both hands in a fluttering motion behind your back.)

Put Your Hands Up in the Air

Let the children do the motions as the song is sung. (If you are facing the children, use your right hand for their left, or they will use the wrong hand.) If children need to move around, this is a good song to use.

Put your hands up in the air. *(Put hands above head.)*
Put your hands down on your nose. *(Put hands on nose.)*
Put your hands in the air. *(Put hands above head.)*
Now bend down and touch your toes. *(Touch toes with hands.)*
Everybody turn around. *(Turn around one time.)*
Now let's all jump up and down. *(Jump up and down.)*
Put your right hand in the air. *(Put right hand above head.)*
Put your right hand on your lips. *(Put right hand on lips.)*
Put your left hand in the air. *(Put left hand above your head.)*
Now put both hands on your hips. *(Put hands on hips.)*
Everybody turn around. *(Turn around one time.)*
Now let's all jump up and down. *(Jump up and down.)*
Walk back quietly to your seat. *(Walk to seat.)*
Don't let the teacher hear your feet. *(Tiptoe quietly.)*
Put your hands down in your lap. *(Put hands in lap.)*
Bow your head and take a nap! *(Put head on chest.)*

Five Little Pumpkins

Five little pumpkins sitting on the gate.
　　(Hold up five fingers of right hand.)
The first one said, "My, it's getting late!"
　　(Hold up pointer finger.)
The second one said, "There's excitement in the air!"
　　(Hold up pointer and middle finger.)
The third one said, "I don't care!"
　　(Hold up ring finger with others.)
The fourth one said, "Let's run, let's run!"
　　(Hold up pinkie finger.)
The fifth one said, "It's only Halloween fun!"
　　(Hold up thumb and all other fingers.)

Then "Whooooo" went the wind.
And crack went the light
　　(Clap hands together.)
And the five little pumpkins rolled out of sight.
　　(Put five fingers behind back.)

My Book

This is my book; it will open wide.
    (Put hands together in front of you as if you are opening a book.)
To show the pictures that are inside.
This is my ball, so big and round
    (Put thumb and pointer fingers in both hands together to resemble a ball.)
To toss in the air *(Act as if throwing ball into the air.)*
Or roll on the ground. *(Act as if rolling ball on the ground.)*
Here's my umbrella to keep me dry *(Put hands together over head.)*
When the raindrops fall from the cloudy sky.
    (Put fingers overhead to trickle down like raindrops.)
This is my kitty; just hear her purr *(Hold out left arm.)*
When I'm gently stroking her soft, warm fur.
    (Stroke left arm with right hand and make purring voice.)

Shape Rhymes and Figures

Suzy Circle
I'm Suzy Circle—
Watch me bend,
Round and round
From end to end.

Tommy Triangle
Tommy Triangle is the name for me,
Tap my sides: one, two, three.

Sandy Square
Sandy Square is my name,
My four sides are just the same.
Count one side and then count more!
Count to two, then three, then four.
Turn me around; I don't care—
I'm always the same. I'm Sandy Square.

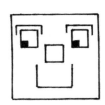

Ricky Rectangle
Ricky Rectangle is my name.
My four sides are not the same.
Two are short and two are long;
Count my sides, come right along.
One, two, three, four.
Turned this way,

The figures should be easily seen. Mine fit on 8½ x 11 pieces of paper. Enlarge as needed.

I look like a door;
One, two, three, four.
Turned this way,
I'm a window in a store;
One, two, three, four.

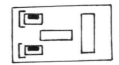

Ollie Oval
Ollie Oval is my name.
Circle and I are not the same.
She's round and round and very stout
I'm tall and thin, and my ends curve out.

Darla Diamond
Two triangles end to end
Make one Darla Diamond
To be your friend.

Snowman

Just do what the rhyme says until you are in a heap on the floor.

Ho, Ho, Ho, Hum, Hum, Hum, you disappear by the minute.
There's one arm gone, now two arms gone
And plop, there goes your head.
Your middle bends, your knees bend, too.
You're smaller by the minute.
Ho, Ho, Ho, Hum, Hum, Hum. Snowman's gone; all gone,
All but your funny hat on the floor.
(The children can do it after you show them how.)

Cookie Jar

Who ate the cookie in the cookie jar, the cookie jar, the cookie jar?
Who ate the cookie in the cookie jar?
(Starting with "who," put both hands on knees and clap on "ate." Repeat, "the cookie jar, the cookie jar…")
___ ate the cookie in the cookie jar. *(Call a child's name to continue the rhythm.)*

You can stop the rhythm when asking the questions and continue with "who" and "ate."
Who me?
Yes, you!
Not me!
Then who?
___ ate the cookie in the cookie jar. *(Repeat)*

Bear Hunt

Teacher or leader says first line, followers repeat, and do the motion.

Let's go on a bear hunt. *(Repeat and slap each leg with each hand.)*
All right, let's go. *(Keep slapping your knees alternately, as if walking.)*
I see a tree. *(Put hand above eyes as if looking.)*
Can't go under it. *(Make motion with right hand as if going under object.)*
Can't go over it. *(Make motion with right hand as if going over object.)*
Have to climb up it. *(Make motions with both hands as if climbing a tree.)*
All right, let's go. *(Slap knees again as if walking.)*
I see a mud puddle. *(Put hands over eyes as if looking.)*
Can't go around it.
Can't go over it.
Have to walk through it. *(Put hands in front of you as if you are walking in mud and make a squish sound with mouth.)*
I see a river.
Can't go over it.
Can't go around it.
Have to swim through it. *(Make the arm motions of swimming.)*
All right, let's go.
I see a wheat field.
Can't go around it.
Can't go over it.
Have to go through it. *(Rub hands together.)*
All right, let's go.
I see a hill.
Can't go under it.
Can't go around it.
Have to run over it. *(Thump fists on chest.)*
All right, let's go.
I see a cave. *(Lightly touch hands together.)*
It's mighty dark in this cave.
I feel something furry. *(Touch someone's hair.)*
It feels like a bear!
It looks like a bear!
It is a bear!
All right, let's go.
Over the hill... *(Thump chest and slap knees.)*
Through the wheat field... *(Rub hands and slap knees)*
Through the river... *(Swim and slap knees)*
Through the mud puddle...*(Squish and slap knees)*

Up the tree… *(Climb with hands)*
Slam! *(Clap hands.)*
Whew! Made it! *(Wipe brow.)*

I Know an Old Lady

I know an old lady who swallowed a fly;
I don't know why she swallowed a fly—
Perhaps she'll die.

I know an old lady who swallowed a spider
That wiggled and jiggled and tickled inside her.
She swallowed the spider to catch the fly;
I don't know why she swallowed the fly—
Perhaps she'll die.

I know an old lady who swallowed a bird—
How absurd to swallow a bird!

She swallowed the bird to catch the spider
That wiggled and jiggled and tickled inside her.
She swallowed the spider to catch the fly;
I don't know why she swallowed the fly—
Perhaps she'll die.

I know an old lady who swallowed a cat—
Think of that…she swallowed a cat!

She swallowed the cat to catch the bird.
She swallowed the bird to catch the spider
That wiggled and jiggled and tickled inside her.
She swallowed the spider to catch the fly;
I don't know why she swallowed the fly—
Perhaps she'll die.

I know an old lady who swallowed a dog.
What a hog to swallow a dog!
She swallowed the dog to catch the cat.
She swallowed the cat to catch the bird.
She swallowed the bird to catch the spider
That wiggled and jiggled and tickled inside her.
She swallowed the spider to catch the fly;
I don't know why she swallowed the fly—
Perhaps she'll die.

I know an old lady who swallowed a goat—
Just opened her throat and swallowed a goat!
She swallowed the goat to catch the dog.
She swallowed the dog to catch the cat.
She swallowed the cat to catch the bird.
She swallowed the bird to catch the spider
That wiggled and jiggled and tickled inside her.
She swallowed the spider to catch the fly;
I don't know why she swallowed the fly—
Perhaps she'll die.

I know an old lady who swallowed a cow;
I don't know how she swallowed a cow!
She swallowed the cow to catch the goat.
She swallowed the goat to catch the dog.
She swallowed the dog to catch the cat.
She swallowed the cat to catch the bird.
She swallowed the bird to catch the spider
That wiggled and jiggled and tickled inside her.
She swallowed the spider to catch the fly;
I don't know why she swallowed the fly—
Perhaps she'll die.

I know an old lady who swallowed a horse;
She's dead...of course!

NAME _Kevin C._

WRITING LETTERS

Do you like to receive letters? You must learn to write them, too. Below Robin Jean has written to her Grandma. Notice the comma (,) placed after her greeting to her Grandma and after her closing:

Dearest Grandma,

Thank you so much for the beautiful doll. I have named her Candy because she is so sweet. I love you very much.

Lovingly,

Robin Jean

Can you write a letter below? Put in the commas. Choose words from these if you want to: (1) Dear Mother, Dad, Grandpa, Aunt June   (2) Write here what you want to say to the person   (3) is the closing. It could be: With love, Love, Sincerely, Your son, Your daughter   (4) is the place for your name.

(1) _Dear Daddy,_

(2) _Thanks for everything. I Love you even though you do spank me._

(3) _Sincerely, your Son_

(4) _Kevin_

Appendix B *Songs*

Ga Goom
Johnny Works with One
   Hammer
Boa Constrictor
Do As I Do
My Head, My Shoulders
Little Wheel a-Turning
   in My Heart
Clap Your Hands
The Old Gray Cat
What Do You Do?
The Little White Duck
The Wheels on the Bus
Sky Bears
Rags
Five in the Bed
Five Little Ducks
Five Elephants
Five Green Frogs
Band of Angels

Animals in the Zoo
I Know Why Dogs
The Alphabet Song
Six Little Ducks
Get Together Song
I Have a Little Rooster
I Have a Little Pussy
The Wordless Book Song
S-M-I-L-E
The Ford Song
Row, Row, Row Your Boat
If All the Raindrops
Little Cabin in the Woods
Jack-O-Lantern Song
Sweetly Sings the Donkey
Oh, How Lovely is the Evening
Land of the Silver Birch
She'll Be Comin' Round
   the Mountain
On a Day Like This

Dr. and Mrs. Wendell Evans with Trent, Trevor, and Ashley Cowling; Simon,
Stephen and Sam Cervantes

Ga Goom

"Ga Goom," went the little green frog one day.
(Stick out tongue and pull in as you say "Ga goom.")
"Ga Goom," went the little green frog.
(Stick out tongue and pull in as you say "Ga goom.")
"Ga Goom," went the little green frog one day
(Stick out tongue and pull in as you say "Ga goom.")
And his eyes went, "Ga, Ga, Goom."
(Blink eyes and bring tongue in and out)

Ga Goom

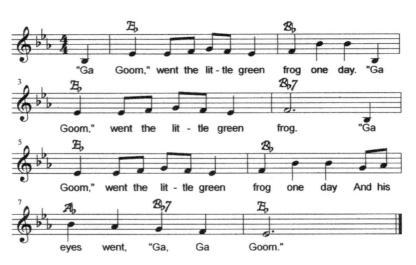

Johnny Works with One Hammer

Johnny works with one hammer, *(Make right arm go up and down after making a fist and pretend you are hammering.)*
One hammer, one hammer. Johnny works with one hammer,
Then he works with two.

Johnny works with two hammers...
(Repeat first verse. Make two fists and go up and down, repeating above)

Johnny works with three hammers... *(Repeat second verse. Make two fists to go up and down and add one foot to above refrain.)*

Johnny works with four hammers... *(Repeat third verse. Make two fists to hammer and use both feet to step up and down.)*

Johnny works with five hammers... *(Repeat previous verse and end with using two fists, step with both feet, and move head up and down.)*

And then he goes to sleep. *(Act as if you are asleep.)*

Johnny Works with One Hammer

John-ny works with one ham-mer, One ham-mer, one ham-mer.
John-ny works with one ham-mer, Then he works with two.

Vs. 2: Johnny works with two hammers...Then he works with three.
Vs. 3-4: *(Repeat, counting up until "...Then he works with five.")*
Vs. 5: Johnny works with five hammers...Then he goes to sleep.

Boa Constrictor

I'm being swallowed by a boa constrictor, a boa constrictor,
    a boa constrictor.
I'm being swallowed by a boa constrictor,
And I don't like it much.

Oh, no! He swallowed my toe! Oh, no! He swallowed my toe! Oh, no!
    He swallowed my toe! *(Put hand on toe)*
And I don't like it very much!

Oh, me! He's up to my knee! Oh, me! He's up to my knee! Oh, me!
    He's up to my knee! *(Put hand on knee)*
And I don't like it very much!

Oh, my! He's swallowed my thigh! Oh, my! He swallowed my thigh!
    Oh, my! He swallowed my thigh! *(Put hand on thigh)*
And I don't like it very much!

Oh, fiddle! He's up to my middle! Oh, fiddle! He's up to my middle!
    Oh, fiddle! He's up to my middle! *(Put hand on waist)*
And I don't like it very much!

What a mess! He's up to my chest! What a mess! He's up to my chest!
    What a mess! He's up to my chest! *(Put hand on chest)*
And I don't like it very much!

Oh, dread! He swallowed my head… *(Put arms on head)*

Boa Constrictor

**Come in at the verse. Do not repeat the beginning of the song.*
Vs. 2: Oh, me! He's up to my knee!...
Vs. 3: Oh, my! He's swallowed my thigh!...
Vs. 4: Oh, fiddle! He's up to my middle!...
Vs. 5: What a mess! He's up to my chest!...
Vs. 7: Oh, dread! He's swallowed my head! *(abrupt ending)*

Do As I Do

Do as I do, do as I do.
Clap your hands. *(Clap your hands.)*
Clap your hands. *(Clap your hands.)*
Let your finger wiggle. *(Hold up all fingers and wiggle them.)*
Let them hide your giggle. *(Put fingers over your mouth.)*
Run away, run away. *(Fingers flutter and go behind you.)*

Do As I Do

My Head, My Shoulders

(Sing to the tune of "Mulberry Bush.")
This song will get the "wiggles" out of children who have been sitting.

My head, my shoulders, my knees, my toes,
My head, my shoulders, my knees, my toes,
My head, my shoulders, my knees, my toes,
Let's all clap hands together!
(Do several times, faster each time)

My Head, My Shoulders

My head, my shoul-ders, my knees, my toes, My
head, my shoul-ders, my knees, my toes, My
head, my shoul-ders, my knees, my toes, Let's
all clap hands to - geth - er!**

**Repeat several times, faster each time.*

Little Wheel a-Turning in My Heart
There's a little wheel a-turning in my heart
   (*Use your pointer finger to make a circle.*)
There's a little wheel a-turning in my heart.
   (*Make heart shape with both hands.*)
   (*Repeat*)

In my heart, in my heart,
   (*Make heart with two hands every time its mentioned.*)
There's a little wheel a-turning in my heart.
   (*Repeat*)

I feel so very happy in my heart.
   (*Repeat as above. Clap on feel so happy and make heart with both hands.*)

Little Wheel a-Turning in My Heart

Clap Your Hands

Any number of movements could be added. Lead the children to do what song says when they are tired of sitting.

Clap, clap,clap your hands, clap your hands together,
Clap, clap, clap your hands, clap your hands together.
Tap, tap, tap your toes,
Blink, blink, blink your eyes,
Nod, nod, nod your head,
Shake, shake, shake your hands,
Jump, jump, jump the rope.

Clap Your Hands

Vs. 2: Tap, tap, tap your toes...
Vs. 3: Blink, blink, blink your eyes...
Vs. 4: Nod, nod, nod your head...
Vs. 5: Shake, shake, shake your hands...
Vs. 6: Jump, jump, jump the rope...

The Old Gray Cat

Choose children to be cat and mice. Can use more than one cat and several mice. Follow the motions of song.

The old gray cat is sleeping, sleeping, sleeping.
The old gray cat is sleeping in the house.
The little mice are creeping, creeping ,creeping.
The little mice are creeping through the house.

The little mice are nibbling, nibbling, nibbling,
The little mice are nibbling in the house.
The little mice are sleeping, sleeping, sleeping,
The little mice are sleeping in the house.

The old gray cat comes creeping, creeping, creeping,
The old gray cat comes creeping through the house.
The little mice all scamper, scamper, scamper,
The little mice all scamper through the house.

The Old Gray Cat

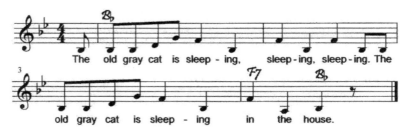

Vs. 2: The little mice are creeping...through the house.
Vs. 3: The little mice are nibbling...in the house.
Vs. 4: The little mice are sleeping...in the house.
Vs. 5: The old gray cat comes creeping...through the house.
Vs. 6: (Increase tempo) The little mice all scamper...through the house.

What Do You Do?

Oh, what do you do when the light turns green,
The light turns green, the light turns green?
Oh, what do you do when the light turns green
On the way to school?

You cross the street when the light turns green,
The light turns green, the light turns green.
You cross the street when the light turns green
On the way to school.

Oh, what do you do when the light turns red?
You stop and wait when the light turns red.

Oh, what do you do when the light turns yellow?
You do not cross when the light turns yellow.

I made a stop light out of a shoebox by cutting three holes in the bottom and putting red over the top hole, yellow in middle, and green on bottom. You can hold a large flashlight behind the color about which the children are singing.

What Do You Do?

Vs. 2: You cross the street when the light turns green...on your way to school.
Vs. 3: Oh, what do you do when the light turns red...on your way to school?
Vs. 4: You stop and wait when the light turns red...on your way to school.
Vs. 5: Oh, what do you do when the light turns yellow...on your way to school?
Vs. 6: You do not cross when the light turns yellow...on your way to school.

The Little White Duck

This story song can be sung, used on the flannel board, or the children can act it out. The figures needed are a white duck, a green frog, a black bug, a red snake, a blue piece of felt to picture water, and a lily pad.

There's a little white duck swimming in the water,
A little while duck doing what he oughta
He took a bite of a lily pad,
Flapped his wings and said, "I'm glad I'm a little white duck
Swimming in the water, 'Quack, Quack, Quack!' "

There's a little green frog jumping in the water,
A little green frog doing what he oughta
He jumped upon the lily pad, croaked and croaked
And said, "I'm glad I'm a little green frog
Jumping in the water, 'Croak, Croak, Croak!' "
There's a little black bug skimming on the water,
A little black bug doing what he oughta
He skimmed around the lily pad
Skimmed and skimmed and said, "I'm glad I'm a little black bug
Skimming on the water, 'Hum, Hum, Hum!' "

There's a little red snake lying in the water
A little red snake doing what he oughta
He frightened the duck and the frog so bad
Ate the black bug and said, "I'm glad I'm a little red snake
Lying in the water, 'Hiss, Hiss, Hiss!' "

Now there's nobody left swimming in the water
Nobody left doing what they oughta
The frog and the duck ran away. It's sad.
The snake ate the bug and crawled away. Too bad!
Now there's nobody left swimming in the water, Boo, Hoo, Hoo!

Enlarge these figures 300% to use with flannel board.

The Little White Duck

There's a lit-tle white duck swim-ming in the wa-ter, A lit-tle white duck do-ing what he ought-a. He took a bite of a lil-y pad, Flapped his wings and said, "I'm glad I'm a lit-tle white duck Swim-ming in the wa-ter, 'Quack, Quack, Quack!'"

Vs. 2: There's a little green frog jumping in the water,
A little green frog doing what he oughta.
He jumped upon the lily pad, croaked and croaked
And said, "I'm glad I'm a little green frog
Jumping in the water, 'Croak, Croak, Croak!'"

The Wheels on the Bus
The wheels on the bus go round and round
    (Roll hands over in front of you.)
Round and round, round and round.
The wheels on the bus go round and round
All around the town.

The windshield wipers go swish, swish, swish.
    (Move open hands from side to side like wipers)

The horn on the bus goes beep, beep,beep.
    (Make fist with right hand and hit open left palm)

The babies on the bus go wah, wah, wah.
    (Act as if holding baby in arms and cry)

The mommies on the bus go yak, yak, yak.
    (Use hands to show talking)

The driver on the bus says, "Move on back."
    (Put hand over shoulder and say "Move on back."

The people on the bus go up and down.
    (Stand up and sit down)

Sky Bears
    (Every time it snowed when our children were little, we sang this song.)
It snowed last night,
It snowed last night.
The sky bears had a pillow fight.
They tore up every cloud in sight
And tossed down all the feathers white.
It snowed last night.
It snowed last night.

The Wheels on the Bus

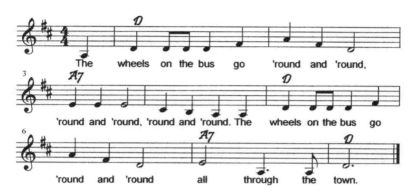

The wheels on the bus go 'round and 'round, 'round and 'round, 'round and 'round. The wheels on the bus go 'round and 'round all through the town.

Vs. 2: The windshield wipers go swish, swish, swish...all through the town.
Vs. 3: The horn on the bus goes beep, beep, beep...all through the town.
Vs. 4: The babies on the bus go wah, wah, wah...all through the town.
Vs. 5: The mommies on the bus go yak, yak, yak...all through the town.
Vs. 6: The driver on the bus says, "Move on back..." all through the town.
Vs. 7: The people on the bus go up and down...all through the town.

Sky Bears

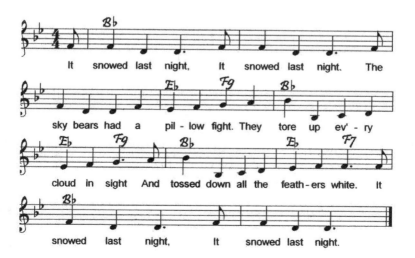

It snowed last night, It snowed last night. The sky bears had a pil-low fight. They tore up ev'-ry cloud in sight And tossed down all the feath-ers white. It snowed last night, It snowed last night.

Rags

I have a dog, his name is Rags.

He ate so much his stomach sags, *(Put hands together under stomach)*

His ears flip flop, *(Put two hands on each side of head and flop like ears)*

His tail wig wags,

    (Put one hand behind you and move from side to side like tail)

And when he walks, he goes zig zag.

    (Bend knees and go first to left and then to right)

Flip flop, *(Use hands as ears)*

Wig wag, *(Use hand as tail)*

Zig zag *(Bend knees to left and right)*

Rags

The next four songs can be used effectively with finger puppets. Art figures are included so you can make your own puppets. I use a manila folder and attach an envelope to hold the puppets for each song. I glue the words on the outside of the envelope and leave on the flaps so the puppets will stay in the envelope.

Five in Bed
There were five in the bed
And the little one said, "Roll over, roll over,"
So they all rolled over and one fell out.

There were four in the bed
And the little one said, "Roll over, roll over,"
So they all rolled over and one fell out.

(Repeat to "one in the bed.")

There was one in the bed
And the little one said, "Come back! Come back!"

There were two in the bed
And the little one said, "Come back! Come back!"

(Repeat until there are five in the bed)

There were five in the bed
And the little one said, "Good Night!"

(Finger puppet art work for this song is on page 359.)

Five in the Bed

There were five in the bed And the lit-tle one said, "Roll o - ver, roll o - ver." So they all rolled o-ver and one fell out.

Vs. 2: There were four in the bed...
Vs. 3-4: *(Repeat, counting down to "There were two in the bed...")*
Vs. 6: There was one in the bed
  And the little one said, "Come back! Come back!"
  So they all rolled over and one came back.
Vs. 7-9: *(Repeat, counting up to "There were four in the bed...")*
Vs. 10: There were five in the bed
  And the little one said, "Good Night!"

Five Little Ducks
Five little ducks went out to play,
Over the hill and far away.
Mother duck said, "Quack, quack, quack,"
Four little ducks came waddling back.

Four little ducks went out to play...
(*Repeat until* **no** *little ducks come waddling back*)

Father duck said, "Quack, quack, quack,"
Five little ducks came waddling back.

(*Finger puppet art work for this song is on page 359.*)

Five Little Ducks

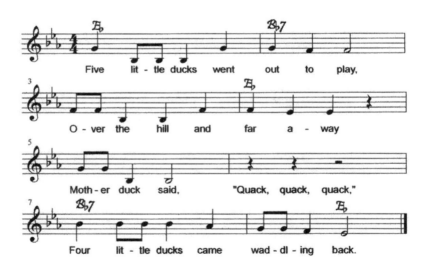

Vs. 2-5: (*Repeat, counting down*
until "**no** little ducks came waddling back.")
Vs. 6: No little ducks went out to play,
Over the hill and far away.
Father duck said, "Quack, quack, quack,"
(*Speed up*) Five little ducks came waddling back.

Five Elephants

The first elephant does a motion an elephant might do such as swing his trunk or stomping his foot. He calls another child who becomes the leader and does a different motion.)

One elephant went out to play
Up on the spider web one day.
He had such enormous fun
He called for another elephant to come.

Two elephants went out to play...
        *Repeat to five. When you reach **five** elephants, the last line is:*
They were too heavy, and they all fell down.

(Finger puppet art work for this song is on page 359.)

Five Elephants

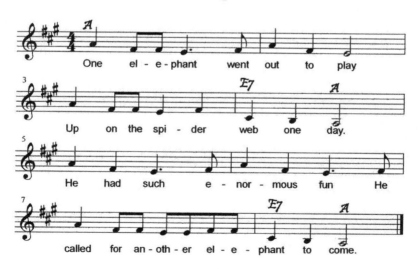

Vs. 2: Two elephants went out to play...
Vs. 3-4: *(Repeat, counting up until reaching "Four elephants went out to play...")*
Vs. 5: Five Elephants went out to play...
    They had such enormous fun
    They were too heavy, and they all fell down.

Five Green Frogs
Five green speckled frogs
Sitting on a speckled log.
Eating some most delicious bugs.
One jumped into the pool
Where it was nice and cool
Now there are four green speckled frogs.
    (Hold up four fingers and repeat until there are no frogs left)

(Finger puppet art work for this song is on page 359.)

ENDING:
Now there are no green speckled frogs
On the log in the bog.

Make a log with your left arm. Put five fingers on the right hand behind the log. Have hand jump over arm. Repeat verse until there are no frogs.

Five Green Frogs

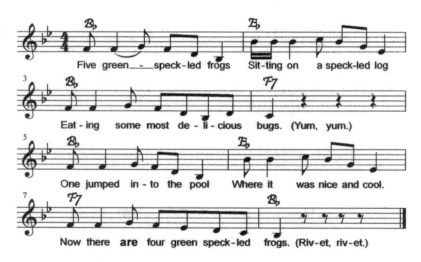

Vs. 2: Four green speckled frogs...
Vs. 3-4: *(Repeat, going down to "Two green speckled frogs...")*
Vs. 5: One green speckled frog
        Sitting on a speckled log
        Eating some most delicious bugs.
        He jumped into the pool
        Where it was nice and cool.
        Now there are no green speckled frogs
        (Same note) On the log in the bog.

Rhythm Instruments

Children love to make noise and rhythm instruments allow them to be noisy—within the limits you set for them. These instruments may be bought or made, and the child will not care which. Stress that the instrument should not be played continually, but you should keep time with the music. The children can march as they play an instrument. Tell a story and remind the children you will select the best five listeners to play an instrument when you sing a song after the story. Instructions for making rhythm instruments are found on pages 92-96. The following is a good song to use with rhythm instruments:

Band of Angels

(Hold up fingers for numbers. Clap for refrain.)
There was one, there were two, There were three little angels
There were four, there were five, There were six little angels.
There were seven, there were eight, There were nine little angels,
Ten little angels in that band.

REFRAIN:
Wasn't that a band, Sunday morning, Sunday morning, Sunday morning.
Wasn't that a band, Sunday morning, Sunday morning soon.
(Have children march and play their instruments.)

Band of Angels

Animals in the Zoo

Sing all lines like the elephant verse. Repeat the chorus after each verse.

Chorus:
Look at the animals in the zoo, in the zoo, in the zoo.
See the different things they do and we can do them too.
(Clap as you sing the chorus.)

Animals in the Zoo

Vs. 2: The tall giraffe can stretch his neck...
Vs. 3: The kangaroo goes jump, jump, jump...
Vs. 4: Monkeys swing in tree tops high...
Vs. 5: Camels march like soldier boys...
Vs. 6: Eagles flap their heavy wings...

The elephant walks and swings his trunk, swings his trunk,
  swings his trunk.
The elephant walks and swings his trunk, and we can do it, too.
  (Put hands together in front and swing like trunk.)

The tall giraffe can stretch his neck. *(Stretch neck.)*

The kangaroo goes jump, jump, jump. *(Put arms together in front and jump.)*

Monkeys swing in tree tops high
  (Put hands over head and act as if swinging in tree)

Camels march like soldier boys *(March in place)*

Eagles flap their heavy wings *(Move both hands up and down like flying)*

I Know Why Dogs

  Develop many verses for this tune by using different animals and their sounds. Teach the children than a fish opens its mouth to allow water to pass over the gills, thus removing oxygen from the water, and allowing the fish to breathe.

I know why dogs go arf, arf, arf. *(Bark 3 times.)*
I know why cats go meow *(Make meow sound.)*
What drives me crazy
  (Use pointer finger and make a circle beside your head like crazy)
And is all so hazy
Is why a fish goes… *(Open mouth twice.)*

I Know Why Dogs

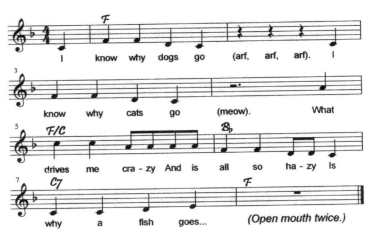

The Alphabet Song
We're marching around the alphabet, round the alphabet
Where we stop no one knows, until the whistle blows (whistle)
Now bend down where you are, choose a letter that's by your toes
When the teacher points to you, tell the teacher which letter you chose.

Put the letters in a circle and have the children march around the letters and sing. Older children can name animals, boys' names, girls' names, fruits, vegetables, people in Bible, or cities in Bible. (Make sure you remove any letter for which you do not know a name.)

Possible Alphabet Animals:
Alligator, bear, cat, dog, elephant, fox, goat, hyena, iguana, jackrabbit, kangaroo, lion, monkey, narwhale, octopus, penguin, quail, rat, stork, tiger, unicorn, viper, whale, xiphosuran, yak, zebra

People in the Bible:
Abraham, Boaz, Chillion, Doag, Elijah, Felix, Goliath, Hezekiah, Israel, Jacob, Korah, Levi, Matthew, Nathan, Obadiah, Paul, Quartus, Rachel, Saul, Timothy, Uriah, Vashti, Woman at the well, Xerxes, (Y), Zachariah

Places in the Bible:
Athens, Babylon, Canaan, Damascus, Egypt, Fair Heavens, Galilee, Haran, Italy, Jerusalem, Kadesh-Barnea, Lodebar, Macedonia, Nazareth, Olivet, Philippi, Quantir, Ramoth-in-Gilead, Samaria, Tyre, Ur of the Chaldees, Vesuvius, Wilderness of Zin, Yehem, Ziklag

The Alphabet Song

We're march - ing a-round the al - pha - bet,
'round the al - pha - bet. Where we'll stop,
no one knows un - til the whist - le blows.
Now bend down where you are; choose a let-ter that's
by your toes. When the teach - er points to you,
tell the teach - er which let - ter you chose.

Six Little Ducks

Teach the children to waddle by holding their left heel with left hand and right holds right. You could pretend as if you were in deep water.

Six little ducks that I once knew, *(Hold up six fingers.)*
Fat ones, skinny ones, fair ones, too, *(Show fat and skinny with hands)*
But the one little duck with a feather on his back,
    (Bend and put hands together on back like a feather)
He ruled the others with a quack, quack, quack,
Quack, quack, quack, quack, quack, quack. *(Clap hands together)*
He ruled the others with a quack, quack, quack. *(Same)*

Six Little Ducks

Get Together Song

The more we get together, together, together
   (Hit knees on "more" and do a rhythm with knees and two claps.)
The more we get together, the happier we'll be.
For your friends are my friends, *(Point to others, then yourself.)*
And my friends are your friends,
The more we get together, the happier we'll be.
   (On "more," hit knees and clap twice.)

The More We Get Together

I Have a Little Rooster

   The verses are repeated each time the song is sung. Use as many animals as you like such as cow, horse, duck, snake, etc. If the children are seated in rows, you can let each row choose an animal and make the sound as they sing the song.

I have a little rooster by the barnyard gate.
And that little rooster is my playmate.
And that little rooster says, "Cock-a-doodle-doo.
De-doodle, de-doodle, de-doodle doo."

I have a little pig at the barnyard gate.
That little pig is my playmate.
That little pig says, "Oink, oink oink."
That little rooster says, "Cock-a-doodle-doo.
De-doodle, de-doodle, de-doo-dle, doo."

I have a little cow by the barnyard gate.
And that little cow is my playmate.
And that little cow says, "Moooo"
And that little pig says, "Oink, oink, oink."
And that little rooster says, Cock-a doodle-do
De doodle, de-doodle, de-doo-dle,doo."

I Have a Little Rooster

**Repeat with other animals and their sounds after
"says," but ending each verse with "de-doodle, de-
doodle, de-doodle-doo."

I Have a Little Pussy
I have a little pussy.
    (Stand up and slowly sink to the floor.)
Her coat is silver gray.
She lives down in a meadow
Not very far away.
She'll always be a pussy;
She'll never be a cat,
For she's a pussy willow
Now what do you think of that?
Meow! Meow! Meow! Meow! Scat!
    (Jump up to a standing position when you say, "Scat!")

I Have a Little Pussy

The Wordless Book Song

Make a wordless book with black, red, white, gold, and green construction paper that is laminated and turn the pages as the song is sung. (For the gold page, use a legal size sheet of seals that is laminated.) To make individual wordless books for each child, cut the laminated sheets into two-inch squares and assemble with a brass brad placed in the upper left corner.

Variation: *Let the children stand each time they are wearing the color that is sung about.*

My heart was black with sin / Until the Saviour came in.
His precious blood I know, / Has washed me white as snow.
And in God's Word I'm told, / I'll walk the streets of gold.
To grow in Christ each day, / I read my Bible and pray.

The Wordless Book

S-M-I-L-E
> *Substitute "L-a-u-g-h" or "Ha, ha, ha, ha, ha!" for additional verses.*

It isn't any trouble just to s-m-i-l-e,
It isn't any trouble just to s-m-i-l-e,
If ever you're in trouble
It will vanish like a bubble,
Just s-m-i-l-e.

S-M-I-L-E

**Substitute "L-A-U-G-H" or "Ha, ha, ha, ha, ha!"
for additional verses.*

The Ford Song
I'm a little piece of tin
    No one knows the shape I'm in
Got four wheels and a running board
    I'm a four door; I'm a Ford.

REFRAIN: *(Repeat refrain four times with motions.)*
Honk, honk *(Tap nose twice with right hand)*
Rattle, rattle, rattle *(Wave hands beside you)*
Crash *(Clap hands once in front of you)*
Beep, beep. *(Hit open left hand with right hand twice)*

The Ford Song

Row, Row, Row Your Boat

Sing through the song, leaving off one word every time you sing through it until no words are left and you end with the word "row."

Row, row, row your boat
Gently down the stream
Merrily, merrily, merrily, merrily
Life is but a dream.

ALTERNATE VERSE:
Propel, propel, propel your craft
Down the liquid solution
Happily, happily, happily, happily
Life is but an illusion.

Row, Row, Row Your Boat

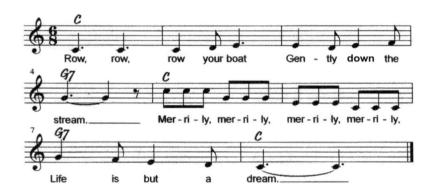

Alternate verse:
Propel, propel, propel your craft
Down the liquid solution.
Happily, happily, happily, happily,
Life is but an illusion.

If All of the Raindrops

Select two children of about the same size and let them have a "big mouth" contest. The winner is the child with the biggest mouth.

If all of the raindrops were lemon drops and gumdrops
Oh, what a rain that would be.
I'd stand around with my mouth open wide
Ah, Ah, Ah, Ah, Ah, Ah, Ah, Ah, Ah, Ah
    (Open mouth as wide as possible)*
If all of the raindrops were lemon drops and gumdrops
    Oh, what a rain that would be.

If all of the rivers were Kool-aid and lemonade
Oh, what a flood that would be
I'd stand around with my mouth open wide
Ah, Ah, Ah, Ah, Ah, Ah, Ah, Ah, Ah, Ah
    (Open mouth as wide as possible)
If all of the rivers were Kool-aid and lemonade
Oh, what a flood that would be.

If all of the snowflakes were chocolate cakes and cupcakes
Oh, what a snow that would be
I'd stand around with my mouth open wide
Ah, Ah, Ah, Ah, Ah, Ah, Ah, Ah, Ah, Ah
    (Open mouth as wide as possible)
If all of the snowflakes were chocolate cakes and cupcakes
    Oh, what a snow that would be.

If All of the Raindrops

Little Cabin in the Woods

Little cabin in the woods (*Make shape of cabin with two hands.*)

Little man by the window stood. (*Put right hand over eyes to look out window.*)

Saw a rabbit hopping by (*Hold up pointer finger and tall finger as rabbit ears and move hand like a rabbit hopping in front of you.*)

Knocking at his door (*Knock with right hand in front of you.*)

"Help me, help me, help," he said. (*Wave your hands up and down.*)

"Or the hunter will shoot me dead." (*Wrap right pointer finger around left thumb and snap fingers of right hand.*)

"Little rabbit, come inside... (*Use pointer finger to beckon toward you*)

Safely you made hide." (*Put up pointer finger and tall finger like rabbit ears on the left hand. Stroke with right hand.*)

Little Cabin in the Woods

Jack-O-Lantern Song
Jack-O-Lantern, Jack-O-Lantern
You are such a funny sight
As you sit there in the window
Looking out at the night.

You were once a yellow pumpkin
Growing on a sturdy vine;
Now you are a jack-o-lantern—
See the candlelight shine!

Jack-O-Lantern Song

The next three songs can be sung in a three-part round.

Sweetly Sings the Donkey (3-Part Round)

Divide group into three parts and ask each to sing the song twice. Bring in each group after singing the line, "Sweetly sings the donkey at the break of day...." When each group has sung the song twice, that group should stop singing until all the groups have finished singing. The last group will finish singing alone.

Sweetly sings the donkey at the break of day (***Enter for round***)
If you do not feed him, this is what he'll say:
Hee-haw, hee-haw, hee-haw, hee-haw, hee-haw.

(Put hands by ears and flap as for ears when you say "hee-haw.")

Sweetly Sings the Donkey
3-Part Round

Oh, How Lovely Is the Evening (3-Part Round)
Oh, how lovely is the evening, is the evening *(Enter for round)*
When the bells are sweetly ringing, sweetly ringing.
Ding-dong, ding-dong, ding-dong.
 (Use the same note for "ding-dong.")

Land of the Silver Birch (3-Part Round)
Land of the silver birch,
Home of the beaver **(Enter for round)**
Where still the mighty moose
Wanders at will.
Blue lakes and rocky shores,
I will return once more.
Boom did e boom boom, boom did e boom boom, boom did e boom
   boom, boom.
   (Use the same note for each "boom did e boom boom....")

She'll Be Comin' Round the Mountain

Verse 1
She'll be comin' round the mountain when she comes. Toot toot!
   (Put right hand up beside head and "pull" the train whistle twice.)
She'll be comin' round the mountain when she comes. Toot toot!
   (Put right hand up beside head and "pull" the train whistle twice.)
She'll be comin' round the mountain, she'll be comin' round the mountain, she'll be coming round the mountain when she comes. Toot toot!
   (Put right hand up beside head and "pull" the train whistle twice.)

Verse 2
She'll be drivin' six white horses when she comes. Whoa, back!
   (Pretend to pull reins of horse.) [Repeat]

Verse 3
We will all go out to meet her when she comes, Hi, Babe!
   (Wave hand like saying "Hi!")
[Repeat]

Verse 4
She'll be wearing red pajamas when she comes. Scratch, scratch!
   (Scratch your upper arm.)
[Repeat]

Verse 5
We will kill the old red rooster when she comes. Hack, Hack!
   (Open right hand and act as if hacking left arm.)
[Repeat]

Verse 6
We will have chicken and dumplings when she comes. Yum, yum!
   (Pat tummy.)
[Repeat]

Verse 7
She will have to sleep with Grandma when she comes. Snore, snore!
   (Snore out loud.)
[Repeat]

   All the motions and sound effects are repeated each time a verse is added.

She'll Be Comin' Round the Mountain

Vs. 2: She'll be drivin' six white horses when she comes.
(Whoa, back!)
Vs. 3: We will all go out to meet her when she comes.
(Hi, Babe!)
Vs. 4: She'll be wearing red pajamas when she comes.
(Scratch, scratch!)
Vs. 5: We will kill the old red rooster when she comes.
(Hack, hack!)
Vs. 6: We will have chicken and dumplings when she comes.
(Yum, yum!)
Vs. 7: She will have to sleep with Grandma when she comes.
(Snore, snore!)

On a Day Like This

Every verse of this ditty has three lines. Repeat the motion and sound every time another verse is sung.

On a day like this...Clap, clap
  (Clap hands together.)
On a day like...Clap, clap
  (Clap hands together.)
On a day like this, O Lord, help me.

VERSE 2
On a day like this...Clap, clap; Toot, toot
  (Clap hands together; act like pulling cord for train whistle, and repeat first line twice.)
On a day like this...O Lord, help me.
  (Act like pulling cord for train whistle.)

VERSE 3
On a day like this...Clap, clap; Toot, toot; Uh, uh
  (Move both elbows to back as make sound. Repeat above using both sounds.)

VERSE 4
On a day like this...Clap, clap; Toot, toot; Uh, uh; Eek, eek.
  (Use hands as if pulling mouth as make sound. Repeat using all sounds.)

VERSE 5
On a day like this...Clap, clap; Toot, toot; Uh, uh; Eek, eek; Ooo, ooo.
  (Use hands under arms like monkey as you make sound. Repeat using all sounds.)

VERSE 6
On a day like this...Clap, clap; Toot, toot; Uh, uh; Eek, eek; Ooo, ooo; Oh, wow!
  (Roll head in circles. Repeat using all sounds.)

On a Day Like This

Vs. 2: On a day like this...(Clap, clap); Toot, toot.
Vs. 3: On a day like this...(Clap, clap); Toot, toot; Uh, uh.
Vs. 4: On a day like this...(Clap, clap); Toot, toot; Uh, uh; Eek, eek.
Vs. 5: On a day like this...(Clap, clap); Toot, toot; Uh, uh; Eek, eek;
       Ooo, ooo.
Vs. 6: On a day like this...(Clap, clap); Toot, toot; Uh, uh; Eek, eek;
       Ooo, ooo; Oh, wow!

Appendix C
Fun Recipes

Kevin, Krysten, and Kelly had been sliding in the mud!

Kevin, Kelly, and Nancy the bear

Cooked Play Dough
Mud Dough
Paste Jewelry Modeling
  Mixture
Salt Dough
Bread Clay
Soap Fingerpaint
Pudding Fingerpaint
Cooked Fingerpaint
Goop #1
Goop #2
Super Bubbles
Silly Putty
Slime
Sidewalk Chalk
Dracula's Blood
Molded Sugar Eggs

David Cowling, Stephen, Simon, and Sam Cervantes

Cooked Play Dough

(This recipe for play dough is my favorite!)

1 cup flour	1 tablespoon oil
1 cup water	Oil of wintergreen
½ cup salt	Powdered or liquid tempera or
2 teaspoons cream of tartar*	food coloring

Mix flour, salt, and cream of tartar together in a heavy pan. Add water, oil, a few drops of oil of wintergreen, and color if desired. Stir all together. Cook for about three minutes, stirring constantly until the mixture pulls away from the side of the pan, making sure the center of the ball is not sticky. Cool and knead. When cool, store in an air-tight container.

*I have found that the best place to buy cream of tartar is Gordon Foods in the large container.

**Oil of wintergreen can be purchased from Wal-Mart at the pharmacy counter. In Indiana, you order it one day and pick it up the next.

Mud Dough

2 cups mud	1-2 cups salt
2 cups sand	

Add enough water to make the dough pliable. Be sure it has a nice texture and is easy to use. The finished product cannot be saved because it crumbles. If used outdoors during warm weather, be sure to have a dishpan of water close by for children to wash off their hands. (I found that power companies are willing to give away used wooden spools. These spools are good to use as child-sized tables.)

Paste Jewelry Modeling Mixture

¾ cup flour	½ cup salt
½ cup cornstarch	warm water

Mix dry ingredients in bowl and add warm water gradually until the mixture can be kneaded into a stiff dough. Dust with flour to reduce stickiness. Mixture may be rolled into balls for beads. Pierce each bead with a toothpick or large needle and allow to dry. Paint the beads with acrylic paint or color the dough when you are mixing it. If you want to make a necklace, use dental floss for thread and a large needle for threading the beads.

Salt Dough

Salt dough, a mixture of flour, salt, and water, is much cheaper to make than bread clay. It is ideal for large projects such as candle holders and baskets. Salt dough is great for allowing the children to make ornaments by rolling them and cutting out shapes with cookie cutters. Salt dough can be baked in an oven or allowed to air dry. A sealer is necessary. Salt dough is more dough-like than clay-like, holds impressions only moderately well, and cannot be shaped with the same precision as bread clay, but the resulting sculptures often tend to be even freer and more spontaneous.

Salt dough does have one distinct drawback. Because of the large quantity of salt in the dough, fully dried items tend to draw moisture from the air, soften, and even disintegrate. The softening is not a problem in dry areas or in artificially heated rooms, but anyone living in a damp climate will have to take measures to preserve the dough sculptures. Sealers such as lacquer or varnish are helpful. Apply one or two heavy coats by brushing or dipping salt dough objects, but these sealers do not guarantee permanence. Sprays are ineffective. If an item starts to soften, it can be rehardened in a low oven, but if the softening has gone too far, cracks are certain to develop. The only foolproof way to counteract persistent dampness is to store items in tightly sealed plastic bags whenever they are not on display.

Salt Dough Recipe

4 cups flour   1½ cups water (or less)
1 cup salt

Stir dry ingredients together in a large bowl; then add water, and mix. Turn out onto a lightly floured surface and knead for approximately ten minutes. The kneading is necessary. The dough should be smooth and pliable. Store in a sealed plastic bag in the refrigerator.

Since the moisture content of flour varies with the weather, it is a good idea to start with a little less water than called for, then add the extra only if it is needed. (Firm dough is easier to work with than soggy dough.) The recipe can be halved, but do not double it unless there is someone to share the kneading—it makes a lot. It is best to avoid the recipe popularized by a prominent salt company if you live in a moist area, since the instructions call for twice as much salt and the finished sculptures are even more susceptible to dampness.

Working with Salt Dough

• Salt dough can be made and colored with acrylic paint, which is permanent when dry.

• When making salt dough with young children, use paste food coloring and let the salt dough air dry. The color bakes out at temperatures over 200°.

• In order to hang a salt-dough item, punch a hole in the damp salt dough. After the ornament is dry, put a ribbon through the hole to hang. A paperclip can also be inserted in the damp dough to be used as an ornament hanger.

• Salt dough can be baked in a 350° oven for one-half hour for one-fourth inch thickness of dough. Air-dried dough is white; oven-baked dough looks like a baked pie crust.

Bread Clay

1 slice white bread, crust removed	1 tablespoon liquid tempera paint or paste food coloring
1 tablespoon glue	

Tear bread into small chunks and add glue. Knead to form a dough that is not too gooey. Add paint or color as desired, mixing to avoid streaks. Make Christmas ornaments, jewelry, etc. This dries well. Store leftover clay in airtight containers (bag or bowl) to keep it from drying out. If you want a hole in your creation, make with a round toothpick before it dries.

Soap Fingerpaint

2 tablespoons dish soap	4 tablespoons warm water

Put water and soap in a bowl and whip with a wire whip until a foam is made. Put a scoop of foam on a baking sheet with edges. Cover the child with a man's short-sleeved shirt buttoned in the back, and let the child make designs in the soap. Color can be added by using liquid or powdered tempera to the soap foam. Print the child's picture when he finishes by putting a paper on top of the design, removing the paper, and letting it air dry. This mixture will return to the liquid as it stands but can be whipped up again.

Pudding Fingerpaint

Mix a box of instant pudding according to package directions. Follow the instructions for soap fingerpaint.

Cooked Fingerpaint

3 cups water	Food coloring or tempera paint
1 cup cornstarch	

Boil water in saucepan and remove from heat. Make a paste with the cornstarch by adding cold water to the cornstarch a little at a time and stirring. Add the cornstarch mixture to the hot water, stirring constantly. Boil until thick and clear, stirring constantly about a minute. Add color.

Goop #1

¾ cup warm water
1 cup white glue
2 teaspoons Borax

½ cup warm water
food color or liquid tempera
    paint

Mix ¾ cup warm water and glue together. In a separate bowl, mix the Borax and ½ cup warm water. Add the two mixtures together, mixing well. Add color if desired. Store in airtight bag or bowl to prevent drying. Children love to punch holes in this. It will reproduce the pictures from cookie cutters.

Goop #2

1 cup liquid starch
1 cup Elmer's glue

Food coloring or tempera paint

Mix ingredients until starch and glue are well blended. If liquid remains, pour off excess. Store in a plastic storage bag.

Super Bubbles

1 cup water
2 tablespoons light Karo syrup

4 tablespoons liquid dish soap

Mix all ingredients together and blow bubbles. Blow slowly for big bubbles.

Silly Putty

4 tablespoons white glue

2 tablespoons liquid starch

Mix glue and starch together. If the mixture stays stringy, add a drop of glue. If it is too brittle, add more starch.

Slime

½ cup water
1 cup cornstarch

food coloring

Pour cornstarch into a big mixing bowl. Slowly add the water and mix until it has the consistency of cream. Add color, using food coloring or liquid or powdered tempera if desired. This "recipe" is fun but messy. Use outdoors or cover the table with newspapers and have a dishpan of water nearby so children can wash hands before touching anything.

Sidewalk Chalk

2 cups water
2 cups Plaster of Paris

2 tablespoons powered tempera
paint

Stir dry ingredients together; then add to water, stirring constantly. Let the mixture set a few minutes until it starts to thicken. Pour into paper towel tubes with one end taped over with silver duct tape. Let dry at least two hours until set. Peel off the paper tube.

Dracula's Blood

2 tablespoons corn syrup
1 tablespoon water

red food coloring
cornstarch or cocoa

Pour corn syrup in bowl. Mix with water and 2 drops of red food coloring. Stir well. Pour into small plastic bag. Add 2-3 pinches of cornstarch. Knead bag. Add more pinches of cornstarch until it reaches a blood-like consistency. Use 1-2 pinches of cocoa for a deeper red color.

Molded Sugar Eggs

2 cups granulated sugar
4 teaspoons water

Paste color

Color water the desired color before adding sugar. Add sugar to bowl and mix well. Place mixture in a plastic mold. Pack moistened sugar firmly into the mold, making sure there are no air pockets. If the mold is to be used repeatedly, dust with cornstarch. Molds come in different sizes. Place a piece of cardboard on top of the mold, then invert. Tap the mold lightly if necessary to loosen the contents, then lift off. Place in 200° oven for 8 minutes. Remove from oven. With a spoon, gently hollow each half by scraping as much sugar as possible from the center of the mold, leaving a ¼-inch shell. Scrape the sugar back into the bowl and use again. Put the shell back into the 200° oven for 5 minutes to dry or let sit out overnight.

Appendix D
Food Recipes

Quick Chocolate Cookies
Bar Cookies
Marshmallow Krispy Treats
Ritz Mint Cookies
Cookie Flowers
Oatmeal Cookies
Sugar Cookies
Peanut Clusters
Chinese Bonbons
Dipped Pretzels
Pastry
Fudge Pie
Fresh Fruit Dip
Caramel Sauce
Caramel Corn
Pumpkin Seeds
Chicken Noodle Soup & Noodles
Zesty Vegetable Beef Soup
Instant Hot Cocoa Mix
Biscuit Doughnuts
Fried Dough
Crispas
Pancakes
Monkey Bread
Strawberry Freezer Jam
Jello
Ice Cream Cone Cake

Trent and Ashley Cowling

Keith

Kevin

*Krysten, Katy Hardy, Keith, and Kelly
looking at Katy's birthday cake.*

Quick Chocolate Cookies

2 cups sugar
6 tablespoons cocoa
Mix sugar and cocoa in sauce-pan and add the following:
½ cup milk
1 stick margarine

Mix well and bring to a full boil, stirring constantly for two minutes. Remove from heat and add:
1 teaspoon vanilla
3 cups oatmeal

Drop by teaspoons on waxed paper while mixture is hot.

Bar Cookies

⅔ cup margarine
4 cups oatmeal
1 cup brown sugar

2 teaspoons vanilla
½ cup light corn syrup

Melt margarine. Add remaining ingredients. Spread in a greased pan, 9 x 13 inches. Bake at 350° for 12 minutes or until mixture is bubbly. Remove from oven and cool 10 minutes. Add:
1 cup semi-sweet chocolate chips
⅔ cup chunky peanut butter
Melt chocolate chips and peanut butter in double boiler or microwave. Spread this mixture over first mixture. Chill to set. Freezes well.

Marshmallow Krispy Treats

¼ cup (½ stick) margarine
6 cups crisp rice cereal

1 package (10½ ounces) miniature marshmallows

Microwave margarine in large microwave-safe bowl on high 45 seconds or until melted. Add marshmallows and toss to coat with margarine. Microwave 1½ minutes or until smooth when stirred, stirring after 45 seconds. Immediately add cereal, mix lightly until well coated. Press into greased baking pan, 9 x 13 inches. Cool; cut into squares. Makes about 24.

Ritz Mint Cookies

2 tablespoons paraffin
   or white shortening
Ritz crackers

1-12 ounce package chocolate chips
9 drops of Peppermint oil or to taste

Melt shortening or paraffin in saucepan and remove from heat. Add chocolate and stir until all chocolate is melted. If not melted, hold over heat, but do not put pan on direct heat. Add peppermint oil. Dip crackers into chocolate, using fork. Tap cracker on side of pan to remove excess chocolate. Place on waxed paper. Chill in freezer or refrigerator.

Cookie Flowers

1 package (18 ounces)
    refrigerated cookie dough
8 wooden ice cream sticks

(Or use the sugar cookie recipe listed below)

Shape cookie dough into eight 2-inch balls. Place four balls at a time on an ungreased baking sheet. Insert wooden sticks into each ball like a lollipop. Flatten dough slightly. Bake in preheated oven at 375° for 13 to 15 minutes or until edges are crisp. Cool on baking sheet for one minute. Put on wire rack and cool completely. Frost, dip in melted chocolate, and decorate with sprinkles.

Oatmeal Cookies

¾ cup butter or margarine,
    softened
1 cup packed brown sugar
½ cup sugar
1 egg
2 tablespoons water

1 teaspoon vanilla extract
3 cups quick-cooking oats
⅔ cups all-purpose flour
1 teaspoon ground cinnamon
½ teaspoon baking soda
⅔ cup golden raisins

In a mixing bowl, cream butter and sugar. Beat in egg, water, and vanilla. Combine the oats, flour, cinnamon, and baking soda; gradually add to the creamed mixture. Stir in the raisins (dough will be stiff). Drop by level tablespoonfuls two inches apart onto ungreased baking sheets. Bake at 350° for 12-15 minutes or until the edges are lightly browned. Remove to wire racks to cool. YIELD: 4 dozen

Sugar Cookies

1½ cups confectioners' sugar
1 cup butter
1 egg
1 teaspoon vanilla

½ teaspoon almond extract
2½ cups flour
1 teaspoon soda
1 teaspoon cream of tartar

Mix butter and sugar. Add eggs and flavorings. Add dry ingredients. Wrap in plastic wrap. Refrigerate at least 2 hours. Divide dough in half. Roll out on floured surface to no more than ¼-inch thickness. Cut with cookie cutter. Place on cookie sheet about 1 inch apart. Bake at 350° for 8 minutes or until golden brown. Cool on rack. Frost.

Peanut Clusters

If you have leftover chocolate in a pan, add peanuts, stir, and drop on waxed paper. You can also save chocolate by putting on waxed paper and reheating.

Chinese Bonbons

2 tablespoons white shortening or paraffin
1 cup salted peanuts

1-12 ounce package butterscotch chips
Chow Mein noodles

Melt shortening or paraffin and remove from heat. Add butterscotch chips and stir until chips are melted. Add peanuts and chow mein noodles. Stir. Drop on waxed paper and cool.

Dipped Pretzels

Melt 2 tablespoons white shortening or paraffin in saucepan. Remove from heat. Stir in white or regular chocolate. You can color white chocolate with paste color. Dip pretzels into chocolate with fork, tap on side of pan to remove excess chocolate, and put on waxed paper.

Pastry

1 cup all-purpose, white flour
⅓ cup white shortening

½ teaspoon salt
3 to 4 tablespoons ice water

Mix flour, salt, and shortening together with a pastry blender, two knives, or fingertips until the mixture resembles meal. Put a cube of ice into ½ cup of water and sprinkle ice water on flour mixture a little at a time until a ball that will not crumble is formed. Do not over mix! Remember that pastry is made by "feel." Never dump in all the water at once. Roll out to a thickness of ⅛ inch to ¼ inch on a floured pastry cloth and rub flour on your rolling pin. Roll until pastry is 1-inch larger than your pie pan. Flute edge.

Every time I make a pie, I let the children make "pastry cookies." They roll out the pastry with a flour-covered rolling pin. They place their cookies on a baking sheet, dot them with butter, and sprinkle sugar and cinnamon on them. Bake at 400° for 10 to 12 minutes until brown.

Fudge Pie

¾ cup margarine (1½ sticks)
¼ cup cocoa powder
1½ cups sugar

3 eggs
1¼ cup flour
1¼ teaspoon vanilla

Melt margarine in heavy saucepan. Add sugar and cocoa powder until blended and stir over low heat until sugar dissolves. Beat eggs in a separate bowl. Remove chocolate mixture from heat. Stir one half of chocolate mixture into beaten eggs, stirring constantly to prevent lumps. Put all of chocolate mixture back into plan, but do not cook. Add flour and vanilla. Stir. Pour into 9-inch greased and floured plan. Bake at 325° for 20 to 30 minutes or until the outside edge is set.

Fresh Fruit Dip

1 8-ounce cream cheese
1 7-ounce jar of marshmallow creme
Combine ingredients and mix until well-blended. Dip fruit into this mixture.

Caramel Sauce

½ cup butter or margarine
1 cup brown sugar
2 tablespoons flour

¼ cup evaporated milk or
   half and half
1 teaspoon vanilla

Melt margarine in saucepan. Add brown sugar, and mix well. Add remaining ingredients, and beat together until smooth. Serve with sliced raw apples or as a topping for ice cream or other desserts.

Caramel Corn

2 cups brown sugar
2 sticks butter (1 cup)
½ cup light Karo syrup

1 teaspoon salt
1 teaspoon baking soda

Put all ingredients except baking soda into a 2-quart pan and boil for 5 minutes. Remove from heat. Add 1 teaspoon baking soda; stir in popped popcorn. Put on cookie sheet. Cook at 200° for 1 hour. Stir once or twice.

Pumpkin Seeds

Remove the seeds from the pumpkin and the orange membrane from the seeds. Toss the seeds with melted butter, spread on a baking sheet, and sprinkle with salt. Toast the seeds in a 300° oven for 20 to 30 minutes, stirring every five minutes. The seeds are done when you taste them, and they are crisp instead of like raw sticks in your mouth. Note: Larger seeds may require 30 minutes or more baking time.

Chicken Noodle Soup and Noodles

Put a whole chicken into a large pot, cover with water, and simmer 1 to 2 hours. Pour off liquid from chicken and chill until fat solidifies on surface. Throw away fat and add onion, celery, carrots, salt, and pepper to the stock. Separate fat and bones from cooked chicken by putting on baking sheet. Add meat, stock, chicken bouillon to flavor, and vegetables of choice. Simmer covered for one hour and serve.

While soup is simmering, let children make noodles. They will need help. Cover kitchen counter with flour as well as rolling pin because noodle dough is sticky.

Noodles

1 egg   2/3 cup flour
1/2 teaspoon salt

Beat egg and salt. Add flour until it makes a stiff dough. Do not add all the flour at once. Knead 3 minutes. Roll out the dough to 1/8-inch thickness with a rolling pin. Cut with a plastic dough scraper or with a dull dinner knife. Let the noodles dry until the soup is done. Drop the noodles one at a time into the boiling soup and cook 3 to 5 minutes or until the noodles are tender.

Zesty Vegetable Beef Soup

Stock   1 teaspoon Worcestershire sauce
2 cups tomato juice   1/4 teaspoon hot pepper sauce
1 celery rib   1/2 teaspoon dried oregano
2 medium potatoes, peeled and   1/2 teaspoon dried basil
  cubed   1/2 teaspoon chili powder
1 carrot, scraped and   Beef bouillon cubes for taste
  sliced into circles   (1 cube per cup)
1 medium onion, peeled
  and diced

Put stock into saucepan after removing fat and bone. Add all other ingredients. Bring to boil. Reduce heat; cover and simmer for one hour or until vegetables are tender.

Instant Hot Cocoa Mix

4 boxes instant chocolate   1 cup cocoa
  pudding   5 cups powdered milk
1 large jar coffee creamer   3 cups sugar

Mix all ingredients together and store in airtight container. Use 3 heaping teaspoons to 1 cup boiling water. Add marshmallows to cup before pouring in boiling water, if desired.

Biscuit Doughnuts

Open a can of refrigerator biscuits and put on a flat surface, separated, for five minutes in a warm place. Stretch and cut holes in the center. Cook in hot, deep fat until brown on both sides. Turn once. Drain and roll in powdered sugar or granulated sugar. Best eaten immediately after they are fried.

Fried Dough

Pinch off pieces of yeast dough or stretch into round circles. Heat oil in an electric skillet or deep-fat fryer to 375°. Fry a few at a time, until brown, and center is not doughy. Drain on paper towels. Brush with melted margarine and sprinkle with cinnamon-sugar (1 tablespoon ground cinnamon to ½ cup sugar).

Crispas

Cut tortillas into 6 wedges. Fry in hot fat until light brown. Drain. Roll in cinnamon sugar.

Pancakes

1 cup flour	1 egg
2½ teaspoons baking powder	1 cup milk
2 tablespoons sugar	3 tablespoons oil
¾ teaspoon salt	

Mix together. Spoon onto greased griddle or skillet. Cook until browned on each side. Makes approximately 1 dozen pancakes.

Monkey Bread

½ cup sugar	1 cup brown sugar
1 teaspoon cinnamon	½ cup margarine
2 (10-ounce) canned biscuits	½ cup of nuts

Sprinkle ½ of the nuts into a greased and floured Bundt pan or angel food pan. Mix sugar and cinnamon. Cut each biscuit into 4 pieces. Roll in sugar-cinnamon mixture and place in pan. Sprinkle remaining sugar on top. Add pecans between layers. Combine brown sugar and margarine. Heat until melted. Pour over biscuits. Bake at 350° for 30 to 35 minutes. Cool in pan for 10 minutes. Invert onto plate.

Strawberry Freezer Jam

2 cups fresh strawberries, crushed
4 cups sugar

2 tablespoons lemon juice
¾ cup water
1 package Fruit Jell pectin

Combine crushed fruit and lemon juice. Add sugar. Mix thoroughly and let stand for 10 minutes. Combine water and 1 package pectin in a small saucepan. Boil hard for 1 minute, stirring constantly. Add cooked pectin to fruit mixture and stir for 3 minutes. Ladle jam into jelly jars, leaving ½-inch head space. Let jam stand at room temperature for 24 hours. Store in freezer for up to one year or keep in refrigerator for up to 3 weeks.

Jello

Make jello letting the children taste the powder (solid), liquid, and jello (solid). Give each child a cup and use ice cubes instead of cold water, and the jello will gel as the children watch. Let the children stir the jello you are making with their help. Children feel very important when they can say at mealtime, "I helped make this," even if you did most of the work!

Flat-Bottomed Ice Cream Cone Cakes

Fill flat-bottomed ice cream cones one half full of cake batter. Bake as for cupcakes on a baking sheet in the center of the oven. If you fill the cone more than half full, it will run over the top of the cone and make a mess. Cool. Frost. Decorate with sprinkles. Children love to decorate cupcakes, cookies, etc., with frosting and sprinkles or chocolate chips. Even "store-bought" cookies can be fun when children frost and decorate them!

Appendix E
Books

Kelly

**Encourage children
to love reading!**

Sara Cervantes,
Kelly's daughter

Developing a Desire
in Children to Read Books

I was privileged to grow up in the "pre-television" era. I was nine years old when I saw my first television program, but by that time, I was already "in love" with reading. Our four children were reared with the television turned off. Instead of watching television, they were encouraged to read. Now these children are encouraging our 16 grandchildren to read and love books. My husband and I encouraged this love of reading by employing the following methods:

1. **Since we enjoyed reading, we kept good books and magazines in many places in our home.** As a young person, I was taught that "readers are leaders," and I cannot remember a time when I did not read. I not only loved reading, I wanted to own books of every kind as long as they contained a philosophy that agreed with Philippians 4:8, "*Finally, brethren, whatsoever things are true, whatsoever things are honest, whatsoever things are just, whatsoever things are pure, whatsoever things are lovely, whatsoever things are of good report; if there be any virtue, and if there be any praise, think on these things.*"

I have found that the vast majority of books for children written before 1968 pass the Philippians 4:8 test. However, many books printed after that date are filled with slang, bad language, sex, or philosophies that disagree with the Bible. These philosophies include justifying unscriptural family life styles, sexual perversion, rebellion against authority, and unacceptable language. These books condone lying, stealing, and cheating—if everything comes out right in the end.

Books always reflect the philosophies of the people who read them. As more and more people support the removal of the Bible from the public schools, attend churches where the Bible is not taught, and listen to the liberal media, the books being published increasingly reflect these worldly philosophies. Most Christian book stores contain many books that would not pass the Philippians 4:8 test. It is true that good books are available, but parents must screen them. I feel if I have a book that I could not recommend on one of my bookshelves in my house, it will send the wrong signal to anyone who looks at these books—especially my children and grandchildren. "*Abstain from all appearance of evil.*" (I Thessalonians 5:22) Every person must make his own decision about what is acceptable reading for a child. If a book contains only a few unacceptable words, I cover them with a silver marker. However, if a book is filled with objectionable material, I would not use it. To me, objectionable material would include the following (but not be limited to): slang, swearing, minced oaths, unpunished rebellion, perversion, and justifying unscriptural family life styles. Many times in a book when the message is right, but the character is dressed immodestly, I use a marker and draw the appropriate clothes on the characters throughout the book. Usually, there are not that many illustrations which need correction.

2. Read aloud to children. When our children were infants in the crib, I put books at the foot of the crib at night so they could look at them when they woke up. I used cloth books and cardboard books so they could not tear them. We read aloud to our children many times a day such as before nap time or bedtime and also scheduled times during the day. I am not opposed to teaching a child the numbers and alphabet before they go to school, but I feel it is more important to give them a love for reading and a desire to read for themselves.

Our oldest daughter Kelly always loved books and loved having someone read to her. When she was four years old, I read *Heidi* to her a chapter at a time, and she would beg me to read longer. In those days, children were not taught to read until they entered first grade, and she could not wait to be able to read a book for herself. She entered first grade in Alcoa, Tennessee, and when she had been in school for about two months, I met her on the front steps of our house. "Sit down, Mom, so I can read you this book," Kelly excitedly said. We sat on the front steps, and she read, "See Jane run. See Dick run. See Dick and Jane run." What an exciting day for both of us. We walked into the house and she said, "My teacher loaned me this book and said I could teach Kevin (who was four years old at the time) to read." I told her it was fine with me if Kevin wanted to learn to read. Every day after that, Kelly came home from school, took Kevin downstairs to the playroom, and built him a desk from hollow blocks in front of the chalkboard. Three weeks went by before Kelly marched Kevin upstairs. "Kevin can read," Kelly announced, "listen to him."

"See Jane run," Kevin read. "See Dick run. See Dick and Jane run." When we visit Kevin and his family in Mesa, Arizona, every night he reads a chapter of a book to his four children—our grandchildren, Ashley, Trent, Trevor, and Trey.

It is my belief that we could solve many reading problems in this country by reading ourselves, turning off the television, and encouraging our children to do the same. As you read to children, you are giving them the most important gift—time. You are also building a close relationship with them and creating memories to last forever.

3. Select books that not only pass the Philippians 4:8 test, but books that are well written. As children read well-written books, they literally "come to life." When I was a child, no one taught me about book selection. Since I loved to read, I read Bible stories, biographies, poetry, mysteries, and even the encyclopedia when I had nothing else to read. While I was in grade school, I read many "series" books such as: The Bobbsey Twins, Nancy Drew mysteries, The Hardy Boys, and Trixie Belden. We could not afford to buy all of these, so I kept a list of the ones I had read and was always looking for a new one.

As an adult when I was asked to teach Children's Literature at Hyles-

Anderson College, I decided to reread some of my favorite childhood books. To my surprise, I found these series to be boring, leaving me with an "If-you-have-read-one, you-have-read-them-all" feeling. I discovered these books are not on outstanding book lists for children because they are not well written. However, they serve a purpose for an elementary student because they increase a child's vocabulary and build reading speed, thereby allowing the child to read more difficult books. Many of these series books have been rewritten and reprinted in the last 30 years. These new versions, in my opinion, are totally unacceptable for children because they reflect a worldly philosophy that is not prevalent in the originals.

Some of the other books I enjoyed as a child were even better when I read them again as an adult. Some of the books I thoroughly enjoyed were *The Secret Garden* by Frances Hodgson Burnett, *The Little House* series by Laura Ingalls Wilder, and *Heidi* by Johann Spyri. I discovered that a well-written children's book which passes the Philippians 4:8 test is just as interesting for an adult to read as a child and leaves you with a desire to read the book again.

4.   Fill your house with good books, making it easy for children to read them. This is easier said than done because of the cost of new books. I realize that books can be borrowed from the library, but I love owning books and I wanted our children to feel the same way. I love bargains and was able to get children's books at the following places:

A.   Books I had as a child that my mother was glad to give to me. Since these were older books, they might be boring, but most would pass the Philippians 4:8 test.

B.   Garage and yard sales. Anyone who is a bargain hunter realizes that you can find many valuable items in these places. When buying books, I check to see if the book pages are torn or missing, if crayon markings fill the book, and if it passes the Philippians 4:8 test. If I am interested in several books at one sale, I group them together and offer a lower price than the total value. Remember no book is a bargain if it is in bad condition, does not have good pictures, lacks biblical philosophies, or is boring.

C.   Library sales. We have two kinds of library sales in our area. "Friends of the Library" donate books to the library which are then sold, and discarded books from the library shelves are sold for a fraction of their cost. Many are old books that have a better value system, making them acceptable for children to read. Our Lake County Library has a sale every August where the public can buy five children's books for a dollar. If you are familiar with the classic children's books, many fine books can be bought for a bargain. Hardback books last much longer if these are used in a Christian school library where a number of children are reading them.

D.   Collection stores. Prices for books vary widely, and there seems to be no rhyme or reason to the way they are priced. Sometimes they are sold separately, and sometimes they are packaged together. I have purchased several "talking" books which did not "talk." Buy a hearing-aid battery, and often the book is as good as new. Bargains are available to you if you know the classic books. You may also need patience if the books are in a big pile, and you must sort through them.

5. Surround your children with books. My first choice for a place of storage is low shelves where the books are grouped by category. The children can be taught to put them back where they belong. The shelves can be built or bought, new or used.

At Christmas I put all of our children's books about Christmas in a basket by the Christmas tree so our grandchildren can easily find the books they want to read and have read to them. Books can be put into cabinets or plastic storage containers. The main requirement is that they are easily accessible to the child—to take down and pick up.

6. Make use of your local library. When our children were younger, we made weekly trips to the public library every place we lived and allowed them to check out books. I had the following rules regarding the books they checked out:

a. I had already read the book and knew it was a good book.

b. The date the book was published had to be before 1968. I taught the children to look for this date on the inside left page of the book. If the book was published after this date, I read the book first to determine if I would allow them to read it.

c. If they found bad language or pictures, I taught them to stop reading and bring the book to me.

7. Encourage them to participate in reading contests and praise them liberally when they read. Our children were always very competitive and responded to challenges in every area of their lives. In second grade, Keith's teacher, Mrs. Doris Smith, held a contest to see which child could read the most pages during a certain period of time with the prize being a trip to the teacher's house for spaghetti. Keith won the reading contest even though he did not like spaghetti because he loved to read and wanted to please his teacher.

The local library had reading contests in the summer our children entered. If your library does not have this, have a contest with your own children and reward the children with a meal, a trip, or a purchase.

8. Make your own book list so you will know which books to encourage your children to read. I had a master's degree in Early Childhood Education, and I did not know which books to encourage our children to read. I noticed our children wanted the same books read over and over again. I noticed also that I did not mind reading some books again, but I groaned inwardly when other books were brought to me to read. I asked the public librarian why that was true, and she told me it was due to the writer's skill. "A well-written book will appeal to all ages and will stand the test of time because it is based on truth." At this point I started compiling book lists for different kinds of children's books. They are listed on the following pages; however, they are not comprehensive book lists and do not

302 | Recipes for Rearing Children

contain all of the good books that are available. I am constantly adding books to these lists. Every person should feel free to add to the list or to mark off those that do not appeal to them. Making a book list requires a lot of time and effort for two main reasons.

     a.   You have to read every book completely to know whether or not you want the book on your list.

     b.   Someone will disagree with every book on the list. There are certainly enough books available because of the great profit made from the sale of children's books. I refuse to argue with anyone over whether or not a book is acceptable for a child to read. I can find something wrong with almost every book, especially when reading illustrated books for older children. If I marked every book with something objectionable in it off the list, I would have a very short list. If we are going to encourage our children to read, we must decide where we will draw the line. Parents are responsible for screening the books their children read.

For instance, one current popular series of books that I do not plan to read are the Harry Potter books. I do not need to read one of these books to know that I could not recommend it for children. Everything that we see and every word we read is recorded in our mind, never to be erased. (I do not want or plan to eat slop from the hog pen to know I would prefer a good meal!) I want every book I read to pass the Philippians 4:8 test: *"Finally, brethren, whatsoever things are true, whatsoever things are honest, whatsoever things are just, whatsoever things are pure, whatsoever things are lovely, whatsoever things are of good report; if there be any virtue, and if there be any praise, think on these things."* I trust the following article will help you decide that we must protect our children from the wrong books.

Dear All,

Here's something that was forwarded to me, and I feel it needs our attention. The film, Harry Potter, is being shown in movie theaters across the United States. I believe this to be a blatant attack against our young people of today. Potentially, this can have a worse effect than the September 11 tragedy because it will influence the minds of our young people and plant in them seeds of being vengeful. This movie teaches, aside from witchcraft, that the right thing to do when someone mistreats you is to get even by using "dark powers."

I pray you will read and forward this open letter to all who may be interested in helping to prevent their kids from watching this evil film.

Concerned for youth,
Nene Legson

Thought you might want to know...

This is the most evil thing I have laid my eyes on in ten years, and no one seems to understand its threat. The Harry Potter books are the number one selling children's books in the nation today. Just look at any major storefront. Go to Internet sites and read the reviews. Hear the touting by educators and even Christian teachers about how, "It's great to see the youth so eagerly embracing the reading experience!" [Some public schools even make this required reading.]

Harry Potter is the creation of a former United Kingdom English teacher who promotes witchcraft and Satanism. Harry is a 13-year-old "wizard." Her creation openly blasphemes Jesus and God and promotes sorcery, seeking revenge upon anyone who upsets him by giving examples (even the sources with authors and titles) of spells, rituals, and demonic powers. I think the problem is that parents have not reviewed the material. The name, Harry Potter, seems harmless enough. But that is where it all ends. Let me give you a few quotes from some of the influenced readers themselves:

"The Harry Potter books are cool, 'cause they teach you all about magic and how you can use it to control people and get revenge on your enemies." –Hartland, Wisconsin

"I want to learn the Cruciatus Curse, to make my 'muggle' science teacher suffer for giving me a D." –a ten year old recent convert to the New Satanic Order of the Black Circle. [A "muggle" is a unbeliever of magic.]

Or how about the **really** young and innocent, impressionable mind of a six year old when asked about her favorite character: "Hermoine is my favorite because she's smart and has a kitty," said six-year-old J.L. of South Carolina. "Jesus died because He was weak and stupid."

And here is nine-year-old Ashley, the typical average reader of Harry Potter: "I used to believe in what they taught us at Sunday school," said Ashley, conjuring up an ancient spell to summon Cerebus, the three-headed hound of Hell. "But the Harry Potter books showed me that magic is real, something I can use right now, and that the Bible is nothing but boring lies."

Does this get your attention? If not, how about a quote from a High Priest of Satanism: "Harry Potter is an absolute godsend to our cause," said High Priest Egan of the First Church of Satan in Salem, Massachusetts. "An organization like ours thrives on new blood—no pun intended—and we've had more applicants that we can handle lately. And, of course, practically all of them are virgins, which is gravy." [Since 1995, open applicants to Satan worship has increased from around 100,000 to now …14 million children and young adults!]

It makes me physically ill, people! But, I think I can offer you an explanation of why this is happening. Children have been bombarded with action, adventure, thrills, and scares to the point Hollywood can produce nothing new to give them the next "high." Parents have neglected to see what their children are reading and doing and simply seem satisfied that 'Little Johnny' is interested in reading." And educators and the NEA [National Education Association] are pushing this with no warning as to the effects or the contents.

Still not convinced? I will leave you with something to let you make up your own mind. Finally, a quote from the author, J. K. Rowling, describing the objections of Christian reviewers to her writings: "I think it's absolute rubbish to protest children's books on the grounds that they are luring children to Satan," Rowling told a London *Times* reporter in a July 17 interview. "People should be praising them for that! These books guide children to an understanding that the weak, idiotic Son of God is a living hoax who will be humiliated when the rain of fire comes,…while, we his faithful servants, laugh and cavort in victory."

My hope is that you will see fit to become involved in getting out the word about this garbage. Please forward this information to every pastor, teacher, and parent you know. This author has now published four books in less than two years of this "encyclopedia of Satanism" and is surely going to write more. [At this writing, Rowlings has published 5 books.] I also ask all Christians to please pray for this lost woman's soul. Pray also for the Holy Spirit to work in the young minds of those who are reading this garbage that they may be delivered from its harm.

Lastly, pray for all parents to grow closer to their children, and that a bond of sharing thoughts and spiritual intimacy will grow between them.

The following lists are ones I have compiled. Please do not crucify me if you find a book of which you would not approve on the list. I would recommend you make your own list, altering these lists in any way you choose. Some books listed will need to have some words and pictures covered or altered before using them with children. If an author is still living and has written over a long period of time, the tendency is for the more recent books to reflect worldly philosophies in order to sell more books. Every book by every author needs to be considered individually. You can never assume that just because one book is acceptable that every book by a particular author will be permissible.

Mother Goose and Nursery Rhymes List for Children

Angeli, Marguerite	*A Pocket Full of Posies*
Angeli, Marguerite	*Book of Nursery and Mother Goose Rhymes*
Baker, Augusta	*Best Loved Fairy Tales*
Baker, Augusta	*Best Loved Nursery Rhymes and Songs*
Beall, Pamela & Susan Nipp	*Wee Sing Nursery Rhymes and Songs*
Bearing-Gould, William	*The Annotated Mother Goose*
Blackwood, Alan	*My Best Book of Rhymes*
Brooke, Leslie	*Ring O' Roses, A Pocket Full of Posies*
Decker, Marjorie	*The Christian Mother Goose Treasury I*
Decker, Marjorie	*The Christian Mother Goose Treasury II*
de Paola, Tomie	*Tomie de Paola's Mother Goose*
Dutton, E. P.	*The Margaret Tarrant Nursery Rhyme Book*
Follett	*Mother Goose Nursery Rhymes*

Fujilikawa, Gyo	*Mother Goose*
Grayson, Marion	*Let's Do Finger Plays*
Greenaway, Kate	*Kate Greenaway's Family Treasure*
Greenaway, Kate	*Kate Greenaway's Mother Goose*
Grover, E.	*Mother Goose*
Hillman, Priscilla	*A Merry-Mouse Book of Favorite Poems*
Kincaid, Lucy	*The Magic of Rhymes*
Langner, Nola	*Hi Diddle Diddle*
Page, Don	*Songs from Mother Goose*
Piper, Watty	*Mother Goose Rhymes*
Provensen, Alice & Martin	*The Mother Goose Book*
Rackham, Arthur	*Mother Goose Nursery Rhymes*
Richardson, Frederick	*Mother Goose*
Rojankovsky, Feodor	*The Tall Book of Mother Goose*
Rojankovsky, Feodor	*A Little Golden Mother Goose*
Scarry, Richard	*Mother Goose*
Schlesinger, Alice	*Baby's Mother Goose*
Smith, Jessie	*The Little Mother Goose*
Stevenson, Robert L.	*A Child's Garden of Verses*
Szekeres, Cyndy	*Mother Goose Rhymes*
Szekeres, Cyndy	*Cyndy Szekeres' ABC*
Taylor, Dorothy & John Taylor	*My Honey Bear Book of Rhymes*
Torrey, Marjorie	*Sing Mother Goose*
Tudor, Tasha	*Mother Goose*
Unknown	*Mother Goose: The Old Nursery Rhymes*
Unknown	*Seventy-Seven Verses with Pictures*
Wildsmith, Brian	*Mother Goose*
Wright, Blanche	*The Real Mother Goose*

Picture Book List for Children

Alexander, Anne	*ABC of Cars and Trucks*
Alexander, Anne	*I Want to Whistle*
Aliki	*The Story of Johnny Appleseed*
Anderson, C. S.	*Pony for Linda*
Aridzzone, Edward	*Little Tim and the Brave Sea Captain*
Baker, Marybob	*My Counting Book*
Beers, V. Gilbert	*The House in the Side of the Tree*
Beers, V. Gilbert	*Honeyphants and Elebees*
Beers, V. Gilbert	*Cats and Bats and Things Like That*
Bemelemans, Ludwig	*Madeline*
Bemelemans, Ludwig	*Madeline's Rescue*
Berenstein, Stan & Jan	*Inside, Outside, Upside Down*
Beskow, Elsa	*Pelle's New Suit*
Brett, Jan	*The Hat*
Bright, Robert	*Me and the Bears*

Eastman, P. D.	*Big Dog, Little Dog*
Eastman, P. D.	*Flap Your Wings*
Ets, Marie Hall	*In the Forest*
Ets, Marie Hall	*Play with Me*
Ets, Marie Hall	*Just Me*
Fatio, Louise	*The Happy Lion*
Field, Rachel	*Prayer for a Child*
Fischer, Alans	*Pitschi*
Fischer, Hans	*Puss in Boots*
Fisher, Aileen	*Going Barefoot*
Flack, Marjorie	*Angus and the Ducks*
Flack, Marjorie	*Ask Mr. Bear*
Flack, Marjorie	*The Story About Ping*
Flack, Marjorie	*Tim Tadpole and the Great Bullfrog*
Flack, Marjorie	*Wait for William*
Francoise	*Jeanne Marie Counts Her Sheep*
Freeman, Don	*Mop Top*
Freeman, Don	*Dandelion*
Gackenbach, Dick	*Claude the Dog*
Gag, Wanda	*ABC Bunny*
Gag, Wanda	*Millions of Cats*
Gag, Wanda	*Nothing at All*
Galdone, Paul	*Henny Penny*
Gay, Z.	*Look!*
Gelman, Rita & Jack Kent	*Why Can't I Fly?*
Graham, Margaret	*Benjy's Dog House*
Gramatky, Hardie	*Hercules*
Gramatky, Hardie	*Little Toot*
Green, Mary McBurney	*Everybody Eats*
Green, Mary McBurney	*Everybody Has a House*
Greenaway, Kate	*A = Apple Pie*
Gregorich, Barbara	*Up Went the Goat*
Grimm, Brothers	*Cinderella*
Heide, Florence	*Benjamin Budge and Barnaby Ball*
Heilbroner	*This Is the House that Jack Built*
Hill, Eric	*The Spot Books*
Holl, Adelaide	*The ABC's of Cars, Trucks, and Machines*
Hoban, Russell	*Bedtime for Frances* (Frances series)
Hoff, Syd	*Oliver*
Hutchins, Pat	*Rosie's Walk*
Jackson, Kathryn	*Tawny Scrawny Lion*
Johnson, Crockett	*Harold and the Purple Crayon*
Jones, J. O.	*Small Rain*
Joslin, Sesyle	*What Do You Say, Dear?*
Keats, Ezra	*The Snowy Day*

Keats, Ezra	*Peter's Chair*
Keats, Ezra	*Whistle for Willie*
Keller, Holly	*Geraldine's Big Snow*
Klein, L.	*Brave Daniel*
Krasilovsky, Phyllis	*Very Little Girl*
Krasilovsky, Phyllis	*Scaredy Cat*
Krasilovsky, Phyllis	*The Man Who Didn't Wash His Dishes*
Krauss, Ruth	*Bundle Book*
Krauss, Ruth	*A Very Special House*
Krauss, Ruth	*The Carrot Seed*
Krauss, Ruth	*The Happy Egg*
Langstaff, John M.	*Over in the Meadow*
Langstaff, John M.	*Frog Went a-Courtin'*
Leaf, Munroe	*The Story of Ferdinand*
Lenski, Lois	*Cowboy Small*
Lenski, Lois	*Little Auto*
Lenski, Lois	*Little Fire Engine*
Lenski, Lois	*Papa Small*
Lenski, Lois	*Surprise for Davy*
Lenski, Lois	*Blueberries for Sal*
Lopshire, Robert	*Put Me in the Zoo*
Lowrey, Janette	*The Pokey Little Puppy*
Maris, Ron	*I Wish I Could Fly*
Mays, Tamar	*Johnny Appleseed*
MacDonald, Golden	*Red Light: Green Light*
MacGregor, Ellen	*Theodore Turtle*
McCloskey, Robert	*Make Way for Ducklings*
Moncure, Jane & Terri Super	*Away Went the Farmer's Hat*
Moncure, Jane & Vera Gohman	*My "I" Book*
Mosel, Arlene	*Tikki Tikki Tembo*
Munari, Bruno	*Bruno Munari's ABC*
Petersham, Maud & Miska	*Christ Child*
Petersham, Maud & Miska	*The Circus Baby*
Piper, Walter	*The Little Engine That Could*
Potter, Beatrix	*The Tale of Peter Rabbit*
Preston, Edna M.	*Squawk to the Moon, Little Goose*
Rojankowsky, Feodor	*Over in the Meadow*
Rey, H.A.	*Curious George*
Rey, H.A.	*Curious George Takes a Job*
Scarry, Richard	*The Bunny Book*
Schlein, Mariam	*Fast Is Not a Ladybug*
Stearns, M.	*Albert and His Adventures*
Seuss, Dr.	*And to Think I Saw It on Mulberry Street*
Seuss, Dr.	*Horton Hatches the Egg*
Seuss, Dr.	*Green Eggs and Ham*

Seuss, Dr.	*One Fish Two Fish Red Fish Blue Fish*
Seuss, Dr.	*How the Grinch Stole Christmas*
Seuss, Dr.	*The Foot Book*
Seuss, Dr.	*Dr. Seuss' ABC*
Seuss, Dr.	*The Cat in the Hat*
Seuss, Dr.	*The Cat in the Hat Comes Back*
Sendak, Maurine	*Where the Wild Things Are*
Skaar, B.	*Very Little Dog*
Slobodkina, Esphyr	*Friendly Animals*
Slobodkina, Esphyr	*Caps for Sale*
Sojo, Toba	*The Animal Frolic*
Stevens, Carla	*Rabbit and Skunk and Scary Rock*
Thayer, Jane	*The Puppy Who Wanted a Boy*
Titus, Eve	*Anatole*
Tresselt, Alvin	*Johnny Maple Leaf*
Tresselt, Alvin	*Hi, Mr. Robin*
Tresselt, Alvin	*Timothy Robbins Climbs the Mountain*
Tresselt, Alvin	*White Snow Bright Snow*
Tresselt, Alvin	*The Beaver Pond*
Tresselt, Alvin	*Hide and Seek Fog*
Tresselt, Alvin	*The Dead Tree*
Tresselt, Alvin	*Rain Drop Splash*
Ungerer, Tomi	*Adelaide*
Udry, Janice	*Moon Jumpers*
Udry, Janice	*A Tree Is Nice*
Wadsworth, O.	*Over in the Meadow*
Walsh, Ellen Stoll	*You Silly Goose*
Ward, Lynd	*The Biggest Bear*
Watake, Shigeo	*What a Good Lunch!*
Watake, Shigeo	*How Do I Put It On?*
Watts, Mabel	*Henrietta and the Hat*
Wells, Joan	*Listen, Listen, Listen*
Wiese, Kurt	*Happy Easter*
Will and Nicolas	*Finders Keepers*
Will and Nicolas	*The Two Reds*
Yashima, T.	*Umbrella*
Yashima, T.	*Village Tree*
Zion, Gene	*Harry and the Lady Next Door*
Zion, Gene	*Harry the Dirty Dog*
Zion, Gene	*No Roses for Harry*

First and Second Grade List for Children

Adler, David A.	*A Picture Book of Benjamin Franklin*
Adler, David A.	*A Picture Book of George Washington*
Alexander, Anne	*I Want to Whistle*

Anderson, C. W.	*Billy and Blaze*
Anderson, C. W.	*Blaze and the Thunderbolt*
Anderson, C. W.	*Blaze and the Forest Fire*
Anderson, C. W.	*Blaze and the Mountain Lion*
Anderson, Hans Christian	*The Ugly Duckling*
Anderson, Hans Christian	*The Steadfast Tin Soldier*
Averill, Esther	*The Fire Cat*
Baker, Augusta	*Best Loved Selections from Children's Classics*
Beers, V. Gilbert	*Honeyphants and Elebees*
Beers, V. Gilbert	*The Hole in the Side of the Tree*
Bemelmans, Ludwig	*Madeline*
Bemelsmans, Ludwig	*Madeline's Rescue*
Bemelsmans, Ludwig	*Hansi*
Benchley, Nathaniel	*Red Fox and His Canoe*
Berenstein, Stan and Jan	*The Bike Lesson*
Bishop, Claire & Kurt Wiese	*The Five Chinese Brothers*
Bonsall, Crosby	*The Case of the Dumb Bells*
Bonsall, Crosby	*And I Mean It Stanley!*
Bonsall, Crosby	*What Spot?*
Bonsall, Crosby	*Piggle*
Bonsall, Crosby	*The Case of the Cat's Meow*
Bonsall, Crosby	*The Case of the Hungry Stranger*
Bond, Michael	*Paddington's Garden*
Brandeis, Madeline	*Little Jeanne of France*
Brooke, Leslie	*The Story of the Three Pigs*
Brown, Margaret Wise	*Shhhhhh...Bang*
Brown, Marcia	*Stone Soup*
Brown, Marcia	*Dick Whittington and His Cat*
Brown, Marcia	*Puss in Boots*
Brown, Marcia	*Once a Mouse*
Bulla, Clyde	*White Bird*
Bulla, Clyde	*The Poppy Seeds*
Carroll, Ruth	*Bounce and the Bunnies*
Chandler, Edna	*Cowboy Sam*
Clark, Ann N.	*In My Mother's House*
Clark, Ann N.	*This for That*
Clark, Margery	*Three Stories from the Poppy Seed Cakes*
Classic Volland Edition	*Great Children's Stories*
Clymer, Eleanor	*Benjamin in the Woods*
Clymer, Eleanor	*Belinda's New Hat*
Coerr, Eleanor	*The Josefina Story*
Cooney, Barbara	*Miss Rumphius*
Cooney, Barbara	*Chanticleer and the Fox*
Cosgrose, Stephen	*Little Mouse on the Prairie*
Corrin, Sara & Stephen	*Stories for Six-Year Olds*

Dalgliesh, Alice	*The Courage of Sarah Noble*
Dalgliesh, Alice	*The Thanksgiving Story*
Daugherty, James	*Andy and the Lion*
DeBrunhoff, Jean	*The Story of Babar*
DeRegniers, Beatrice Shenk	*May I Bring a Friend?*
DeRegniers, Beatrice Shenk	*Snow Party*
Dennis, Wesley	*Flip*
Dennis, Wesley	*Flip and the Morning*
Disney, Walt	*Bambi Grows Up*
Disney, Walt	*Peter and the Wolf*
Disney, Walt	*Cinderella*
Duvoisin, Roger	*Veronica and the Birthday Present*
Duvoisin, Roger	*The House of Four Seasons*
Eastman, P. D.	*Are You My Mother?*
Fatio, Louise	*The Happy Lion*
Flack, Marjorie	*The Story of Ping*
Freeman, Don	*Mop Top*
Freeman, Don	*Corduroy*
Freeman, Don	*A Pocket for Corduroy*
Freeman, Don	*Beady Bear*
Freeman, Don	*The Night the Lights Went Out*
Friskey, Margaret	*Indian Two Feet and His Horse*
Friskey, Margaret	*Indian Two Feet and His Eagle Feather*
Gag, Wanda	*Millions of Cats*
Gant, Elizabeth & Katherine	*Little Red Riding Hood*
Gelman, Rita	*Why Can't I Fly?*
George, Jean C.	*All Upon a Stone*
George, William & Lindsay	*Winter at Long Pond*
Goldberg, Martha	*Big House, Little House*
Gool, Van	*Jack and the Beanstalk*
Goudey, Alice E.	*Here Come the Bears!*
Goudey, Alice E.	*Here Come the Elephants!*
Gramatky, Hardie	*Little Toot on the Mississippi*
Green	*Splash and Trickle*
Green, Nancy	*The Bigger Giant*
Grimm, Brothers	*Snow White and Rose Red*
Hader, Berta & Elmer	*The Mighty Hunter*
Hall, Donald	*Ox-Cart Man*
Handforth, Thomas	*Mei Li*
Hays, Wilma Pitchford	*The Little Horse that Raced a Train*
Heide, Florence	*Benjamin Budge and Barnaby Ball*
Himmelman, John	*Ibis, A True Whale Story*
Hoban, Lillian	*A Sorely Trying Day*
Hoban, Russell	*Bedtime for Frances*
Hoban, Russell	*Baby Sister for Frances*

McGovern, Ann	Stone Soup
McPhail, David	The Bear's Toothache
Milne, A. A.	Winnie the Pooh
Minarik, Else H.	Little Bear
Minarik, Else H.	Little Bear's Visit
Minarik, Else H.	A Kiss for Little Bear
Minarik, Else H.	Father Bear Comes Home
Minarik, Else H.	Little Bear's Friend
Minarik, Else H.	Cat and Dog
Moore, Lillian	The Ugly Duckling
Mosel, Arlene & Blair Lent	Tikki Tikki Tembo
Newell, Hope	The Little Old Woman Who Used Her Head
Ormondray, Ed	Theodore's Ritual
Owens, Jeff	Character Lessons for Children
Owens, Jeff	The Ant that Made His Burden a Bridge
Parish, Peggy	Amelia Bedelia
Parish, Peggy	Come Back, Amelia Bedelia
Payne, Emmy	Katy No-Pocket
Perkins, Al	The Ear Book
Petersham, Maud & Miska	Joseph and His Brothers
Petersham, Maud & Miska	Moses
Peterson, John	The Littles Take a Trip
Peterson, John	The Littles Go to School
Potter, Beatrix	The Tale of Benjamin Bunny
Potter, Beatrix	The Tale of Peter Rabbit
Preston, Edna	Squawk to the Moon, Little Goose
Rayner, Mary	Mrs. Pig's Bulk Buy
Rey, H.A.	Curious George series
Rumsey, Mariam	Beaver of Weeping Water
Runyan, Catherine	All-Wrong Mrs. Bear
Sendak, Maurine	Where the Wild Things Are
Seuss, Dr.	The 500 Hats of Bartholomew Cubbins
Seuss, Dr.	Horton Hatches the Egg
Seuss, Dr.	Daisy-Head Mayzie
Seuss, Dr.	Happy Birthday to You!
Schlein, Mariam	Laurie's New Brother
Schlein, Mariam	Elephant Herd
Shannon, Terry	Where Animals Live
Shannon, Terry	"…and Juan"
Silverstein, Shel	The Giving Tree
Simon, Norma	Benjy's Bird
Slater, Cecilia	The Pied Piper
Slobodkin, Esphyr	Excuse Me Certainly
Slobodkin, Esphyr	Caps for Sale
Slobodkin, Esphyr	Too Many Mittens

Stearns	*Albert and His Adventures*
Steig, William	*Sylvester and His Magic Pebble*
Stevens, Carla	*Stories from a Snowy Meadow*
Stolz, Mary	*Belling the Tiger*
Tazewell, Charles	*The Littlest Angel*
Thayer, Jane	*The Puppy Who Wanted a Boy*
Thurber, James	*Many Moons*
Tousey, Sanford	*Little Bear's Pinto Pony*
Tower	*Bark, Beetles, and Birthdays*
Tresselt, Alvin	*White Snow, Bright Snow*
Tresselt, Alvin	*Hide and Seek Fog*
Turkle, Brinton	*Thy Friend, Obadiah*
Ungerer, Tomi	*Crictor*
Vance, Marguerite	*The Boy on the Road*
VanStockum, Hilda	*Patsy and the Pup*
Waber, Bernard	*An Anteater Named Arthur*
Waber, Bernard	*You Look Ridiculous*
Wahl, Jan	*Pleasant Fieldmouse*
Ward, Lynd	*The Biggest Bear*
Watts, Monte	*The Adventures of Winnie the Minnie*
Watts, Monte	*The Adventures of Fuzzy*
Wayne, Jenifer	*Sprout*
Will and Nicholas	*Finders Keepers*
Will and Nicholas	*The Little Tiny Rooster*
Williams, Margery	*The Velveteen Rabbit*
Wise, William	*The Cowboy's Surprise*
Wiseman, Bernard	*Iglook's Seal*
Young, Ray & Debi	*The Oak Tree and the Tumbleweed*
Zion, Gene	*Harry, the Dirty Dog*
Zion, Gene	*No Roses for Harry*
Zion, Gene	*Harry and the Lady Next Door*
Zolotow, Charlotte	*Mr. Rabbit and the Lovely Present*
Zolotow, Charlotte	*The Storm Book*
Zweifel, Frances	*Bony*

Third and Fourth Grade List for Children

American Girls series	
Atwater, Richard	*Mr. Popper's Penguins*
Anderson, Hans Christian	*The Ugly Duckling*
Anderson, Hans Christian	*The Snow Queen*
Barrie, Sir James	*Peter Pan*
Baum, Frank	*The Wizard of Oz*
Baum, Frank	*Dorothy and the Wizard of Oz*
Binns, Archie	*Sea Pup*
Bly, Stephen	*Nathan T. Riggins Western Adventure*

Boston, Lucy	*The Children of Green Knowe*
Boston, Lucy	*An Enemy at Green Knowe*
Bray, Marian	*Lassie* series
Brink, Carol	*Caddie Woodlawn*
Brock, Emma	*Drusilla*
Browning, Robert	*The Pied Piper of Hamlin*
Bulla, Clyde	*Squanto, Friend of the Pilgrims*
Bulla, Clyde	*Star of Wild Horse Canyon*
Bulla, Clyde	*White Bird*
Bulla, Clyde	*Pirates' Promise*
Bulla, Clyde	*Sword in the Tree*
Bulla, Clyde	*Conquista*
Burnett, Frances Hodgson	*Sara Crewe*
Carroll, Lewis	*Through the Looking Glass*
Carroll, Lewis	*Alice in Wonderland*
Caudill, Rebecca	*Did You Carry the Flag Today, Charlie?*
Chaucer, Geoffrey	*Chanticleer and the Fox*
Cleary, Beverly	*Henry Huggins*
Cleary, Beverly	*Ribsy*
Cleary, Beverly	*The Mouse and the Motorcycle*
Cleary, Beverly	*Ramona, the Pest*
Cleary, Beverly	*Ellen Tebbits*
Cleary, Beverly	*Henry and the Paper Route*
Cleary, Beverly	*Henry and Ribsy*
Cleary, Beverly	*Henry and Beezus*
Cleary, Beverly	*Ramona Quimby, Age 8*
Cleary, Beverly	*Beezus and Ramona*
Cleary, Beverly	*Otis Spofford*
Cleary, Beverly	*Socks*
Coatsworth, Elizabeth	*Away Goes Sally*
Coatsworth, Elizabeth	*Five Bushel Farm*
Coatsworth, Elizabeth	*The Fair American*
Coerr, Eleanor	*The Josefina Quilt*
Collins, David	*Frances Scott Key*
Collodi, C.	*The Adventures of Pinocchio*
Dalgliesh, Alice	*The Bears on Hemlock Mountain*
Dalgliesh, Alice	*The Columbus Story*
Dalgliesh, Alice	*The Courage of Sarah Noble*
d'Aulaire, Ingri & Edgar	*Abraham Lincoln*
Davis, Tim	*Mice Books - Tales of Dust River Gulch* series
DeJong, Meindert	*A Horse Came Running*
DeJong, Meindert	*Along Came a Dog*
Dejong, Meindert	*Hurry Home Candy*
Edmonds, Walter	*The Matchlock Gun*
Edmonds, Walter	*Cadmus Henry*

Ellison, Lucille	*Butter on Both Sides*
Ellison, Lucille	*The Tie that Binds*
Elmer, Robert	*Promise of Zion*
Elmer, Robert	*Young Underground*
Enright, Elizabeth	*Thimble Summer*
Enright, Elizabeth	*The Saturdays*
Estes, Eleanor	*Ginger Pye*
Estes, Eleanor	*Pinky Pie*
Estes, Eleanor	*The Middle Moffat*
Estes, Eleanor	*The Moffats*
Estes, Eleanor	*The Hundred Dresses*
Fellings, Muriel	*Samani Goes to Market*
Fritz, Jean	*The Cabin Faced West*
Fritz, Jean	*Brady*
Gates, Doris	*Blue Willow*
Grafton, Tom	*I Wear Long Trousers*
Grafton, Tom	*The Skinner Mill Fire*
Grafton, Tom	*True Stories Especially for Boys*
Grafton, Tom & Jane	*True Stories for Boys and Girls*
Grahame, Kenneth	*Wind in the Willows*
Gruelle, Johnny	*Raggedy Ann and the Golden Ring*
Hale, Lucretia	*The Peterkin Papers*
Handford, Elizabeth	*Those Kids in Proverbsville*
Haywood, Carolyn	*Robert Rows the River* (a series of 30 books)
Henry, Marguerite	*King of the Wind*
Henry, Marguerite	*Brighty of Grand Canyon*
Henry, Marguerite	*Misty of Chincoteague*
Henry, Marguerite	*Benjamin West and His Cat Grimalkin*
Hess, Donna	*Dust of the Earth*
Hess, Donna	*A Father's Promise*
Hill, Elizabeth	*Evan's Corner*
Hooker, Bob	*Who Told Mama?*
Hooker, Bob	*Just One More Lap*
Hooker, JoBeth	*Where Troubles Hide*
Hutchins, Paul	*The Sugar Creek Gang* (series)
Jackson, Dave & Neta	*Trailblazers*
Johnson, Lois	*Northwoods* (series)
Johnson, Ruth	*Joy Sparton* (series)
Kipling, Rudyard	*The Jungle Book*
Kjelgaard, Jim	*Big Red* series
Lawson, Robert	*Ben and Me*
Lawson, Robert	*Mr. Revere and I*
Lawson, Robert	*Rabbit Hill*
Lenski, Lois	*Cotton in My Sack*
Lenski, Lois	*Strawberry Girl*

Landis, Mary	*Trouble at Windy Acres*
Leodhas, Horch	*Always Room for One More*
Lines, Kathleen	*Dick Whittington*
Lois, Grandmother	*The Missing Popcorn*
Lois, Grandmother	*Grandmother's Secret and Other Stories*
Lorenzini, Carlo	*Adventures of Pinocchio*
MacMullen, Grace	*A Reward for Jerry*
McCloskey, Robert	*Homer Price*
McCloskey, Robert	*Centerburg Tales*
Meadowcroft, Enid	*Silver for General Washington*
Milne, A. A.	*The House at Pooh Corner*
Milne, A. A.	*Winnie the Pooh*
Milne, A. A.	*Three Stories from Winnie the Pooh*
Norton, Mary	*The Borrowers*
Ogle, Robin	*This Is the Day! (The Adventures of Sheriff Ogle and His Deputies)*
Palmer, Bernard	*Danny Orlis (series)*
Palmer, Bernard	*Felicia Cartwright (series)*
Palmer, Bernard	*Lori Adams (series)*
Peterson, John	*The Littles (series)*
Porter, Eleanor H.	*Pollyanna*
Pyle, Hugh	*Adventures in Animal Land*
Pyle, Hugh	*More Adventures in Animal Land*
Pyle, Hugh	*The Crooked Cave Caper*
Richardson, Arleta	*Treasures from Grandma*
Richardson, Arleta	*Away from Home*
Richardson, Arleta	*At Home in North Branch*
Richardson, Arleta	*Grandma's Attic (series)*
Richardson, Arleta	*New Faces, New Friends*
Robertson, Keith	*Henry Reed, Inc.*
Salten, Felix	*Bambi*
Salten, Felix	*Bambi's Children*
Seredy, Kate	*The Good Master*
Sperry, Armstrong	*Call It Courage*
Spyri, Johanna	*Heidi*
Steele, William	*Winter Danger*
Strong, Phil	*Honk, the Moose*
Stockum, Hilda	*The Cottage at Bantry Bay*
Stolz, Mary	*A Dog on Barkham Street*
Stolz, Mary	*The Bully on Barkham Street*
Taylor, Sydney	*All-of-a-Kind Family*
Tazewell, Charles	*The Littlest Angel*
Thompson, George	*The Cricket in Times Square*
Titus, Eve	*The Basil of Baker Street Mystery (series)*
Travers, Pamela	*Mary Poppins*

Twain, Mark	*The Adventures of Huckleberry Finn*
Walker, Kevin L.	*Children's Bible and Prayer Guide (Volume 1-Old Testament)*
Walker, Kevin L.	*Children's Bible and Prayer Guide (Volume 2-New Testament)*
Warner, Gertrude	*The Boxcar Children* (series of 20 books)
West, Jerry	*The Happy Hollisters* (series)
White, E. B.	*The Trumpet of the Swan*
White, E. B.	*Charlotte's Web*
White, E. B.	*Stuart Little*
Wiggin, Kate Douglas	*Rebecca of Sunnybrook Farm*
Wilder, Laura Ingalls	*The Little House on the Prairie* (series)
Witter, Evelyn	*Abigail Adams*

Fifth and Sixth Grade List for Children

Alcott, Louisa	*Little Women*
Alcott, Louisa	*Little Men*
Alcott, Louisa	*Rose in Bloom*
Alcott, Louisa	*Eight Cousins*
American Adventure series	
Brink, Carol	*Caddie Woodlawn*
Brown, Marion & Ruth Brown	*The Silent Storm*
Bulla, Clyde	*Lion to Guard Us*
Bunyan, John	*The Pilgrim's Progress*
Burnford, Sheila	*The Incredible Journey*
Burnett, Frances Hodgson	*The Secret Garden*
Burnett, Frances Hodgson	*The Little Princess*
Camp, Norma	*George Washington*
Carroll, Lewis	*Alice in Wonderland*
Carroll, Lewis	*Through the Looking Glass*
Chute, Marchettte	*The Wonderful Winter*
Collins, David	*Abraham Lincoln*
Dahl, Roald	*Charlie and the Chocolate Factory*
Dahl, Roald	*James and the Giant Peach*
Dalgliesh, Alice	*The Silver Pencil*
DeAngeli, Marguerite	*The Door in the Wall*
Defoe, Daniel	*The Life and Adventures of Robinson Crusoe*
DeJong, Meindert	*The House of Sixty Feathers*
Dickens, Charles	*A Christmas Carol*
Dodge, Mary Mapes	*Hans Brinker or the Silver Skates*
Doss, Helen	*The Family Nobody Wanted*
Estes, Eleanor	*The Middle Moffatt: The Moffats*
Evans, Dr. Wendell	*Some Thoughts on American History*
Farley, Walter	*The Black Stallion* (series of 21 books)
Forbes, Esther	*Johnny Tremain*

Forbes, Kathryn	*Mama's Bank Account*
George, John & Jean	*Vulpes, the Red Fox*
George, John & Jean	*My Side of the Mountain*
Gipson, Fred	*Old Yeller*
Gray, Elizabeth	*Adam of the Road*
Gray, Elizabeth	*I Will Adventure*
Hale, Lucretia	*The Peterkin Papers*
Henry, Marguerite	*King of the Wind*
Henry, Marguerite	*Misty of Chincoteague*
Hilton, James	*Goodbye, Mr. Chips*
Hunt, Irene	*Across Five Aprils*
James, Will	*Smokey the Cowhorse*
Jenkins, Jerry	*Global Air Troubleshooters* (series)
Kauffman, Christmas Carol	*Hidden Rainbow*
Kerr, Judith	*When Hitler Stole Pink Rabbit*
Keith, Harold	*Rifles for Watie*
Kipling, Rudyard	*The Jungle Book*
Kjelgaard, James	*Big Red* (series)
Krumgold, Joseph	*…And Now Miguel*
Lamb, Harold	*Genghis Khan and the Mongol Horde*
Latham, Jean Lee	*Carry on, Mr. Bowditch*
Lee, Albert	*Thrilling Escapes by Night*
Marshall, Catherine	*Christy*
McNear, May & Lynn	*Armed with Courage*
McNear, May & Lynn	*John Wesley*
Montgomery, Lucy Maud	*Anne of Green Gables* (series)
Montgomery, Rutherford	*Gray Wolf*
Morey, Walt	*Kavik, the Wolf Dog*
Morey, Walt	*Gentle Ben*
Morrow, Honore	*Seven Alone* or *On to Oregon*
Mowat, Farley	*Owls in the Family*
O'Dell, Scott	*Island of the Blue Dolphins*
O'Dell, Scott	*Sing Down the Moon*
O'Dell, Scott	*The Hawk That Dare Not Hunt by Day*
Otis, James	*Toby Tyler*
Politi, Leo	*Song of the Swallows*
Pyle, Howard	*Men of Iron*
Pyle, Howard	*Otto of the Silver Hand*
Rawlings, Marjorie Kinnane	*The Yearling*
Ridle, Julia	*Christopher Columbus*
Ridle, Julia	*Mohawk Gamble*
Roddy, Lee	*Robert E. Lee*
Rugh, Bella	*Crystal Mountain*
St. John, Patricia	*Treasures in the Snow*
St. John, Patricia	*Tanglewood Secrets*

Schaefer, Jack	Old Ramon
Seredy, Kate	The Good Master
Sewell, Anna	Black Beauty
Sharp, Margery	Miss Bianca
Sheldon, Charles	In His Steps
Sidney, Margaret	Five Little Peppers
Sorenson, Virginia	Miracles on Maple Street
Speare, Elizabeth	The Witch of Blackbird Pond
Speare, Elizabeth	Calico Captive
Speare, Elizabeth	The Bronze Bow
Speare, Elizabeth	The Sign of the Beaver
Sperry, Armstrong	Call It Courage
Spyri, Johanna	Heidi
Stevenson, Robert Louis	Treasure Island
Suhl, Truitt	A Boy and His Shadow
Sutcliff, Rosemary	Dawn Wind
Tiner, John	Isaac Newton
Tiner, John	Johannes Kepler
Thompson, George	The Cricket in Times Square
Thurber, James	Many Moons
Travers, P. L.	Mary Poppins
Ullman, James	Banner in the Sky
Verne, Jules	A Journey to the Center of the Earth
Vogel, Thomas	Growing Up in Vietnam
Witter, Evelyn	Abigail Adams
Wier, Esther	The Loner
Wojokowska, Maia	Shadow of a Bull
Wyss, J. D.	The Swiss Family Robinson
Yates, Elizabeth	Amos Fortune, Free Man

Poetry, Fables, and Folk Tale List for Children

Aesop	Aesop's Fables
Alexander	Poems that Touch the Heart
Anderson, Hans Christian	Anderson's Fairy Tales
Anderson, Hans Christian	The Nightingale
Anderson, Hans Christian	The Ugly Duckling
Anderson, Hans Christian	Thumbelina
Anderson, Hans Christian	The Snow Queen
Arkhurst, Joyce	Adventures of Spider
Arkhurst, Joyce	More Adventures of Spider
Arno, Ed	The Gingerbread Man
Asbjornsen, P.	The Three Billy Goats Gruff
Baker, Augusta	Best Loved Fairy Tales
Bennett, Jill	Days Are Where We Live
Blake, William	Songs of Innocence

Brooke, Leslie	*The Golden Goose Book*
Brooke, Leslie	*The Story of the Three Bears*
Brown, Marcie	*Stone Soup*
Brown, Margaret W.	*Nibble Nibble*
Browning, Robert	*Pied Piper of Hamlin*
Cavanah, Frances	*Family Reading Festival*
Chute, Marchette	*Around and About*
Ciardi, John	*The Reason for the Pelican*
Ciardi, John	*I Met a Man*
Cooney, Barbara	*Chanticleer and the Fox*
Dalgliesh, Alice	*Enchanted Book*
Davidson, Gladys	*Sinbad's Seven Voyages*
Disney, Walt	*Peter and the Wolf*
Disney, Walt	*Cinderella*
Disney, Walt	*Snow White and the Seven Dwarfs*
Evans, Katherine	*A Camel in the Tent*
Evans, Pauline	*Best Book of Fairy Tales*
Felton, Harold	*John Henry and His Hammer*
Felton, Harold	*Legends of Paul Bunyan*
Field, Eugene	*Poems for Children*
Fisher, Aileen	*Cricket in a Thicket*
Frederick, Robert	*My Book of Fairy Tales*
Fujikawa, Gyo	*Fairy Tales and Fables*
Goldsmith, Oliver	*Treasury of Aesop's Fables*
Galdone, Paul	*Three Aesop Fox Fables*
Gool, Van	*Jack and the Beanstalk*
Greenaway, Kate	*Kate Greenaway's Family Treasury*
Greenaway, Kate	*Under the Window*
Greenaway, Kate	*Marigold Garden*
Grimm, Brothers	*Sixty Fairy Tales of the Brothers Grimm*
Grimm, Brothers	*Grimm's Fairy Tales*
Grimm, Brothers	*The Shoemaker and the Elves*
Gross, Ruth	*Hansel and Gretel*
Haddock, Peter	*Jack and the Beanstalk*
Hicks, Laurel	*Aesop's Fables*
Hopkins, Lee	*Go to Bed*
Hyman, Trina Schart	*Little Red Riding Hood*
Ingpen, Roger	*1000 Poems for Children*
Irving, Washington	*Legend of Sleepy Hollow*
Jacobs, Joseph	*English Fairy Tales*
Jacobs, Joseph	*The Best Loved Fables of Aesop*
Kellogg, Steven	*Paul Bunyan*
Kincaid, Lucy	*The Magic of Rhymes*
Kipling, Rudyard	*Just So Stories*
Kramer, Nora	*Grimm's Fairy Tales*

Lang, Andrew	Tales from the Green Fairy
Lang, Andrew	The Andrew Lang Fairy Tale Treasury
Larrick, Nancy	Piper, Pipe That Song Again
Lawrie, Robin	Children's Class Poetry
Lear, Edward	Whizz!
Lindsay, Vachel	Springfield Town is Butterfly Town
Lobel, Arnold	Fables
Luckhardt, Mildred	Spring World Awake
Marshall, Helen L.	A World That Sings
Milne, A. A.	When We Were Very Young
Milne, A. A.	Now We Are Six
Modern	Sleeping Beauty
Moore, Clement	The Night Before Christmas
McCormick, Dell	Paul Bunyan Swings His Axe
McGovern, Ann	Aesop's Fables
Nash, Ogden	The Moon Is Shining Bright as Day
O'Mara, Michael	Classic Children's Poetry
O'Neil, Mary	Hailstones and Halibut Bones
Parker, Elinor	100 More Story Poems
Perrault, Charles	Perrault's Complete Fairy Tales
Perrault, Charles	Puss in Boots
Picard, Barbara	The Faun & the Wood Cutter's Daughter
Rackham, Arthur	The Arthur Rackham Fairy Book
Rackham, Arthur	Aesop's Fables
Rasmussen, Knud	Beyond the High Hills
Riley, James Whitcomb	Joyful Poems for Children
Sechrist, E. & J. Woosley	It's Time for Story Hour
Shepherd, Esther	Paul Bunyan
Silverstein, Shel	A Light in the Attic
Silverstein, Shel	Where the Sidewalk Ends
Slater, Cecelia	The Pied Piper
Spriggs, Ruth	The Fables of Aesop
Stevenson, Robert L.	A Child's Garden of Verses
Stoutenbury, Adrien	American Tall Tales
Tall, Tony	Nursery Rhymes
Tarcov, Edith	Three Famous Stories
Tarcov, Edith	The Frog Prince
Tudor, Tasha	The Tasha Tudor Book of Fairy Tales
Untermeyer, Louis	The Golden Treasury of Poetry
Wadsworth, Wallace	Henny Penny
Weigle, Oscar	Hansel and Gretel
Werner, Jane	The Golden Book of Poetry
Weygant, N.	It's Winter
Wong, Jeanyee	Chinese Fairy Tales
Wortman, Arthur	Father, We Thank Thee

Biography List for Children

Adler, David	*A Picture Book of George Washington*
Adler, David	*A Picture Book of Benjamin Franklin*
American Heritage	*Andrew Jackson, Soldier and Statesman*
Auebaucher, Inge	*I Am a Star*
Averill, Esther	*Cartier Sails the St. Lawrence*
Bailey, Carolyn	*Children of the Handicrafts*
Barrett, Ethel	*John Welch, The Man Who Couldn't Be Stopped*
Barrett, Marvin	*Meet Thomas Jefferson*
Barton, Thomas	*Patrick Henry*
Bell, Margaret	*Kit Carson, Mountain Man*
Boylston, Helen	*Clara Barton, Visiting Nurse*
Bragdon, Lillian	*Meet the Remarkable Adams Family*
Bulla, Clyde	*Squanto, Friend of the Pilgrims*
Bulla, Clyde	*Pocahontas and the Strangers*
Camp, Norma	*George Washington*
Carey, Barbara	*Meet Abraham Lincoln*
Collier, Edmund	*The Story of Buffalo Bill*
Collins, David	*Abraham Lincoln*
Collins, David	*Frances Scott Key*
Collins, David	*Florence Nightingale*
Collins, David	*George Washington Carver*
Collins, David	*Christopher Columbus*
Collins, David	*Benjamin Franklin*
Collins, David	*George Washington*
Commager, Henry	*America's Robert E. Lee*
Daugherty, James	*Daniel Boone*
Daugherty, James	*Poor Richard*
d'Aulaire, Ingri	*Abraham Lincoln*
d'Aulaire, Ingri	*Pocahontas*
d'Aulaire, Ingri	*Columbus*
Davidson, Margaret	*Helen Keller*
DeKay, James T.	*Meet Christopher Columbus*
DeKay, Ormonde & Davis	*Meet Theodore Roosevelt*
Dolson, Hildegarde	*William Penn: Quaker Hero*
Dugan, James	*Undersea Explorer*
Eaton, Jeannette	*That Lively Man, Benjamin Franklin*
Every, Dale & Tracy	*Charles Lindberg, His Life*
Forbes, Esther	*America's Paul Revere*
Garst, Shannon	*Crazy Horse, Great Warrior of the Sioux*
Garst, Shannon	*Kit Carson, Trail Blazer and Scout*
Graff, Stewart & Polly	*Helen Keller*
Graham, Shirley	*Dr. George Washington Carver, Scientist*
Graham, Shirley	*Booker T. Washington*
Henry, Marguerite	*Benjamin West and His Cat Grimalkin*

Reynolds, Quentin	*The Wright Brothers*
Rhodes, Bennie	*Christopher Columbus*
Rockwell, Anne F.	*Silippo's Dome*
Roddy, Lee	*Robert E. Lee*
Sadler, Bennie	*I'm a Lucky One*
Santrey, Laurence	*John Adams, Brave Patriot*
Seymour, Flora	*Pocahontas, Brave Girl*
Shippen, Katherine	*Leif Erikson: First Voyage to America*
Sperry, Armstrong	*The Voyages of Christopher Columbus*
Smith, Kathie B.	*George Washington*
Steele, William	*The Story of Leif Erickson*
Sterling, Dorothy	*Freedom Train, The Story of Harriett Tubman*
Stevenson, Augusta	*Anthony Wayne, Daring Boy*
Stevenson, Augusta	*Andy Jackson, Boy Soldier*
Streatfield, Noel	*Queen Victoria*
Tappan, Eva	*American Hero Stories*
Tiner, John	*Johannes Kepler*
Tiner, John	*Isaac Newton*
Vinton, Iris	*We Were There with Jean Lafitte at New Orleans*
Vogel, Tom	*Growing Up in Vietnam*
Wagoner, Jean	*Jessie Fremont, Girl of Capitol Hill*
Well, Ann	*John Quincy Adams, Boy Patriot*
Wheeler, Opal	*The Adventures of Richard Wagner*
White, Paul	*Jungle Doctor to the Rescue*
Whitridge, Arnold	*Simon Bolivar*
Weddemer, Mabel	*Washington Irving*
Wilbur, William	*The Making of George Washington*
Wilson, Hazel	*Mad Anthony Wayne*
Winwar, Frances	*Napoleon and the Battle of Waterloo*
Witter, Evelyn	*Abigail Adams*
Wollheim, Donald	*Lee de Forrest*
Yates, Elizabeth	*Amos Fortune*

There are many books in the "Heroes of the Faith" series, "Men of Faith" series, and "Women of Faith" series by different authors which may be ordered from the Library and Educational Service Company or the Christian Book Distributors listed on the library resource page. However, every book must be considered individually.

Historical List for Children

Allen, Merritt	*The Wilderness Way*
Beatty, John & Patricia	*At the Seven Stars*
Brink, Carol Ryrie	*Caddie Woodlawn*
Bruton, Hester	*Beyond the Weir Bridge*
Bruton, Hester	*Time of Trial*

Lawson, Robert	*Mr. Revere and I*
Lawson, Robert	*Ben and Me*
Lee, Albert	*Thrilling Escapes by Night*
Mathieu, Joe	*The Olden Days*
McGovern, Ann	*If You Sailed on the Mayflower*
Meader, C. W.	*Boy with a Pack*
Meadowcroft, Enid	*Silver for General Washington*
Meadowcroft, Enid	*By Secret Railway*
Miers, Earl S.	*When Washington Won at Yorktown*
Morrow, Honore	*Seven Alone* or *On to Oregon*
O'Dell, Scott	*Island of the Blue Dolphins*
O'Dell, Scott	*The King's Fifth*
O'Dell, Scott	*Sing Down the Moon*
O'Dell, Scott	*Carlotta*
Pyle, Howard	*Otto of the Silver Hand*
Pyle, Howard	*Men of Iron*
Reece, Colleen	*Plymouth Pioneers*
Speare, Elizabeth	*The Witch of Blackbird Pond*
Speare, Elizabeth	*The Bronze Bow*
Speare, Elizabeth	*Calico Captive*
Sutcliff, Rosemary	*The Lantern Bearers*
Vinton, Iris	*We Were There with Jean Lafitte at New Orleans*
Wilder, Laura Ingalls	*The Little House on the Prairie* (series)

Informational List for Children

Adler, Irving	*The Wonders of Physics*
Aliki	*My Five Senses*
Andrews, Mary	*The Perfect Tribute*
Andrews, Roy	*All About Whales*
Ardley, Neil	*How Birds Behave*
Ayer, Margaret	*Getting to Know Thailand*
Bailey, Bernadine	*Pennsylvania*
Bailey, Carolyn	*Children of the Handcrafts*
Barnhardt, John	*Indiana: The Hoosier State*
Beard, Charles A.	*The Presidents in American History*
Beard, Isobel	*Frogs*
Beers, Gilbert	*Cats, Bats, and Things Like That*
Bendick, Jeanne	*Names, Sets, and Numbers*
Bleeker, Sonia	*The Eskimo*
Blough, Glenn	*The Birds in the Big Woods*
Boulton, Rudyard	*Traveling with the Birds*
Branley, Franklin	*The Milky Way: Galaxy Number One*
Brindze, Ruth	*All About Courts and the Law*
Brewster, Benjamin	*The First Book of Baseball*

Hausman, Leon & Felix Sutton	The Illustrated Book of the Sea
Heller, Ruth	How to Hide a Polar Bear
Henry, Marguerite	Birds at Home
Henry, Marguerite	Album of Dogs
Hinton, Sam	Exploring Under the Sea
Hish, Duane T.	Dinosaurs, Those Terrible Lizards
Howland, Deborah	Heart of the Arctic
Horfinde, Robert	Indian Sign Language
Holden, Raymond	All About Fire
Holling, Clancy	Paddle to the Sea
Hunnelmann, John	Ibis, A True Whale Story
Huntington, Harriet	Praying Mantis
Hutchinson, William	The Sea and Its Mysteries
Johnson, Thomas	When Nature Runs Wild
Johnson, Spencer	The Value of Believing in Yourself
Johnson, Spencer	The Value of Dedication
Johnson, Spencer	The Value of Friendship
Johnson, Spencer	The Value of Sharing
Johnson, Spencer	The Value of Curiosity
Johnson, Spencer	The Value of Learning
Johnson, Spencer	The Value of Giving
Johnson, Gerald	The Presidency
Joy, Charles	Getting to Know Costa Rica
Joy, Charles	Getting to Know El Salvador
Joy, Charles	Getting to Know Nicaragua
Karen, Ruth	The Land and People of Central America
Keen, Martin	Let's Experiment
Kettelkamp, Larry	Drums, Rattles, and Bells
Klein, Leonore	What Is an Inch?
Knight, James E.	Seventh and Walnut
Kuchalla, Susan	Now I Know Baby Animals
Lancaster, Bruce	The American Revolution
Lauber, Patricia	Who Discovered America?
Leaf, Monro	Geography Can Be Fun
LeBar, Mary	How God Gives Us Jelly
Lewellen, John	The True Book of Moon, Sun, Stars
Lineweaver, Charles & Marion	Canada
Livermore, Elaine	One to Ten Count Again
Loder, Dorothy	The Land and People of Belgium
Malkus, Alida	The Story of Good Queen Bess
Marr, Moly	I Wonder Where Butterflies Go in Winter
Marx, Richard	About Mexico's Children
Mayer, Albert I.	The Story of Old Glory
Meyer, Jerome	Picture Book of the Sea
McClung, Robert	Thor: Last of the Sperm Whales

Meltzeh, Milton	*Into Their Own Words*
Meltzeh, Milton	*A Light in the Dark: Story of Samuel G. Howe*
Miller, J. P. & Katherine Howard	*Do You Know Colors?*
Miller, Natalie	*The Story of the Liberty Bell*
Miller, Natalie	*The Story of the Star-Spangled Banner*
Miller, Natalie	*The Story of the Lincoln Memorial*
Miller, Natalie	*The Story of the Statue of Liberty*
Nighbert, Esther	*The True Book of Cloth*
Miers, Earl	*The Story of Thomas Jefferson*
O'Neill, Hester	*The Picture Story of the Philippines*
O'Neill, Hester	*The Picture Story of Denmark*
Pallazzo, Janet	*What Makes the Weather*
Paton, Alan	*The Land and People of Belgium*
Paton, Alan	*The Land and People of South America*
Payne, Elizabeth	*Meet the Pilgrim Fathers*
Peterham, Maud	*The Story of the Presidents of the U.S.A.*
Podendoz, Illa	*The True Book of Sounds We Hear*
Podenorf, Illa	*Animal Homes*
Pollard, Josephine	*Christopher Columbus and the Discovery of the New World*
Pratt, Fletcher	*The Civil War*
Prime, Derek	*Tell Me About Becoming a Christian*
Prime, Derek	*Tell Me About the Lord Jesus Christ*
Prime, Derek	*Tell Me About the Holy Spirit and the Church*
Prolman, Marilyn	*The Story of the Constitution*
Prolman, Marilyn	*The Story of the Capitol*
Prolman, Marilyn	*The Story of Mount Rushmore*
Prolman, Marilyn	*The Story of Jamestown*
Price, Willadene	*Bartholdi and the Statue of Liberty*
Rabinowicz, R. A.	*The Land and People of Israel*
Renfro, Alfred	*The World of Insects*
Rey, H. A.	*Find the Constellations*
Rich, Louise	*The First Book of New England*
Richards, Kenneth	*The Story of the Conestoga Wagon*
Richards, Kenneth	*The Story of the Gettysburg Address*
Richards, Norman	*The Story of the Declaration of Independence*
Richards, Norman	*The Story of the Mayflower Compact*
Richards, Norman	*The Story of Monticello*
Richards, Norman	*The Story of the Bonhomme Richard*
Ross, Edward	*The Ants*
Sands, George	*Why Glasses? The Story of Vision*
Santrey, Laurence	*What Makes the Wind?*
Scott, Foresman, and Co.	*All Around Us*
Selsam, Millicent	*Ants*
Selsam, Millicent	*All Kinds of Babies*

Shannon, Terry	*Where Animals Live*
Shuttlesworth, Dorothy	*The Story of Spiders*
Schlein, Marian	*Fast Is Not a Ladybug*
Smith, Kathie	*George Washington*
Spencer, Cornelia	*Let's Read About China*
Stein, Conrad R.	*The Story of the Arlington National Cemetery*
Stein, Conrad R.	*The Story of The Little Bighorn*
Stein, Conrad R.	*The Story of the Erie Canal*
Stein, Conrad R.	*The Story of the Monitor and the Merrimac*
Stein, Conrad R.	*The Story of the Powers of the Presidency*
Stein, Conrad R.	*The Story of the Trail of Tears*
Stein, Conrad R.	*The Story of the Oregon Trail*
Stein, Conrad R.	*The Story of Ellis Island*
Stein, Conrad R.	*The Story of Valley Forge*
Stein, Conrad R.	*The Story of the Homestead Act*
Stein, Conrad R.	*The Story of the Pony Express*
Stein, Conrad R.	*The Story of the Smithsonian Institution*
Stein, Conrad R.	*The Story of the Lafayette Escadrille*
Stein, Conrad R.	*The Story of the Battle of the Bulge*
Stein, Conrad R.	*The Story of the Golden Spike*
Stein, Conrad R.	*The Story of the Spirit of St. Louis*
Stein, Conrad R.	*The Story of the Battle for Iwo Jima*
Stein, Conrad R.	*The Story of D-Day*
Stein, Conrad R.	*The Story of the San Francisco Earthquake*
Stein, Conrad R.	*The Story of the U.S.S. Arizona*
Stein, Conrad R.	*The Story of Wounded Knee*
Stone, Harris	*The History of a Lemon*
Stoutenburg, Adrien	*Changing Cultures*
Sterling, Dorothy	*Trees and Their Story*
Szekeres, Cyndy	*Little Bear Counts His Favorite Things*
Tor, Regina	*Getting to Know Puerto Rico*
Tresselt, Alvin	*The Beaver Pond*
Tunis, Edwin	*Frontier Living*
Tunis, Edwin	*Colonial Living*
Van Blarcom, Wayne	*To Get to Heaven*
Vandivert, Rita	*Favorite Pets: How to Choose and Care for Them*
White, Anne	*All About the Stars*
Wilson, Phoebe	*Young Readers Book of Presidents*
Wilson, Walter	*Animal Stories*

The following are series that are interesting for children, but each book must be considered individually.

- Leaders of America series
- Life and Time series
- World at War series

- Cornerstones of Freedom series
- American Biographies series
- We Were There... series

Our children enjoyed working to fulfill the requirements for the following reading clubs. Now, our grandchildren are involved in these exciting reading clubs.

Children's Reading Clubs

- **Great Classics.** These famous books or famous authors have withstood the test of time. Ten of the following sixteen books listed must be read:

  Little Women (Alcott)
  House of Sixty Fathers (Dejong)
  Hans Brinker or the Silver Skates (Dodge)
  Sherlock Holmes (Doyle)
  Wind in the Willows (Grahame)
  Hidden Rainbow (Kaufmann)
  Anne of Green Gables (Montgomery)
  Where the Red Fern Grows (Rawls)
  Five Little Peppers and How They Grew (Sidney)
  The Bronze Bow (Speare)
  The Witch of Blackbird Pond (Speare)
  Call It Courage (Sperry)
  Treasure Island (Stevenson)
  Gulliver's Travels (Swift)
  The Prince and the Pauper (Twain)
  Rebecca of Sunnybrook Farm (Wiggins)

- **Literary.** These books are children's favorite selections. Ten of the eleven books listed must be read. If the books are part of a series, no more than two books from the series may be read.

  The Boxcar Children (Warner)
  The Black Stallion (Farley)
  Charlotte's Web (White)
  Island of the Blue Dolphins (O'Dell)
  Heidi (Spryi)
  Old Yeller (Gibson)
  On to Oregon (Morrow)
  Ribsy (Cleary)
  The Secret Garden (Burnett)
  Treasures of the Snow (St. John)

- **Principal's Club.** Two principals listed their favorite childhood stories, books about the states in which they were born, and books pertaining to their interests, such as photography, the Marines, wildflowers, etc. A total of ten books must be read.

Book of Proverbs
John Paul Jones
Robert E. Lee
Lewis and Clark
Francis Marion
Charles Finney
Herbert Hoover
Dreamers and Doers
The Texas Rangers
America the Beautiful
(Any state)

Photography
Wildflowers
Rifles for Watie (Harold)
Black Beauty (Sewell)
Chariots to China (Williamson)
*The Hawk That Dare Not Hunt
by Day* (O'Dell)
Any *Big Red* book
(Jim Kjelgaard)

• **Dr. Watson's Mystery Club.** Only three favorites from a series will count toward the mystery club requirements. The rest must be by other authors, such as three Boxcar Children books, three Sugar Creek Gang books, and so forth. To be eligible for Dr. Watson's Mystery Club, the requirements for Dr. Jack Hyles' Club, Leaders of America Club, and the Literary Club must first be completed. Three books from each of the following mystery series must be read:

*The Hardy Boys (Dixon)
*Nancy Drew (Keene)
*The Bobbsey Twins (Hope)
The Sugar Creek Gang (Hutchins)
The Boxcar Children (Warner)
The Happy Hollisters (West)

(*Only the old editions of the Hardy Boys, Nancy Drew, and Bobbsey Twins series are acceptable.)

• **Dr. Jack Hyles' Club.** These selections are biographies of great Christians, preachers, or missionaries. Ten of the following twelve books must be read. (The book starred is required reading.)

Exploring Prayer with Jack Hyles
In His Steps (Sheldon)
Adoniram Judson
D. L. Moody
*The Little Woman—
Gladys Aylward*
David Livingstone

John Newton
Billy Sunday
Hudson Taylor
Mary Siessor
George Mueller
Wilderness Rider (N. Fidler)

• **Leaders of America.** These selections are from people who helped shape and build America. Ten of the following eleven books must be read:

Albert Einstein, Betsy Ross, Christopher Columbus, Thomas A. Edison, Helen Keller, Abraham Lincoln, Simon Kenton, Clara Barton, John Wesley, William H. McGuffey, George Washington

- **Historian's Club.** This club includes books on war, ancient times, or biographies of famous historical people. All 14 books listed must be read:

  1 – Life and Times
  5 – World at War
  5 – Cornerstones of Freedom
  2 – American Biographies
  1 – We Were There (JF)

- **Thomas A. Edison Science Reading Club.** Books must be selected from various scientific subjects, such as mammals, reptiles, space, etc. One 50-page book from each category listed must be read:

  Aviation (629); Birds (598); Insects (592); Mannals (599); Plants (580); Pollution (628); Reptiles (597); Sea (508); Space (520); Weather (550)

- **Boys' Club ~ Girls' Club.** Books pertaining to activities boys enjoy such as fishing, sports, and camping, as well as biographies are included on the boys' list. The girls' book lists include those with a girl's name for the title or included in the title such as Mandie, Miss Pickerell, Anne, etc.

  To be a member of the **Girls' Club**, a total of 10 books, two of which must be biographies, from the following list must be read:

Mandy (Leppard)	*Emily* (Montgomery)
Grandma's Attic (Richardson)	*Alice in Wonderland* (Carroll)
Molly (Tripp)	*Miss Pickerell* [1] (McGregor)
Kirsten (Shaw)	*Betsy* [1] (Harwood)
Samantha (Adler)	*Pippi Longstocking* (Lindgren)
Addy (Porter)	*Abigail Adams* (Witter)
Nancy Drew (Keene)	*Molly Pitcher* (Stevenson)
Joy Sparton (Johnson)	*Louisa May Alcott* (Howard)
Pollyanna (Porter)	*Martha Washington* [1] (Wagoner)

To be a member of the **Boys' Club**, books will be read according to grade level. This club is divided into two divisions: the "Light-Weight Club" for grades 3 and 4 only, and the "Heavy-Weight Club" for grades 5 and 6 only. Boys must read a total of 10 books, one of which must be a "how-to" book.

"Light-Weight" Book List	"Heavy-Weight" Book List
2 Baseball Heroes	1 Baseball Hero
1 Soccer book	2 Baker Street Sports Club
1 Basketball book	Ty Cobb
1 Baker Street Sports Club	Billy Sunday
Jim Thorpe (Santrey)	Willie Mays
Mickey Mantle Slugs It Out (May)	Babe Ruth
Jesse Owens (Sabin)	Cubs Win!
Babe Ruth (Brandt)	Track and Field
Jackie Robinson (Sabin)	*Better Boxing* (Sullivan)
Better Fishing for Boys (Kenealy)	*The Real Book about Sports* (Bonner)
Football Rules Illustrated (Sullivan)	

A list of required books for each club is posted on the wall of the library. More than the required number of books to be read is listed giving the student the opportunity to make his own choices. An oral or written report must be presented on the material read. Students may complete the requirements for any club from third through sixth grade. When a student completes the requirements, his name is read in chapel, he is presented with a certificate to keep, and his name is displayed with other club members in the library.

Keeping records is important. A file box is kept with a card for each student. After the student reads a book, prepares a report, and turns it in, the librarian records the book under the proper club. Students always have access to this file box so they can see how many more books are needed to complete a club. The goal is for them to be a well-rounded reader in each particular area.

Library Policies

1. Open stacks are necessary for a children's library.
2. Books must be proofread before placing on the library shelf. Books must be censored for unacceptable words, philosophies, and pictures. A few improper words can be covered with a silver pen, and a few improper pictures may be covered. If a book cannot pass the philosophy test, reject it. Keep in mind that it is almost impossible to find a book that has nothing objectionable in it, so you must decide where you will draw the line according to biblical principles. You will not know whether or not you can approve the book unless you read it, and someone will disagree with something in every book. It takes a lot of time to build a book list, but it is essential if children are encouraged to read.
3. The children should pay fines and costs for lost or damaged books to teach responsibility and character.
4. The loan period will vary according to the age of the children and the number of books available to be loaned.
5. Any book promoted by the teacher will create a desire for children to read the book.

Children's Library Resources

Foliate Library Resources
1340 Ridgeview Dr.
McHenry, Illinois 60050-7048
1-800-435-6170
This big company has everything but Christian books.

Library and Educational Services
P. O. Box 146
Berrien Springs, Michigan 49103
1-616-695-1800
This company has Christian books at great prices, but not every book would be usable.

Christian Book Distributors
P. O. Box 7000
Peabody, Mass. 01961-7001
978-977-5000
This company has Christian books but not all are usable.

Internet
    Check under e-bay.
    Check for books which are out of print.

Bound-to-Stay-Bound Books
West Morton Road
Jacksonville, Illinois 62650
1-800-637-6586

Perma-Bound Books
Hertzberg-New Method, Inc.
Vandalia Road
Jacksonville, Illinois 62650
1-800-637-6581
This company will convert paperbacks into hardbound books.

Demco Educational Corporation
P.O. Box 7488
Madison, Wisconsin 53707-7488
Order library supplies and a catalog is sent free of charge.

Puppet Scripts
For puppet scripts and information on obtaining puppets, contact Evangelist Kevin Walker, 8400 Burr Street, Crown Point, Indiana 46307.

Appendix F
Flannel Board Stories

The Pancake Man
The Bremen Town Musicians
The Big Turnip
The Three Wishes
The Three Billy Goats Gruff

*Keith, Kevin,
Kelly, and Krysten
dressed for
"Pioneer Day"*

*Grandpa
& Stephen*

*Grandpa
with Stephen,
Trent, and Ashley*

See additional information on how to make flannelboard figures in the Toddler section on pages 65-67.

The Pancake Man
(Norse Folk Story)

The story can be told or acted out by children. For flannel board, the following props are needed: an old man, an old woman, a pancake, a dog, a bear, and a fox. Pictures are on page 360.

Once upon a time there was an old woman and an old man who lived in a cottage in the forest. One day the old man had been cutting wood and asked his wife to make him a pancake. The old woman made the batter and poured it in the pan. "Hurry up, old woman, I can't wait to eat the pancake," the old man said.

The woman replied, "I'll turn it over to cook on the other side." However, as she flipped the pancake over, the pancake jumped out of the pan and rolled across the floor and out the door. The old man and old woman ran after the pancake and said, "Come back, pancake. We want to eat you."

The pancake rolled down the road and sang, "Run, run as fast as you can. You can't catch me. I'm the Pancake Man."

The old man and the old woman ran fast, but the pancake ran faster, and they had to stop to rest. The pancake rolled down the road past a black dog who woofed, "Come here, Pancake. I want to eat you."

The pancake rolled on and said, "Run, run as fast as you can. You can't catch me, I'm the pancake man. I ran away from an old woman and an old man, and I can run away from you, I can!"

The black dog ran fast, but the pancake rolled faster, and the dog stopped to rest.

Before long, the pancake rolled by a brown bear who growled and said, "Come here, Pancake. I want to eat you."

The pancake rolled on down the road and sang, "Run, run as fast as you can. You can't catch me, I'm the pancake man. I ran away from an old woman, an old man, and a black dog, and I can run away from you, I can."

The brown bear ran fast, but the pancake ran faster, and the bear had to stop and rest.

The pancake rolled on down the road until he saw a gray fox. Being quite sure he could outrun everyone, the pancake started singing his song, "Run, run as fast as you can. You can't catch me, I'm the pancake man."

The fox said, "Eh? Speak a little louder; I can't hear you."

The pancake rolled closer to the fox and said in a louder voice, "Run, run as fast as you can. You can't catch me! I'm the pancake man."

"Eh? Speak a little louder. I can't hear you," said the fox.

In his loudest voice, the pancake sang in the fox's ear. "Run, run as fast as you can. You can't catch me. I'm the pancake man."

The fox went, "GULP!" and that was the end of the pancake man—but pancakes are made to be eaten!

As you tell the story, you can teach the principle of Proverbs 16:18, "Pride goeth before destruction, and an haughty spirit before a fall."

The Bremen Town Musicians

This story can be told to children, acted out by children, or told using the flannel board. If the flannel board is used, the following characters are needed: a donkey, a dog, a cat, a rooster, and a cabin with a removable roof. The children can help repeat the refrain and make the animal sounds to help keep their attention. The templates are on page 360.

Once upon a time there was an old donkey *(Put donkey on flannel board.)* who had worked hard for his owner for many years. However, one day he overheard his owner say that he was planning to take the donkey to the glue factory because he was too old to work. The donkey decided that he would run away from his home and become a musician in Bremen. As he went down the road he sang, *(Use a low voice.)* "My master's driven me away from home, away from home, away from home. My master's driven me away from home because I'm too old to work."

As he went down the road, he saw a dog *(Put dog on the flannel board.)* howling beside the road. *(Howl and use a different voice from donkey.)*. "My master's driven me away from home, away from home, away from home. My master's driven me away from home because I'm too old to watch like a watchdog."

The donkey replied, "You have a wonderful voice! Why don't you come to Bremen Town and become a musician with me?"

The dog hopped on the back of the donkey *(Put dog on the donkey's back.)*, and they went on their way to Bremen. They had not gone far when they saw a cat beside the road making a mournful sound. "Meow, meow, meow."

They stopped and asked why the cat should be so sad. She replied, "My master's driven me away from home, away from home, away from home. My master's driven me away from home because I'm too old to catch mice."

The animals replied, "You have a lovely voice. Why don't you go to Bremen and be musicians with us?" The cat got on the back of the dog *(Put flannel cat on back of dog)* on the donkey, and they continued toward Bremen.

They had not gone far when they saw a rooster in a tree crowing in the middle of the day. "Cock-a-doodle-doo. Cock-a-doodle-doo. Cock-a-doo-dle-doo."

Our friends asked, "Why are you crowing in the middle of the day in such a sad way?"

The rooster replied, "My master's driven me away from home, away from home, away from home. My master's driven me away from home because I'm too old to crow in the morning."

"Why you have a lovely voice," the animals said. "You can go to Bremen and be a musician with us."

The rooster hopped on the back of the cat, the cat on the back of the dog, and the dog on the back of the donkey; and they went down the road. However, our friends were old. Since it was still a long way to Bremen, they decided to sleep that night and continue on the next day. The rooster flew to a tree to roost, the donkey stood under the tree, and the cat and dog were resting by the donkey's feet when the rooster crowed, "Cock-a-doodle-doo. I see a light."

Our friends said, "Maybe there are people there who could give us something to eat." They had been traveling a long way and were very hungry. They crept quietly toward the light, and the donkey looked in the window of a small cabin. Inside he saw robbers around a table piled high with money. Another table was filled with delicious food.

Our friends said, "If we sing for them, maybe they will give us food." (*Divide children into four groups. Let one group practice being donkeys who say, "Hee-haw." Let another group practice being dogs who howl, "Oh oooh." Let another group practice saying, "Meow," like the cat. The last group should practice saying, "Cock-a-doodle-doo" like the rooster. After the children have been divided so each can be an animal, tell them you are going to count to three, and all will make their sound.*)

When the robbers heard this terrible noise in the middle of the night, they were so frightened they jumped up and ran out the door far away from the cabin. Our friends waited and when the robbers did not return, the rooster flew up to a tree to roost, the donkey went to sleep under the tree, the dog went to sleep inside the cabin behind the door, and the cat curled up on the hearth beside the fire. Soon all were sound asleep.

When the robbers stopped running, one said, "We were foolish to run away and leave all our money and food. Nothing could have been so terrible as that sounded. I'm going back to see what it was." However, none of the others were willing to go with him.

The lone robber crept back to the cabin, carrying a torch that he planned to light from a coal in the fire. He silently stole across the floor of the cabin to light his torch, but instead of striking the torch on a coal, he struck it into the glowing eyes of the cat. The cat jumped to the head of the robber, clawing and scratching him. This frightened the robber, and as he tried to run back out the door of the cabin, the dog woke and bit him on the back of the leg as he ran by. This noise woke the donkey who kicked the robber with his hind legs. This woke the rooster, who began to crow with all his might, "Cock-a-doodle-doo! Cock-a-doodle-doo!"

The robber ran until he found his fellow robbers. He declared, "We can **never** go back to that cabin. When I tried to light my torch, a terrible witch tried to claw out my eyes. When I tried to run out the door, a man stabbed me in the leg with a knife. When I ran into the yard, a monster hit me with a club; another monster was in a tree saying, "Throw the rascal up here. Throw the rascal up here. We can never go back." The robbers left, and since no one returned, our friends decided that they would stay near the cabin and live happily ever after instead of going to Bremen. However, every night after supper they would sing because, after all, they were musicians.

("When I count to three, sing the part of your animal.")

The Big Turnip

The story can be told or acted out by children. For the flannel board, a farmer, a farmer's wife, a daughter, a turnip, a dog, a cat, and a mouse are needed for props. The templates for this story are on page 361.

A farmer once planted a turnip seed. It grew, and it grew, and it grew. The farmer saw it was time to pull the turnip out of the ground. So he took hold of it and began to pull. He pulled, and he pulled, and he pulled, and he pulled, but the turnip wouldn't come up. So the farmer called to his wife who was preparing dinner, "Fe, fi, fo, fum. I pulled on the turnip, but the turnip wouldn't come."

The wife came running, and she took hold of the farmer, and they pulled, and they pulled, and they pulled, and they pulled. But the turnip wouldn't come up. So the wife called to the daughter who was feeding the chickens nearby, "Fe, fi, fo, fum. I pulled on the turnip, but the turnip wouldn't come."

The daughter came running. The daughter took hold of the wife. The wife took hold of the farmer. The farmer took hold of the turnip. And they pulled, and they pulled, and they pulled, and they pulled. But the turnip wouldn't come up. So the daughter called to the dog who was chewing a bone, "Fe, fi, fo, fum. I pulled on the turnip, but the turnip wouldn't come."

The dog came running. The dog took hold of the daughter. The daughter took hold of the wife. The wife took hold of the farmer. And the farmer took hold of the turnip. And they pulled, and they pulled, and they pulled, and they pulled. But the turnip wouldn't come up. So the dog called to the cat who was chasing her tail, "Fe, fi, fo, fum. I pulled on the turnip, but the turnip wouldn't come."

The cat came running. The cat took hold of the dog. The dog took hold of the daughter. The daughter took hold of the wife. The wife took hold of the farmer. And the farmer took hold of the turnip. And they pulled, and they pulled, and they pulled, and they pulled. But the turnip wouldn't come up. So the cat called to the mouse who was nibbling spinach nearby, "Fe, fi, fo, fum. I pulled on the turnip, but the turnip wouldn't come."

The mouse came running.

"That little mouse can't help," said the dog. "He's too little."

"Phooey," squeaked the mouse. "I could pull up that turnip by myself, but since you have all been pulling, I'll let you help, too."

So the mouse took hold of the cat. The cat took hold of the dog. The dog hold of the daughter. The daughter took hold of the wife. The wife took hold of the farmer. And the farmer took hold of the turnip. And they pulled, and they pulled, and they pulled, and they pulled. And UP came the turnip! The mouse squeaked, "I told you so!"

The Three Wishes

The story can be told or acted out by children. For flannel board, an old man, an old woman, a fairy, and a sausage are needed for props. The templates are on pages 360 and 361.

Once upon a time there was an old man and an old woman who had worked hard all their lives and had little to show for their efforts. They lived in a small cabin in the woods, and the man was a wood-cutter. One day as he was cutting down a tree, a beautiful fairy appeared before him. She said, "I have noticed your hard work through the years, and I have come to reward you by granting you three wishes. Make the wishes with care because when they are made, no more will be given."

The old man was very excited and hurried home at once to tell his wife of their good fortune. They couldn't decide if they should wish for riches, an impressive home, a fine carriage, or beautiful clothes. Since this was such an important decision, the old man said, "I'm hungry. Why don't we eat, and then we can decide what we should wish for."

The old woman bustled about getting the food on the table and when she sat the bowl of soup in front of her husband he exclaimed, "Soup again! I am becoming very tired of soup. How I wish I had a nice hot sausage to eat with this soup." Before the old man realized what he had said, a sizzling hot sausage was on the table before him.

"Look what you have done," the old woman shrieked. "You have wasted one of our precious wishes on a sausage. How could you have been so foolish? We could have had a fine carriage, a castle, or money to provide for our needs the rest of our lives, and you wished for a sausage."

The old man felt very sorry about his unwise wish, and his wife's words only made him feel worse as he attempted to eat his soup. Finally in desperation he said, "Old woman, I am very tired of your words. In fact, I wish that sausage were stuck to the end of your nose." In a flash the sausage was hanging from her nose; and the old man, in horror, realized what he had done. *(Make a fist with one hand and put the fist on the end of your nose.)*

"Old man, what have you done? Now I have a sausage stuck to the end of my nose." They pulled the sausage, but to no avail. The sausage was permanently attached to her nose. The old man, wanting to make the best of a bad situation, said, "Never fear, my dear, we can still wish for riches, fine clothes, or a castle."

She replied, "What good would those things be to me if I had a sausage stuck on the end of my nose? I would be too humiliated to show my face."

The old man sadly realized there was no other remaining choice, so he said, "I wish the sausage was off your nose." Instantly, the sausage disappeared. The old man and old woman had used their three wishes and had nothing to show for them—not even a hot sausage to eat with their soup.

The Three Billy Goats Gruff
The templates for these characters are on page 361.

Once upon a time there were three billy goats, and the surname of the three was "Gruff." They lived on a green hillside were they would eat the green grass and become fat. One day they noticed another hillside where the grass was greener than their own. However, in order to reach it, they had to cross over a bridge; and under the bridge lived a mean and ugly troll whose eyes were as big as saucers and whose nose was as long as a poker.

By and by the small billy goat decided that he would cross the bridge. *(Make a noise by drumming fingers on a desk.)* When the small billy goat reached the center of the bridge, the troll said, "Who's that tripping on my bridge?"

"It's I, the small billy goat crossing the bridge to the green pasture so I can get fat."

"I'm going to come and gobble you up," said the troll.

"Oh, no, wait for my brother. He's much bigger, " said the billy goat.

"Be off with you then," replied the troll.

By and by the second billy goat saw his brother on the greener grass and decided that he too would cross the bridge. *(Make a louder noise with hands to simulate the goat crossing the bridge.)*

"Who's that tripping on my bridge?" said the troll.

"It's I, the second billy goat going to join my brother."

"I'm going to come and gobble you up," said the troll.

"Oh, no, wait for my brother. He's much bigger," replied the billy goat.

"Be off with you then," said the troll.

By and by the big billy goat decided to cross the bridge and join his brothers. He started across the bridge. *(Make a loud sound with hands.)*

"Who's that tripping on my bridge?" said the troll.

"It's I—the biggest billy goat," he said.

"I'm going to come and gobble you up," replied the troll.

"Come ahead then," said the big billy goat. "I've got two spears, and I'll poke your eyeballs out your ears. I've got two big bones, and I'll crush you to bits—body and bones."

344 | R<small>ECIPES FOR</small> R<small>EARING</small> C<small>HILDREN</small>

That's what the billy goat said, and that is what he did. He crossed over the bridge where he joined his brothers on the green hillside where they all got fat. If the fat hasn't fallen off them, they're still fat. Now snip, snap, snout, this tale's told out!

Appendix G
Story Telling

The Tongue on the Slide
The Boar Hunt

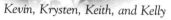

Stories Suitable for Storytelling

Moon Bear by Frank Asch

The Animal by Lorna Balian

Kevin, Krysten, Keith, and Kelly

Sometimes It's Turkey, Sometimes It's Feathers
    by Lorna Balian

Peter's Pocket by Judi Barrett

The Five Chinese Brothers by Claire Bishop

Good Night Moon by Margaret Wise Brown

The Runaway Bunny by Margaret Wise Brown

Peter and the Wolf by Walt Disney

Corduroy by Don Freeman

Millions of Cats by Wanda Gag

The Three Chinese Brothers by Paul Galdone

Henny Penny by Paul Galdone

The Carrot Seed by Ruth Krauss

The Little Drummer Boy by Ezra Jack Keats

Jennie's Hat by Ezra Jack Keats

Frog and Toad Are Friends by Arnold Lobel

Where Can an Elephant Hide? by David McPhail

Winnie the Pooh by A. A. Milne

Little Bear by Else Minarik

Peace At Last by Jill Murphy

Mrs. Pig's Bulk Buy by Mary Rayner

Caps for Sale by Esphyr Slobodkina

Crictor by Tomi Ungerer

You Look Ridiculous by Bernard Waber

How Do I Put It On? by Shigeo Watanabe

Mr. Rabbit and the Lovely Present by Charlotte Zolotow

The Tongue on the Slide

When I was in grade school, our playground had swings, a jungle gym, a merry-go-round, and monkey bars. I loved the monkey bars, and as soon as recess was announced, I ran to get in the "monkey bar" line. On one particular fall morning, it was cold outside and I remember blowing puffs of frost from my mouth as I ran toward the playground. I got in line, and I advanced to the monkey bar ladder. At this point, I must have been possessed with a case of "temporary insanity" because I decided to lick the ladder that led to the jungle gym. The moment my tongue touched the cold ladder, it stuck.

I could not pull my tongue off the ladder, and it was a miserable experience. The child behind me said, "Go on, it's your turn." It was impossible to move with my tongue stuck, so I just shook my head "No." Finally someone noticed that I had a problem and ran for the teacher. She sent a child into the school building for a cup of warm water to pour on my tongue. Immediately my tongue was "unstuck." I learned a valuable lesson—keep your tongue in your mouth—not on the ladder—when climbing the monkey bars.

The Boar Hunt

When I was eight and my brother David was four, we took our summer vacation in the Cherokee National Forest with the Parks family who lived next door. They had a boy and girl the same age as my brother and me. This part of the Smoky Mountains was undeveloped, and in the fall people would go wild boar hunting. We had a friend who owned a cabin, and he offered to let us stay there for a week in the summer. It was a rustic cabin with no electricity, and every night we would build a fire in the large fireplace. My dad would tell stories because there was nothing else to do.

One night he was pretending to be a wild boar. He rolled up two pieces of paper to be his tusks, crawled around the room making snorting noises, and chasing us. We were having so much fun.

The next day, after we had eaten lunch, the two mothers took the four children for a walk down a path behind the cabin. We had been walking for about ten minutes when we heard a wild boar snort behind us. We were immediately frightened because the sound was between us and our cabin.

The two boys started to cry, and I could tell my mother was frightened. She began frantically looking around to see where we could go to escape from the wild boar. She announced that we all had to climb trees. That sounded like an exciting adventure to me because I loved to climb trees. My friend Barbara found a dogwood tree and climbed to a low limb. My mother sat my brother David on a limb of another tree and ordered, "Stop crying and hold to the tree. Do you want the wild boar to get you?" He wailed on.

Finally my mother and Barbara's mother each began climbing a tree. I'm not sure how long this took, but as I remember, it was a considerable time. Whenever it became quiet, the boar would make a snorting noise. We sat in our trees for a little while with my brother still crying.

Soon I noticed my mother climbing down from her tree and walking down the path toward the cabin—straight toward the sound of the boar. She was out of sight when we heard her scream, "Bill White, the very idea! You scared us half to death."

We heard my dad laughing hysterically and saw him rolling on the ground. Eventually, he came to rescue us from the wild boar!

Frieda Cowling with three of her "Oregon" grandchildren at their story wall.

"I Found the Story Wall!"

Every vacation time in August, my husband and I visit our daughter and son-in-law, Krysten and Chris Vestal, in Oregon where he is an assistant pastor at the Grand View Baptist Church. One highlight of the trip is the time I spend with our grandchildren—Derek, Karissa, Wesley, and Ryan. Since I only see them twice a year, I plan things to help them remember me. Last summer we walked around their subdivision daily smelling flowers, looking for dogs, and picking blackberries. On the corner of one street, there was a retaining wall where we sat, and I told them stories.

During the Christmas holidays, Krysten called to say they were driving around their subdivision, looking at the lights when Derek yelled, "Stop, Dad! I've found it!"

Chris stopped the car in surprise. "What have you found, Derek?"

"I've found the story wall where we stopped for stories when Grandma was here," Derek happily explained. "I never want to lose it again."

It does not take a lot of time to build lasting memories in the hearts and minds of children. Sometimes all it takes is a story wall!

Appendix H
Games

Animal Dominos
Memory
Husker Du
Candyland
Chutes and Ladders
Concentration
Following Directions
Red Light,
   Green Light
The Name Game
Doggie, Doggie!
   Where's Your Bone?
I See Something
Simon Says
Duck, Duck, Goose
Alphabet Sign Game
7-Up
Bible Verse Game
Steal the Bacon
Mother, May I?
Over and Under
Black Magic
Popcorn Scramble
Musical Chairs
Relay Shoe Race
Suitcase Relay
Pictionary
Streets and Alleys

Hot Potato
Telephone
Memory Game
Word Scramble
Squirrel in a Tree
Murder
Ballon Stomp
Spoon & Bean Relay
Siamese Relay
What Did You Eat?
Charades
Paper Ball
Backward Get Up
Three Deep
Huckle, Buckle,
   Beanstalk
Dodge Ball
Catch the
   Handkerchief
Bean Bag Relay
Hot Seat
Lost Child
Blind Tiger
Hunter
Numbers
Friends
Shadow Tag

Right:
Trey, Trent,
& Trevor

Top center:
Keith
Center: Kevin
Bottom center:
Trent &
Trevor

- **Animal Dominos.** This is a quick matching game that even very young children can play.
- **Memory or Lotto.** These take a little longer to play, but are also matching pictures.
- **Husker Du.** A matching game where children must remember how to match identical pictures. Children have excellent memories, and I had to concentrate to beat them.
- **Candyland.** A board game that teaches children their colors.
- **Chutes and Ladders.** A board game with a race to the finish that teaches children their numbers and patience.
- **Concentration.** A game in which a child fits shapes in the corresponding space before the buzzer goes off.
- **Following Directions.** Have the child or several children listen to directions and do what they are told. Start with a one-stage command and proceed to a four-stage command. Praise the child who follows directions correctly.
    1. Clap your hands two times. Ready, go!
    2. Tap your foot three times. Ready, go!
    3. Clap your hands once and then touch your head. Ready, go!
    4. Touch your head, touch your elbow. Ready, go!
    5. Stand up, sit down, and clap your hands twice. Ready, go!
- **Red Light, Green Light.** Have all of the children line up along a wall or in a straight line side by side. One child stands against the opposite wall about 25 feet away from the other children with his back to them. When he says "Green Light," all of the other children begin to **walk** toward him. However, as soon as he says "Red Light," and turns to face the children, they must stop. If any child moves after the leader says "Red Light," they must go back to the starting line. The first one to reach the child who is the leader becomes the new leader.
- **The Name Game.** Everyone gets in a circle with one person standing in the middle with a roll of paper in his hand. One person in the circle starts off by saying, "I like **Stephen**," (or any other person's name who is in the circle). The person in the middle has to run to the person whose name was called and try to tap him on the head before he can say, "I like **Sam**," (using the name of someone else in the group). You cannot call the same name twice in a row. This game will help the children learn each other's names.
- **Doggie, Doggie, Where's Your Bone?** One child is seated in the front of the room facing a wall. One child is chosen to come up and steal the "bone" (any object you choose) from under the chair. After the child has hidden the bone, the children say in unison, "Doggie, Doggie, where's your bone? Somebody stole it from your home. Guess who!"
    The "doggie" turns around and has three guesses to discover who has the bone. If the "doggie" guesses the right person, he can sit down with the other children, and the person with the bone is now the "doggie."
- **I See Something.** Choose one child to begin the game. That child will look around the room and pick something saying, "I see something blue."

(Or whatever color he chooses) Everyone tries to guess the object, and the first person to guess the object is the next person to choose.

• **Simon Says.** Have children stand in straight lines in front of the teacher. If the teacher says, "Simon says, 'Pat your head' " or some other command beginning with "Simon says...." the children are to do what the teacher says. If the teacher does not include "Simon says" in his command, then the children are not supposed to obey. If they do, the child or children must sit down until the end of that game. The winner is the last child standing who has obeyed all the commands correctly.

• **Duck, Duck, Goose.** Everyone sits in a circle. One child walks around the outside of the circle saying, "Duck, duck, duck." When he taps another child on the head using a paper towel roll and says "Goose," the "goose" must get up and race him back to the spot where he was seated. The loser walks around the circle saying, "Duck, duck, duck..." and the game continues.

• **Alphabet Name Game.** Start with the letter "A," and let the children take turns thinking of a boy's name or a girl's name that starts with that letter. If they cannot think of one, go to the next child. You can also think of animals, starting with each letter of the alphabet.

• **Alphabet Sign Game.** While driving have the children look for the alphabet letters in order on signs or billboards until they have found all of the letters.

• **7-Up.** All children sit down, close their eyes, and put their thumbs up. Select three children who walk around the room and each pushes down one thumb. When this is done, those whose thumbs were put down, must try and guess who pushed down their thumbs. The first three to guess correctly are the next three to put down thumbs, and the three who did it have to sit down.

• **Bible Verse Game.** Divide all the children into two teams. Choose a Bible verse and have the two teams line up in single file an equal distance from the blackboard where the verse will be written. The first child from each team goes to the board and legibly writes the first word of the verse and returns to the end of the line. The next child writes the second word, and so on until the entire verse is written on the board. The team who finishes the verse first wins the game.

• **Steal the Bacon,** Divide the children into two teams. Number both teams beginning with "1," so there is a number "1" on each team and so on. Have teams line up on opposite sides of the room and place an item such as a handkerchief or rag, in the center of the room. When you call a number, the child from each team with that number will run to the center of the room and try to get the "bacon" back to his starting line before the other child can steal it and get it back to his starting line. Every time a team retrieves the bacon and gets it back to their side, they get a point. The team with the most points in the end wins. (If the children do not listen for their number, they will lose the chance to win the point.)

• **Mother, May I?** Have the children line up and face the "mother." She tells each child how many steps to take such as: baby steps, giant steps, hops, skips, leaps, scissors steps, backward steps, sideway steps, squat steps, etc. Each time she gives a command, the child must say, "Mother, May I?" before he starts. If he does not say it, he is out. The first child to reach the mother is the winner.

• **Over and Under.** Divide children into two teams. Have two rows of chairs, one row per team or let the children stand in a line, one behind the other. Have five objects for each team to pass over and under consecutively from the front to the back and then back to the front. The team that has all five objects back first wins.

• **Black Magic.** Two people must know how to play this game in advance—a leader and a person who will leave the room. The object of this game is for the group to figure out how the person who leaves the room can always identify the object they have chosen. The leader stays in the room while the group chooses the object that everyone can see whether it is in the room or on a person. The person who left the room is then asked to return. The leader asks questions like, "Is it the chair?" "Is if the desk?" etc. The person who has returned to the room answers the questions, "No," until the appropriate cue.

  The Secret: In order to pick the correct object each time, the leader will ask if several objects in the room are the chosen object. Then he will ask about an object that is black. The object that the group has chosen will always be the very next item named after the black object. As soon as someone thinks he has caught on, he is the next to exit the room and guess the chosen object.

• **Popcorn Scramble.** Divide children into two teams and place popcorn in two bowls, one for each team. Put one Lifesaver® per team member in each bowl. Each child has to dig for a Lifesaver® using his mouth and eat it without using his hands. Each member passes the bowl and holds it for the next team member. This continues until each team member has found a Lifesaver®. Each member of the winning team must have a Lifesaver® in his mouth.

• **Musical Chairs.** Place chairs in a circle, one chair fewer than the number of children participating. Have the children walk around chairs while music is playing or the leader is singing. When the music stops, the children must sit in the nearest chair to them. One child will be left without a chair. This child is out of the game. Take one chair from the circle, and repeat until only one child is left. This child is the winner.

• **Relay Shoe Race.** Divide children into two teams and have each team line up in single file, one behind the other. A team member from each team will run to a designated point, take off his right shoe and leave it, run to another point, take off his left shoe and leave it, and then run back to his team's starting line. Each team member will follow suit until all their shoes are in designated piles. They will repeat this procedure in reverse until every team member is wearing his shoes. Shoes with buckles or laces must be put on completely. The first team with all their shoes back on properly is the winning team.

• **Suitcase Relay.** Divide children into two teams with each team standing single file in a straight line, one behind another. Have two suitcases or grocery bags filled with various articles of clothing. Each member must run to the suitcase (or bag), open it, put on all of the articles, then take off all the articles, return them to the suitcase, close the suitcase, and run back to his team. Each team member does the same, and the last member takes the suitcase with him to the starting line. The first team who finishes wins.

• **Pictionary.** Choose a person to come to the board and tell that person to draw a picture which describes an object or a phrase, without using numbers or letters. The person has a set amount of time to draw before the others try to identify the picture being drawn. The person who guesses correctly first is the next illustrator. You can also divide the children into teams and let one person draw from each team with the team identifying the picture first receiving a point for his team.

• **Streets and Alleys.** Everyone stands in rows with his arms stretched out. Someone calls "streets," and everyone must do a 90-degree turn, making rows in the opposite direction. Then the person calls out "alleys," and everyone returns to his original position, making rows in the original direction. While this is going on, a designated "cat" is chasing a designated "mouse" up and down the rows, trying to tag that person. They must go up and down the streets and alleys, not under the arms of the players. (This game works like a maze.)

• **Hot Potato.** Everyone stands or sits in a circle. A very "hot" potato or an object is passed around the circle as quickly as the player can get rid of it while music is being played or the leader hums or sings. The person in charge suddenly stops the music, and whoever has the object in his hands has to leave the circle. The last one remaining in the circle is the winner.

• **Telephone.** Choose one person to make up a sentence. Have all children sit in a circle. The child who made the sentence up may whisper it to the child sitting next to him. He may not repeat it. That child then whispers it to the next child and so on. When all have heard the sentence, the last child should say what he has heard out loud. The child who made up the original sentence should say it out loud to see how close the end result was to the actual sentence.

• **Memory Game.** Place several unrelated items on a tray and have one person walk with the tray through the rows of children. Then have the person with the tray cover it. When the leader says, "Go," everyone writes down every object that he can remember from the tray. The person who remembers the most objects that were on the tray wins.

• **Word Scramble.** Write a word on a chalk board or choose an object that everyone in the room can see. Tell everyone to form as many different words from that one word as they are able. The person with the most words spelled correctly is the winner. (Set a time limit before beginning the game

354 | Recipes for Rearing Children

and tell them the letters in the word can only be used one time.)

• **Squirrel in a Tree.** Children are divided into groups of three of the same gender. Two of the children face each other, forming a "tree." The third child stands between them; he is a squirrel. One child is designated as "it" who does not have a "tree." When the leader calls, "squirrel in a tree," all of the children in the middle of the trees who are "squirrels" have to change trees before the child without a tree gets to a tree. The child who does not get to a tree becomes "it." The children who are the two sides of the tree should be rotated periodically so they have a chance to be a squirrel.

• **Murder.** The object of the game is to reveal the murderer. Each player will choose a paper from a cup. All the papers are blank except one piece which has an "X" on it. Whoever gets the paper with the "X" marked on it is the murderer, but he must not let anyone else know. Players sit in a circle, facing each other. The murderer has to wink to "kill" someone. His goal is not to be seen by another player when he winks at his victim. The victim waits for a second after being winked at and says, "I am dead." Once "dead," the player is out of the game. The goal of each player who is not the "murderer" is to spot the murderer in the act of winking and reveal his identity before being "killed." The last person left in the circle or the one who reveals the murderer wins, and the game can start again.

• **Balloon Stomp.** You will need some large balloons and string or yarn cut into 18-inch lengths. Each child blows up a balloon and securely ties a string onto it. This string is then tied around the child's ankle, and the contest is ready to begin. In an area marked off with boundaries, the children are to stomp each other's balloon. They must stay within the boundaries, and the last one left with a blown-up balloon is the winner. Children are not allowed to hold their balloon or to protect it between their legs.

• **Spoon and Bean (or Potato) Relay.** Divide the children into two teams and have them form two lines, one behind the other. Give the first child in each team a spoon with a bean or potato on it. Each child must carry the spoon with the bean or potato on it to the goal line and back. If he drops the bean (or the potato), he must pick it up and start over. The team who finishes first wins.

• **Siamese Relay.** Teams of two boys and teams of two girls pair off and one of their legs is tied to one of their partner's legs with torn material or old hosiery. (If you wish, you can use a burlap sack and let each child put one leg into the sack. One child uses his right leg and one his left leg.) Each team of two will run together to the goal line, racing another team. The team who reaches the finish line first is the winner.

• **What Did You Eat?** You need two blindfolds and various kinds of food. Divide the group into two teams. Blindfold the first player from each side. Place a bite of the same food in the mouth of each player at the same time. The first to say the correct name of the food wins a point for his team.

• **Charades.** With the children seated, choose one to go first. He is to think of something such as playing ball, riding a bicycle, being a teacher, etc., that he can act out without making any sounds. After whispering his idea to the teacher, he acts out his charade in front of the group. Children must raise their hands when trying to guess. The first one to guess correctly gets to do the next charade. Teams can be used. Different ideas for the charades can be put into a paper sack, and the children can draw an idea out of the bag if they have trouble thinking of ideas to act out. If the children are divided into teams, the team will receive a point for each charade they guess correctly first.

- **Paper Ball.** You will need music and a paper ball made as follows: Put several pieces of candy inside a clear plastic sandwich bag. Around this, wad a sheet of newspaper and secure it with masking tape. Continue to add more newspaper and tape until you have made a good-sized ball. In fact, the bigger the better! The children stand in a large circle. Explain what is on the inside of the paper ball. The ball is then passed around the circle while music is playing. When the music stops, the child holding the ball begins tearing off the newspaper and tape. As soon as the music starts, he must continue to pass the ball around the circle. This continues until someone gets down to the candy. The last person keeps the prize.

- **Backward Get Up.** Everyone chooses a partner of the same gender. The partners sit on the floor back to back. They hook elbows and draw their feet up close to their bodies. Both start pushing against the lower part of the back. The object is to rise and stand by pushing and using each other as leverage. The partners sit down again, without moving their feet. This can be played in teams with the team who finishes first winning.

- **Three Deep.** One person is chosen to be "it," and one person is chosen to be chased. The rest of the group is divided into groups of three. If this does not work out evenly, two groups may have four. The groups scatter around a large area. The children in each group must form a line facing the same direction so that one person is clearly in the front. The person who is "it" then begins to chase his "victim." They may run anywhere around the groups of three. The person being chased may be "safe" if he simply stands in front of one of the groups. As soon as he does this, he becomes part of that group; and the last person in that line begins running from "it." Whenever "it" succeeds in tagging someone, that person then becomes "it."

- **Huckle Buckle Beanstalk.** You will need one small item, such as a thimble or a button, to be hidden. This game is best if played indoors. Two children are chosen as players, and a third is picked to hide the thimble. The rest of the group is seated together on the floor. The two players must leave the room and wait to be called. The person with the thimble must hide it somewhere that is visible from at least one position. He then returns to the group, and the two players are called in. The players begin searching for the thimble as the group gives hints by telling them when they are "hot" (close) and "cold" (far away). As soon as one of the players sees the thimble, he says, "Huckle Buckle Beanstalk" and runs to be seated with the group. He does not point out the thimble in any way to the other player.

Although the other person has already lost, he must continue to hunt until he also sees the thimble. The game then starts over with the winner of the last game hiding the thimble. The loser of the game and person who first hid the thimble will choose the next two players. (Putting the thimble in the teacher's ear is a favorite hiding place!)

• **Handkerchief Race.** You will need two handkerchiefs or two pieces of material or two cloth napkins for this game. Divide the group into two teams. Form two straight lines about 12 feet apart. The first person from each side comes to the center and lies down flat on his back. The leader centers an open handkerchief over each player's face. Upon a given signal, the two contestants attempt to remove their handkerchief using only their face muscles and tongue. The first one to move the handkerchief so that his nose is revealed wins a point for his team.

• **Dodge Ball.** You will need a large foam ball. Divide the group into two teams. One team should form a large circle. The other team gets in the center of this circle. The members of the outside circle try to hit those in the center. The ball must be thrown low so the child is hit below the waist. They may not catch or push the ball. They must stay within the circle. When a child is hit, that child is eliminated from the game. The game continues until only one person is left in the center. That child is the winner. The teams change position with those in the outside circle becoming the inside group for the next game.

• **Catch the Handkerchief.** You will need an old handkerchief or a piece of cloth of similar size. One student is designated as the starter, and the rest of the students stand in a circle. The starter will stand in the center of the circle, call out a student's name and throw the handkerchief in the air. The student whose name was called must catch the handkerchief before it hits the floor. The starter is changed only when a student fails to catch the handkerchief. For a variation, each student could be assigned a number or letter and thus respond to it instead of his name.

Bean Bag Relay. One bean bag for each row of students or a wadded-up paper ball. The entire class will be participating while seated in rows. At the teacher's signal, the first player in each row passes the bean bag over his head and into the hands of the student directly behind. This is continued until the last student in the row receives the bean bag. At that point, the last student will hop on one foot to the front, and each student in that row will move back one seat. This will continue in the same manner until the all of the students have returned to their own chairs. The first row to complete this relay is declared the winner.

• **Hot Seat.** One child is designated as the "hunter," and all others are seated in chairs placed very close to each other in a circle. The teacher will make sure there is one more chair than there are seated students. The "hunter" stands in the circle and heads for the empty chair. The person to the right of the empty chair slides into that chair, thus leaving another empty chair until the "hunter" finally manages to get to an empty chair first.

• **Lost Child.** You will need a blindfold. One student is chosen to be the "detective," and the balance of the class will remain seated in chairs placed in a semi-circle. The "detective" will go to the front of the semi-circle and put on a blindfold. The teacher will point to one student who is to be the "lost child." At a signal, that student will leave the room while all other students will change places. After everyone is again seated, the blindfold is removed and the "detective" has three guesses in which to name the "lost child." If the "lost child" is determined, the "detective" is seated, and the "lost child" becomes the new "detective." If the "lost child" is not detected, the student returns to his chair; and the game begins again.

• **Blind Tiger.** You will need a blindfold. The teacher should choose one student to be the "tiger." The balance of the class will form a circle around the "tiger," and the "tiger" is then blindfolded. The students walk around the circle so the "tiger" does not know where the students are. After the students in the circle stop, the "tiger" points. The child pointed to growls, "Grrr." The "tiger" has three chances to try to guess the child who has growled. Each time the "tiger" guesses wrong, the player growls again. If the child is correctly identified, that child becomes the "tiger" for the next game. If the identity is not guessed, the circle revolves, and the same "tiger" has one more chance to guess.

• **Hunter.** One student is designated as the "hunter." The "hunter" will go to the front of the class and say, "Who wants to go hunting with me?" All of the other students will then form a line behind the "hunter," and the hunt will begin. Students will follow the "hunter" until the "hunter" spots a bird, raises his invisible gun, and shoots. When shooting, the "hunter" says, "Bang." At this signal, all students hurry toward their seats. The first student properly seated in his seat becomes the new "hunter."

• **Numbers.** One child is chosen to be the "leader" and stands in the center of the room. The balance of the class forms a circle around the leader who has been chosen. All the players count off beginning with the "leader," who is number one. Remind the students that they will keep this number for the entire game. The teacher calls out two numbers, and the "leader" tries to get in one of those two places before the change is completed. The player without a place becomes the "leader," and the teacher calls out two different numbers.

• **Friends.** One child is designated as the "lost soul" while all other children are seated in a circle. The "lost soul" will approach any student and say, "Where can I find a friend?" The reply would be with the names of two other students. When those students hear their names called, they must switch places immediately, and the "lost soul" will attempt to get into one of their chairs before they do. When this happens, students exchange places; and the game now has a new "lost soul."

• **Shadow Tag.** Have the children try to step on your shadow outside on a sunny day.

"There should be enough love
in a Christian home
to spill over into the lives of all
children who need it,
for love grows by giving—
and never ends."

Top: Joseph Cowling
with infant son, Pete
Cowling
Left: Pete Cowling
Center: Joseph Cowling (Joey), 1 month old
Right: Peter Cowling (Petey), 2 years
(Joey and Petey are Keith's children named in honor
of his dad and grandfather.)

Templates for Finger Puppets, Songs, and Flannel Board Stories

The faces are used with the song, "Five in the Bed." Choose five. (Enlarge 200%)

Use with the song, "Five Elephants." (Enlarge 130%)

Use with the song, "Five Little Ducks." Enlarge 130%)

Roll the template into a circle. Glue the finger puppet to the tip of the circle.

Use with the song, "Five Green Frogs."

Left:
Templates for the story,
"The Pancake Man."
(Enlarge 200%)

Below:
Templates for the story,
"The Bremen Town
Musicians"
(Enlarge 200%)

Templates for
"The Big Turnip"
(Enlarge 200%)

Templates for
"Three Billy
Goats Gruff"
Make the goat 3
different sizes.
(Enlarge troll
200%)

Left: Templates
for "The Three Wishes"
story. Use the old man and old
woman from the pancake man
story. (Enlarge 200%)

Learning Disability (Dyslexia)

To some degree, dyslexia affects approximately seven children out of every one hundred children. This learning disability is more common among boys and lower-income families. Dyslexia is a coordination problem, and the children who have it, have average or above-average intelligence. They are neither slow nor retarded, but this disability can prevent them from doing well in school if this problem is not identified and corrected before the child sees himself as unable to learn normally.

The Importance of Early Detection

The longer a child has the problem before it is detected, the greater the degree of emotional disturbance in addition to the learning disability. When a child gives his best effort and fails to perform satisfactorily, he usually becomes discouraged and stops trying. If the problem is detected before the child starts school, the emotional damage may be eliminated. Some children learn to cope with this problem by the time they enter the fourth grade. Though the learning disability does not disappear, they learn to adapt and be successful in learning.

The Symptoms

1. An inability to print, write, or draw for the child's age and intelligence
2. General coordination problems, such as mixed dominance which is no preference for the right or left hand
3. Hyperactivity (extreme activity)
4. Hypokinetic (lack of activity)
5. Impulsiveness (temper tantrums, little or no self-control)
6. Transient strabismus–the eyes do not work together, poor hand-eye coordination, and some mild or delayed speech may be present.
7. Irritability and distractibility–perseveration, the inability to finish what the child starts
8. Misbehavior and inattention are frequent signs.
9. Poor auditory perception–poor understanding of the spoken command

Tests to Detect Dyslexia

1. **Ask the child to stand with his back to a wall and walk away from the wall ten times.** Watch which foot the child uses to step away from the wall. In most cases a right-handed person will step out from the wall with the right foot the majority of the time. A left-handed person will step out from the wall using the left foot the majority of the time. This test reveals mixed dominance or no preference for the right or left hand if a learning disability is present.
2. **Have the child walk a balance beam or put a 20-foot piece of masking tape on the floor.** Have the child walk on the beam or on the tape

by putting his heel to toe all the way to the end. A child with dyslexia will not be able to do this easily.

3. Observe the child's ability to cut with scissors which is the most difficult small motor skill. I have found the most effective way to teach a child to cut with scissors is to get a pair of child-sized scissors that will cut. You cut a strip of paper one-inch wide and six-inches long. Show the child how to hold the scissors by putting his thumb in the top hole and his pointer finger and tall finger in the bottom hole of the scissors. Let him practice snapping the scissors like a mouth and stress that the scissors should not be turned to the side because they will not cut.

You hold the strip of paper taut and let the child snip the paper in half. If he is holding the scissors correctly, and you are holding the paper taut, he will succeed. Praise him for his effort. Save the strips of paper and ask him to glue them on a large paper which says, "I cut this." Brag on him for succeeding in cutting.

• *Observe the child's ability to skip, the most difficult large motor skill.* I have found the most effective way to teach a child to skip is to stand beside the child and hold the child's hand. Slowly teach him to step, then hop on one foot, then step and hop with the other foot. Go slow and be patient if he has difficulty. (What seems very easy to you may be very difficult for him, regardless of his age.) If he tries, praise him, and stop before he becomes frustrated. I have never had a child who did not learn to skip by using this method, even if it took a week or two. Always stop before the child gets tired. Use praise liberally when he succeeds and let him show everyone how he can skip with you after he masters it.

• *Observe the child's ability to draw.* A child will usually draw symbol drawings (something you can recognize, like a face) just before the age of three. Until this time, he scribbles (something you cannot recognize), but the scribbling is developing his small motor skills. The child needs to scribble, but not on your walls and floors. Provide plenty of paper, crayons, and washable markers to encourage his scribbling. A child with a learning problem will be behind in drawing symbols. If the other children are drawing objects you can recognize, and every time he scribbles you ask, "What is that?" he will usually stop trying. Every person desires success, and we need to work hard to help the child be successful on his level if he is giving his best effort.

• *Observe the child's ability to print his name.* A child with dyslexia will be behind the other children his age. The person who knows the child best should make the evaluation.

4. Ask the child to fold the dog and cat made from 8½ x 11-inch paper. (See the paper folding instructions at the end of this section.) Have the child fold one step at a time and give assistance where needed. You can have the child draw faces on the dog and cat and praise him for his efforts.

5. Watch to see if he is hyperactive or inactive as compared to the other children his age.

6. **Watch to see if he has a poor attention span and poor concentration for a child his age.** Can he listen to a story without walking away? Can he follow instructions? Search for a book that will appeal to the child and put yourself into reading it or telling the story so you can fight for the child's attention.

7. **Have the student follow a line on the blackboard with a piece of chalk.** Draw a line on paper or chalkboard and ask him to trace with chalk or a pencil. Draw a car and a garage. Ask the student to drive the car into the garage.

A child can have one or more of these problems without having dyslexia, but if several symptoms are present, he should be professionally tested. If this is impossible, work with him on improving his small and large motor skills. When these skills improve, his learning ability will improve.

Treatment of a Learning Disability

If at all possible, the child should be left in a regular classroom if the problem is discovered after he starts to school. The younger the child is when you suspect a learning disability, the better for you and the child. This way you can help prevent his feelings of failure before he enters school. If his motor skills—both large and small—improve, the child's learning disability will improve. The parents can do the following at home which will help the child:

A. Read stories to him every day, starting with simple books and gradually moving to longer books. (See the preschool list in Appendix E.)

B. Have a five to fifteen-minute time period, depending on the child's age, when you sit with him and practice drawing, cutting with scissors, coloring and staying within the lines, etc. Make it fun by adding new items frequently and praise him when he succeeds. Make sure the child succeeds.

C. Have a five to fifteen-minute time period when you work on large motor skills every day. Have the child hop, skip, ride a tricycle, throw bean bags, and build with blocks.

D.   Play simple games with the child like Lotto, Husker Du, simple Domino games, or Memory. Make sure the child finishes the game.

E.   Have the child walk the balance beam four or five times a day.

F.   Toys or games or puzzles with shapes to fit in specific holes would be helpful. Start with simple puzzles with a few pieces so the child can be successful.

G.   Use praise liberally if the child is doing his best, even though his best may not be up to your expectations. Any action the child does that achieves positive results will recur.

To help us understand what a child faces in dealing with a learning problem hold this dot-to-dot paper in front of a mirror and connect the dots by looking in the mirror. It should be difficult for you because your brain tells your hand to go in one direction, and you must force your hand to go in the opposite direction. We are told the child must learn to turn his words around in his mind if he learns to read.

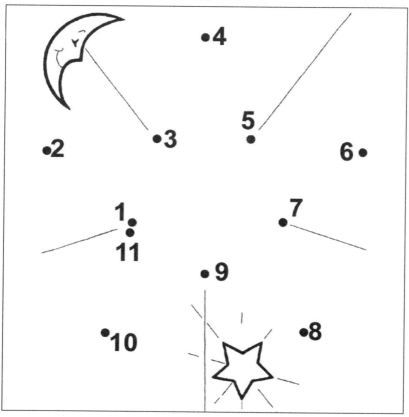

No one really knows why a child has a learning disability. Usually it does not affect every child in a family. Usually the child either learns to cope by the time he is in fourth grade or he sees himself as a failure at school. If a child is trying and the parent feels he is not trying, it can be a problem.

Over 30 years ago, I was hired by the University of Tennessee to do a series of classes for grade school teachers on identifying learning disabilities in children. I wrote the material you have just read to accomplish this goal. I remember one of the first classes I taught was in a classroom with about 40 teachers present with the only door to the classroom behind me. I was explaining how to determine if a child had a learning disability when I noticed a woman on my left side staring at me in a funny way. She made me feel uncomfortable, and I tried to identify her problem as I continued to talk. "Maybe she is ill," I thought, "and is embarrassed to walk out the door with everyone looking at her." "Maybe she has a personal problem." "Maybe she has had a hard day at school."

It was difficult for me to concentrate with these kinds of questions flooding my mind and her piercing stare on me as if she were looking through me. I took it as long as I could and stopped and questioned her. "Are you ill? Is there something I can do to help you?"

Without saying a word, the woman started sobbing uncontrollably. She was crying so hard, we could not talk to her so we just sat there. Finally when she began to regain control, I asked if I could help. She said, "That's what is wrong with my little boy." She told us she was an elementary teacher and her husband was a high school teacher and coach. Obviously her husband wanted a son who was athletic, so he tried to teach the son to bat, but the son always missed the ball. She said they had accused the child of not trying to play ball, but the more they talked, the worse the child's performance became. She told us her six year old had just failed first grade and seemed withdrawn. She said that she always had the feeling that her child was trying but had no explanation for his failure to learn to read and for his poor motor skill performance.

"Now that I know how to help him, I'm certainly going to try," she ended.

I often wonder what happened to that boy, and if he was able to lead a normal life. I have known many others who had a learning disability as a child but who learned to cope. When I asked them about the lasting effects of the learning disability, they mentioned that when they were driving and someone said, "Turn left," a feeling of panic overwhelmed them. They forced themselves to stop and say, "My watch is on my left arm. There is no need to panic."

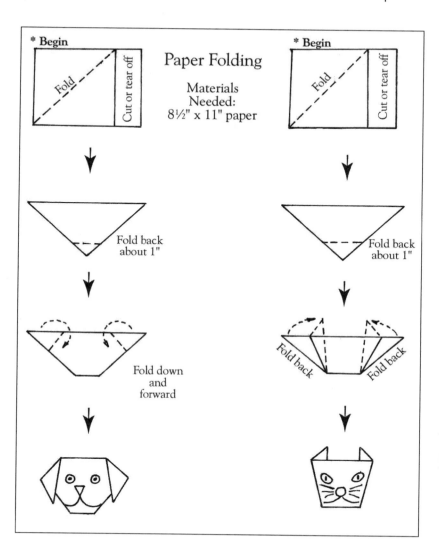

* Begin

Fold

Cut or tear off

Paper Folding

Materials
Needed:
8½" x 11" paper

* Begin

Fold

Cut or tear off

Fold back
about 1"

Fold back
about 1"

Fold down
and
forward

Fold back

Fold back

368 | RECIPES FOR REARING CHILDREN

Without God, there could be no recipe for rearing children. The Bible has all the answers and provides the truths for today, as well as for the future, if we know Christ in a personal way. The most important decision my husband and I have ever made is accepting the gift of salvation by faith in Christ. This gift is available to everyone. Are you 100% sure of a home in Heaven? There are four simple facts that you need to know in order to go to Heaven.

1. **We are all sinners.** Romans 3:23 says, *"For all have sinned, and come short of the glory of God."*

2. **Sin came from Adam.** Romans 5:12 says, "Wherefore, as by one man sin entered into the world, and death by sin; and so death passed upon all men, for that all have sinned." The word *death* in this verse means Hell.

3. **God has a price on sin.** Romans 6:23 says, *"For the wages of sin is death; but the gift of God is eternal life through Jesus Christ our Lord."*

4. **God made a way out.** Romans 5:8 says, *"But God commendeth his love toward us, in that, while we were yet sinners, Christ died for us."* Romans 10:13 says, *"For whosoever shall call upon the name of the Lord shall be saved."*

If you believe these four points, pray this sample prayer: "Dear Jesus, I know I am a sinner. Right now, by faith, I am trusting You as my personal Saviour and my only hope for Heaven. Thank You for dying for me and for saving me from Hell. In Jesus' name, Amen."

If you did pray this prayer and really meant it, God says you can be 100 percent sure you will go to Heaven. Please let us know that you made this decision by writing to Pete and Frieda Cowling, 540 Iroquois, Schererville, Indiana 46375.